HOLY LAND AS HOMELAND?

The Social World of Biblical Antiquity, Second Series, 7

Holy Land as Homeland?

Models for Constructing the Historic Landscapes of Jesus

edited by

Keith W. Whitelam

Sheffield Phoenix Press

2011

Copyright © 2011 Sheffield Phoenix Press

Published by Sheffield Phoenix Press
Department of Biblical Studies, University of Sheffield
45 Victoria Street, Sheffield S3 7QB

www.sheffieldphoenix.com

A CIP catalogue record for this book
is available from the British Library

Typeset by the HK Scriptorium
Printed by Lightning Source

Hardback 978-1-907534-32-4

CONTENTS

CIL	*Corpus inscriptionum latinarum* (Berlin: G. Reimer, 1968–)
Clement of Alexandria	
Protr.	*Protrepticus*
Eunapius	
Vit. soph.	*Vitae sophistarum*
FRLANT	Forschungen zur Religion und Literatur des Alten und Neuen Testaments
Horace	
Ep.	*Epistulae*
Josephus	
Ant.	*Antiquities of the Jews*
Life	*Life of Josephus*
War	*Jewish War*
JSOT	*Journal for the Study of the Old Testament*
Meleager	
Anth. Palat.	*Anthologia Palatina*
Pliny	
Nat. hist.	*Naturalis historia (Natural History)*
Papyri	
P.Oslo	*Papyri osloenses*
PSI	*Papiri greci e latini*
P.Tebt.	*The Tebtunis Papyri*
P.Wisc.	*The Wisconsin Papyri*
Rabbinic literature	
b.	Babylonian Talmud
m.	Mishnah
t.	Tosefta
y.	Palestinian Talmud
Tractates of the Talmud and Mishnah	
B. Meṣ.	*Baba Meṣi'a*
B. Qam.	*Baba Qamma*
Dem.	*Demai*

Giṭ.	*Giṭṭin*
M. Qaṭ.	*Moʿed Qaṭan*
Ned.	*Nedarim*
Peʾah	*Peʾah*
Pes.	*Pesaḥim*
Šeb.	*Šebiʾit*
Cant. R.	*Canticles Rabbah*
Gen R.	*Genesis Rabbah*
Lam. R.	*Lamentations Rabbah*
Lev. R.	*Leviticus Rabbah*
Num. R.	*Numbers Rabbah*
Ruth R.	*Ruth Rabbah*
Sifre Deut.	*Sifre Deuteronomy*
Strabo	
Geog.	*Geographica (Geography)*
Suetonius	
Tib.	*Tiberius*
WUNT	Wissenschaftliche Untersuchungen zum Neuen Testament

CONTRIBUTORS

RENE BAERGEN is a PhD candidate at Emmanuel College, University of Toronto, and an Adjunct Instructor in New Testament Studies at the Toronto School of Theology. His research interests include the social and cultural projects of early Christianity within the context of the ancient Mediterranean, historical Jesus studies, and the role of the Bible in contemporary identity politics.

JONATHAN C.P. BIRCH has taught New Testament and Christian Origins at the University of Glasgow, where he is currently completing his PhD. He has contributed to the periodicals *Philosophy Now* and the *Reformation and Renaissance Review*. His research interests include the history of biblical studies and philosophy in the European Enlightenment.

JAMES G. CROSSLEY is Reader in Bible, Culture and Politics in the Department of Biblical Studies, University of Sheffield. His publications include *Why Christianity Happened* (Westminster/John Knox Press, 2006), *Jesus in an Age of Terror* (Equinox, 2008) and *Reading the New Testament* (Routledge, 2010). His research interests include Christian origins and political and ideological readings of scholarship, religion and receptions of the Bible.

BURKE O. LONG is the Kenan Professor of Religion and the Humanities Emeritus at Bowdoin College in Brunswick, Maine. He is the author of *Planting and Reaping Albright: Ideology, Politics, and Interpreting the Bible* (Pennsylvania State University Press, 1997) and *Imagining the Holy Land: Maps, Models and Fantasy Travels* (Indiana University Press, 2003). His most recent research focuses on popular representations of the Bible. He also publishes short fiction.

DAVINA C. LOPEZ is Assistant Professor of Religious Studies at Eckerd College (St. Petersburg, Florida, USA) where she coordinates the Religious Studies and Women's & Gender Studies programs. She is the author of *Apostle to the Conquered: Reimagining Paul's Mission* (Fortress Press, 2008). Her research interests include Pauline discourses, visual representation, and methodologies in New Testament studies. She is currently working on *De-Introducing the New Testament* with Todd Penner.

HALVOR MOXNES is Professor of New Testament in the Faculty of Theology at the University of Oslo. Among his publications are *Putting Jesus in his Place: A Radical Vision of Household and Kingdom* (Westminster/John Knox Press, 2003), *Jesus and the Rise of Nationalism* (I.B. Tauris, 2011), and he is co-editor of *Jesus beyond Nationalism* (Equinox, 2009). His main research interests include the New Testament and Early Christianity in the cultural context of the Mediterranean in Antiquity, the history of interpretation of the historical Jesus in modern societies, and gender and masculinity studies in religion.

TODD PENNER is the Gould H. and Marie Cloud Associate Professor (and Chair) of Religious Studies and Director of the Gender Studies Program at Austin College. He is author of *In Praise of Christian Origins* (T. & T. Clark International, 2004) and co-author of *Contextualizing Gender in Early Christian Discourse* (Society of Biblical Literture, 2009). He is currently working on *De-Introducing the New Testament* with Davina Lopez.

LEIF E. VAAGE is Associate Professor of New Testament Literature and Exegesis at Emmanuel College of Victoria University (and the Toronto School of Theology) in the University of Toronto. He is the author of *Galilean Upstarts* (Trinity Press International, 1994) and of a book of poems, *Schooled in Salt* (The St. Thomas Poetry Series, 2003) as well as, most recently, the editor of *Religious Rivalries in the Early Roman Empire and the Rise of Christianity* (Wilfrid Laurier University Press, 2006). He contributes regularly to the *Revista de interpretacion biblica latinoamericana*, and otherwise is busy with Paul's biographical problems, including the question of where and how to find them.

KEITH W. WHITELAM is Emeritus Professor in Biblical Studies at the University of Sheffield. His publications include *The Invention of Ancient Israel: The Silencing of Palestinian History* (Routledge, 1996), *The Emergence of Early Israel in Historical Perspective* (with Robert B. Coote, reprinted Sheffield Phoenix Press, 2010). He is joint editor of *The Journal for the Study of the Old Testament*. His major research interests are in the history and archaeology of ancient Palestine, cartography and travel narratives of Palestine, and the social and political influences that have shaped the development of biblical studies as a discipline.

INTRODUCTION

Keith W. Whitelam

The papers collected in this volume were presented over two very enjoy-able days in Oslo at a seminar on 'Holy Land as Homeland? Models for Reconstructing the Historic Landscapes of Jesus'. The seminar was the latest in a series of events organized by the 'Jesus in Cultural Complex-ity: Interpretation, Memory and Identification' project directed by Halvor Moxnes at the University of Oslo.[1] Halvor was an extremely gracious and generous host, providing a supportive and relaxed environment in which participants from a range of backgrounds and disciplines were able to exam-ine the ideological and cultural understandings that underpin constructions of the landscapes of Jesus within biblical studies.

It was a refreshing antidote to the way in which many national and inter-national meetings have become overblown with very little time for ques-tions or discussion of the various presentations. While such meetings have become imperative for a scholar's CV in order to justify travel funds or demonstrate scholarly esteem—particularly in the UK, where research assessment and now 'impact' have become the determining factors driving research—they have, in my opinion, been little short of disastrous for the nature of research and scholarship. Too many conferences have become so large, with multiple parallel sessions, that the constraints on scheduling have all but eliminated time for questions or discussion, effectively absolving the presenter from any need to justify assertions or arguments. The chance to present and listen to papers in such a relaxed environment, with ample time for the discussion of individual papers as well as plenary sessions looking

1. The Project is located at the Faculty of Theology at the University of Oslo and is financially supported by the Norwegian Research Council (http://www.tf.uio.no/english/research/projects/jcc/). The papers collected in this volume are a sample of the pre-sentations made at the seminar. A number of papers have not been included because the authors deemed them to be works in progress or had already agreed to have them published elsewhere.

at overlapping themes, was a welcome relief from the frantic scramble to move between parallel sessions that are the feature of so many conferences.

Constructing Homelands

'The past is a foreign country: they do things differently there.' L.P. Hartley's now near-immortal phrase is oft repeated to emphasize the temporal and cultural gulf between our contemporary world and the ancient past we seek to recover. Yet the quest for the historical Jesus has invariably tried to make sense of his world by constructing what it considers to be the historic landscapes that he inhabited. Powerful images of 'Holy Land' and 'homeland' have been used to close the temporal and cultural gulf exposed by Hartley so that we can feel safe and at home in a landscape inhabited by Jesus. It is part of a sly move that denies that we are not capable of reclaiming what has been lost in the past. Yet, however hard we strive, we do not create an actual past or rediscover an actual landscape with its towns and villages. What we discover in place of these actual towns and villages are 'imaginary homelands', to use Salman Rushdie's phrase; powerful constructs that allow us to inhabit and possess the past.

These imaginary homelands have seldom if ever lived up to the expectations of western visitors: 'a hopeless, dreary, heart-broken land' as Mark Twain described it in 1867. It is the present that the visitor experiences that seems strange and alien where they do things differently. The real homeland, where we can feel familiar and safe, is in the past. But it is a past that conforms to the visitor's or scholars own present at home, an imaginary homeland. The pursuit of the historical Jesus and a historical Galilee or Palestine within biblical studies exemplifies Rushdie's claim that it is clear that redescribing a world is the necessary first step towards changing it. And it is particularly at times when the State takes reality into its own hands, and sets about distorting it, altering the past to fit its present needs, then the making of the alternative realities of art, including the novel of memory, becomes politicized' (Rushdie 1992: 13-14). The papers in this volume explore the wordly affiliations of the numerous different homelands that have been created by biblical scholars in their quest for the historical Jesus.

A number of the papers in this volume explore the ways in which constructions of the Holy Land as homeland in the nineteenth century were mediated through history textbooks, geographies and maps and continue to exert an influence on contemporary scholarship. The complex interrelationships between the scholarship and its national settings is a constant thread throughout the papers. Moxnes traces these influences in the work of many of the iconic figures of nineteenth- and twentieth-century European biblical scholarship: from the romanticized geography of Renan and George Adam

Smith, Schleiermacher's notion of 'Volk' as the basis of nation, Strauss's views of mixed race as a positive, the attempts of Nazi scholarship to deny the Jewishness of Jesus, to Vermes's search for a Galilean Judaism and Sanders's reinstatement of a Jewish Jesus.

Birch is concerned to trace the roots of European constructions of homeland beyond its usual starting point in the nineteenth century. Although it is Reimarus who emerged as the great innovator in Schweitzer's classic account of the quest for Jesus, Birch traces the intellectual currents from the Enlightenment that help to reveal the significant roles played by Thomas Chubb, Matthew Tindal, Anthony Collins, and John Toland in shaping later debates. What emerges from the seventeenth and eighteenth centuries is a group of writers who 'broke new ground by daring to take the most iconic figure in Western culture, and Christian piety, as one of those historical subjects. Whether Jesus was wholly and only human or, as Christian orthodoxy insists, wholly human and wholly divine, his human story and his human legacy could now be studied like any other person of his time.' The homelands that have been built by nineteenth- and twentieth-century biblical scholars have foundations set deep in the Enlightenment.

The various essays also highlight the competing national constructions of Holy Land that were fundamental to Western expansion into and exploitation of Palestine. While Moxnes and Birch trace the roots of European scholarship, Long is concerned with what was happening across the Atlantic. He focuses on three towering figures of American biblical scholarship to show how they each constructed very different homelands: For Albright, it was a source of empirical rationalism and true religion; for McCown, a source of democracy and defence against socialism and communism; while for Margolis, it was a homeland in which the nationalistic dreams of Zionism could be realized.

Long poses the question at the end of his essay: 'But suppose that even the most scientifically and historically accurate maps of the Holy Land were themselves vehicles of Holy Land myth and articulators of holy lands at home?' It is a question taken up by Whitelam, who explores how the same intellectual currents and assumptions about nation and ethnicity explored by Moxnes and Long are inscribed behind the seeming scientific objectivity of cartographers such as Jacotin, Seetzen, Kiepert, Burckhardt, Conder and Kitchener. The models that underpin these maps are revealed in the texts that often accompanied them.

While nineteenth- and twentieth-century scholarship constructed a Galilaean homeland for Jesus, Baergen and Vaage seek to shift the focus from Lower Galilee to the geographical 'fringe' or 'border region' otherwise known as the Lake Region. In so doing, they take up a challenge at the end of Whitelam's paper to remove the conceptual lock on the history of the region that has been imposed by notions of nationality and ethnicity that are bounded and stress that which separates different regions or communities. Baergen and Vaage show that the lake is an aid to connectivity—cultural, intellectual, and economic—rather than the barrier that it has traditionally been represented as being. Baergen follows Horden and Purcell (2000) in questioning the fragmentation of the Mediterranean, seeking to stress the connectivity, mobility and interdependence of the population around the lake. This 'inside-out geography' of the lake brings together the opposite shores while the land around becomes increasingly peripheral with its distance from the water. As he notes, 'scholarship has chosen to remember Jesus elsewhere—inland—in a discursive space more conducive to neat categorization and abstraction than cultural complexity.'

Vaage reinforces many of these arguments through his exploration of a Cynic Jesus; again he highlights the interconnectivity around and across the lake that this would entail. He challenges recent scholarship on Galilee and the historical Jesus that continues to take the Roman administrative divisions around the lake as though they were concrete boundaries, as though they were a wall between the eastern and western sides of the rift valley. Recent descriptions of Jesus the 'Galilaean' and 'the Galilee of Jesus' are at odds with the material and cultural environment that he reveals. Baergen and Vaage, in different but overlapping ways, challenge the conceptual lock on the history of the region—which fragments and divides—by effectively integrating the Lake Region into the history of Jesus and Palestine

Just as Long demonstrates how American scholars constructed holy lands at home, Crossley analyses the academic work of the controversial British Conservative politician Enoch Powell to show how this was achieved in mid-twentieth-century Britain. Powell's idiosyncratic views derived from his reconstructed text of the Gospel of Matthew, in which the Galilee of the Gentiles and the Gentile mission were central. Crossley emphasizes how Powell's downgrading of Judaism was part of a broader social and intellectual trend within the 'racializing' roots of modern biblical scholarship. He concludes that one imagined homeland, Galilee, is replaced by another Empire in support of Powell's contemporary imagined homeland, England, and refracted through the memory of Powell's homeland at its peak, the British Empire. All this was fought out in the text of the Gospel of Matthew.

The volume ends with a methodological reflection that brings together many of the complex and interrelated issues that are woven through the different essays. Penner and Lopez take up the themes of 'home', 'homeland' and 'homelessness' to reflect on the methods and models that underpin contemporary scholarship, including those who critique more traditional forms of scholarship. They question the easy assumption that methods are neutral in origin and are used in order to show that they are the means by which we construct self-identity and social relations. Their examination of the contemporary work of Nanos and Frey reveals how contemporary discourses continue to project notions of the self and home into the past. This final essay and the volume as a whole show how the scholarly task is a continuing questioning—and self-questioning—of the models and methods with which we are most at home.

THE CONSTRUCTION OF GALILEE AS A PLACE FOR THE HISTORICAL JESUS: THE HERITAGE OF THE NINETEENTH CENTURY*

Halvor Moxnes

Why is it that the quest for the historical Jesus has become a quest for the historical Galilee? There seems to be a conviction that is not discussed, but is taken for granted, that the more we can know about Galilee, the more we know about Jesus. Hans Dieter Betz points out that some scholars attributed 'Jesus uniqueness . . . to his origin in Galilean Judaism. Jesus appeared to be unique because his Judaism was non-normative or regionally conditioned by Galilee' (Betz 1991: 100). That added an almost existential dimension to information about ancient Galilee that went beyond a general interest in the ancient history of various regions of the Mediterranean.

It is this relationship between Galilee and Jesus research that I would like to explore. How have scholars understood and constructed Galilee in discussions of the historical Jesus? What are the presuppositions behind the attempts to describe Galilee as the home or background for Jesus? And what aspects of Galilee are considered to be important? Moreover, what do we mean by Galilee? Place is not something that can be taken for granted, as something that has an existence independent of viewers; it is always something that is *posited*. We do not have an immediate, unmediated access to Galilee but approach it only through maps, films, photos and books that are produced by somebody. To say that Galilee is socially constructed is, therefore, to question whether it is 'natural,' whether the categories used to understand it can be taken for granted, as self-evident. What are the presuppositions that color an interpretation, and what are the powers implied in the creation of an image of Galilee? Moreover, they create not only Galilee but

*This essay was first published as "The Construction of Galilee as a Place for the Historical Jesus—Part I," *Biblical Theology Bulletin: A Journal of Biblical Theology* 31 (2001), pp. 26-37. It is published here with permission of SAGE Publications.

also 'the other', that is, what is outside and in contrast to Galilee (Duncan and Ley 1993: 330-31).

To follow some of the traditions of interpretations of Galilee, I will start with the construction of Galilee as part of the 'Holy Land' in the nineteenth century. The idea of the 'Holy Land' is of course much older; it goes back at least to the fourth century, with the establishing of Christian churches and monasteries and the start of pilgrimages (Wilken 1992: 101-25). But the nineteenth century represented a new beginning. It started with European political and military engagement, followed by scientific explorations and archaeological investigations, as well by individual adventurers and eventually 'mass' tourism and pilgrimages (Shepherd 1987). Finally, towards the end of the century the Zionist movement focused its attention on Palestine. As a result of these activities, the 'Holy Land' became part and parcel of the imagination of Western Christians (Obenzinger 1999). And the development of historical-critical Bible studies as well as Jesus research created a market for histories, geographies and atlases of the Holy Land.

What were the cultural context for these studies and their underlying presuppositions? First, they originated in the context of the Western colonizing influence in the Middle East and therefore represented a form of Orientalism. Moreover, since geography and history were an integral part of the scientific development of the nineteenth century, they shared many presuppositions about culture and race with disciplines like anthropology and biology. One such presupposition was the idea of a close relationship between physical geography and the character of the inhabitants of the area. Finally, ideas of nationality, ethnicity and race were all of major concern in nineteenth-century Europe and North America. I will use these presuppositions to establish the main issues in the images of Galilee from the nineteenth century: Holy Land as colony; geography as shaping personality, nationality and race and ethnicity. Since the nineteenth century was so influential in establishing biblical scholarship, these paradigms of understanding continued to exert their influence on studies in the twentieth century. Consequently, it is relevant to ask how these questions developed, which ones declined in interest, and which continued to play a role. It is also pertinent to ask whether new perspectives were brought into the attempt to construct the 'Holy Land' and Galilee in the twentieth century

Setting the Agenda
Nineteenth-Century: Galilee, Geography, and Nationalism

Colonialism and the Creation of the Holy Land
The political, economic and religious history of nineteenth-century European expansion into the Near East was important for the construction of

Palestine in historical Jesus research. Thus, the picture of Palestine and Galilee was shaped by the cultural and intellectual categories of this period of colonialism (Ben-Arieh 1989). It started with Napoleon's unsuccessful military expedition to Egypt, which was accompanied by a large scientific expedition. This became the beginning of a military and scholarly competition for influence in the Ottoman Empire throughout the nineteenth century—mainly between England and France, but with Germany, Russia and other European powers also playing a role. This competition extended to Palestine, which became the destination for innumerable visitors, scholars and also modern pilgrims. Many of these visits resulted in eyewitness reports, as well as in scientific, especially geographical, studies that were often carried out by scholars as part of or in conjunction with military expeditions. That was true of the first French surveys following in the steps of Napoleon I as well as Ernest Renan's archaeological expedition under the reign of Napoleon III (Gavish 1994). Officers from the Royal Engineers did the surveys undertaken by the British Palestine Exploration Fund (PEF).

This was not a mere coincidence, but corresponded to a mentality about the relations between the great European powers and the region. This mentality was summed up in one of the PEF publications: 'The Ordnance Survey of Palestine was so obvious a duty for the English nation to undertake, that it is needless to dwell on its importance' (Stanley 1871: xxii). This comment could be read as an illustration of how the maps and descriptions of Palestine made it a familiar place to the English, so to speak naturalized it as an English place. But the statement could also be given a less benign and a more colonizing interpretation. It illustrates the points made by David Ley and James Duncan regarding a drawing by Joanne Sharp titled *Topographical Survey*, which juxtaposes a surveyed area with the cartographer's large eye. Topography claims to be an objective science, but it is actually a 'science of domination', and the surveyor has the power of observation. 'In practice', moreover, 'it is usually a white, male elite, Eurocentric observer who orders the world he looks upon, one whose observations and classifications provide the rules of representation, of inclusion and exclusion, of precedent and antecedent, of inferior and superior' (Duncan and Ley 1993: 2). Thus, we might say that to undertake the survey of Palestine was a colonizing effort to make it a part of England, emphasizing the importance of Palestine as the Holy Land for the English nation. Surveillance and map making went hand in hand with collecting Near Eastern antiquities, proudly displayed in the major museums of European capitals as symbols of the continuity between these nations and the great nations of the past (Silberman 1997: 105). Yet even if Palestine did not have a memorable past as a great power in the same way as Egypt, because it was the scene of biblical history and especially the life of Jesus, it still had a very important role.

The main interest behind many of the descriptions of Palestine was to provide background information for Western readers of the Bible. As a result the authors' interest was primarily historical, and the present inhabitants and their conditions hardly entered into the picture—at least not in a positive way. The region was part of the declining Ottoman Empire and was divided into various administrative subregions. But these divisions were of no interest to Western visitors, who were interested in Palestine as the 'Holy Land' and who based their picture of the land on their readings of the Bible. Since the 'Holy Land' did not correspond to any political or administrative region, there were no agreed-upon, fixed borders. However, there was widespread agreement about what were the central parts of the 'Holy Land' (Ben-Arieh 1989: 71). A comparison of various nineteenth-century sources shows that the areas could be ranked according to degrees of holiness: Jerusalem was the most holy, then followed the core areas of Judea, Samaria and Galilee, that is, Western Palestine. Eastern Palestine, the area on the eastern side of the Jordan and the Negev, was considered secondary in holiness.

Geography and Character
Within this constructed Holy Land, after Jerusalem, Galilee held a special place. This is summed up by the British cartographer Captain Wilson in his introduction to the survey of the Sea of Galilee: 'With the exception of Jerusalem, there is no place in Palestine which excites deeper interest than that lake district in which our Lord passed so large a portion of the last three years of his life, and in which he performed so many of his mighty works.' But it was not easy to describe this place in light of expectations of its uniqueness:

> What is the Sea of Galilee like? Is one of the first questions a traveller is asked on his return from the Holy Land, and a question which he finds it extremely difficult to answer satisfactorily. Some authors describe its beauties in glowing terms, whilst others assert that the scenery is tame and uninteresting; neither perhaps quite correct, though perhaps representing the impression produced at the time on the writer's mind (Wilson 1871: 337).

This is an interesting observation, because it seems to question one of the main presuppositions of human geography until the middle of last century: that descriptive fieldwork, based on observation, could give an accurate understanding of the area under study (Duncan and Ley 1993: 2). Instead, Wilson appears to represent a different approach to representation, where there is no 'objective' truth underneath. He appears to point towards a hermeneutical approach in which the interpreter is engaged with the data in an act of interpretation. Here the uniqueness of the place, for the visitor, is attributed to its role as the place where Jesus lived and worked. It is because *he* is unique that the place becomes so interesting.

The observations by Wilson on 'the lake district' shows what first caught the interest of the visitor: the geography of the Galilee: what it looked like and its relationship to Jesus' life and activities. Thus, we shall ask: how did the nineteenth-century authors conceive of the relations between geography and human life, landscape and character? They perceived that there was a close relationship between place as nature, landscape, geography and the human situation, in particular the human mind (Ben-Arieh 1989: 76-77). This becomes visible especially in Renan's 1863 work *La vie de Jésus*. The way in which Renan makes place, the Galilean countryside, into gospel, is quite extraordinary in its explicit expression of a position that in a weaker form was shared by many scholars of historical geography. Historical geography combined many elements that played a part in the general cultural climate in the middle and later part of the nineteenth century. Social biology, philology and ethnography shared a set of presuppositions about the interdependence between race, nature and character. It was taken for granted that nature and landscape made an impression on the character of an individual.

Renan is explicit about the role of geography; he finds in the landscape of Galilee nothing less than a 'fifth gospel'. But he also comments on the present state of the area, which he sees as desolate and disappointing; this makes him describe Galilee as a gospel that is 'torn, but still legible'. Renan presents himself, then, as a person who is able to read this landscape. His descriptions of Jesus in Galilee are now perhaps best known through Albert Schweitzer's (1998: 181-82) scathing criticism of his romantic pictures of a sun-drenched Galilee peopled by Jesus and his happy group of disciples. The main theme that runs through these descriptions is the correspondence between nature and the people in Galilee (Renan 1927: 85-86). When Renan describes Nazareth, it is as a representation of the ideal state: 'Even in our times Nazareth is still a delightful abode, the only place, perhaps, in Palestine in which the mind feels itself relieved from the burden which oppresses it in this unequalled desolation.' Nazareth was an exceptional place in that it had escaped the contemporary desolation and showed the same correspondence between charming environment and a happy population that characterized its situation in antiquity. Thus, Renan could conclude: 'The people are amiable and cheerful, the gardens fresh and green.' In a way, the Nazareth of the present was living in an idealized past.

There is a statement that encapsulates Renan's view on the ideal relations between nature and populations: 'The environs, moreover, are charming and no place in the world was so well adapted for dreams of perfect happiness.' He elaborates on that in the following section on the view from the mountains overlooking Nazareth, concluding with the observation that 'such was the horizon of Jesus'. Renan's interpretation of this scene of natural grandeur and beauty as well as of historical reminiscences is that these mountains formed an 'enchanted circle'. To this circle, moreover, is attributed a new meaning: it is the 'cradle of the kingdom of God'. Here description and interpretation are mixed, and the movement from 'enchanted circle' to 'cradle of the kingdom of God' is so swift that it appears obvious—natural—that this meaning should be attached to the scene that Renan draws up before his readers with the authority of 'us' who have seen it. He concludes that this 'was for years his [i.e. Jesus'] world'. Thus, on the basis of his belief in a correspondence between nature and the character of the inhabitants, Renan has established a unity between Jesus and the nature of Galilee.

This type of picture of Galilee was not just a romantic idea of Renan. In his famous *Historical Geography of the Holy Land,* the Scottish theologian and geographer George Adam Smith draws a broad picture of the benefits of combining a vision of the land as a whole and its history (Butlin 1988). He thinks that students can

> discover from the 'lie of the land' why the history took certain lines and the prophecy and the gospel were expressed in certain styles—to learn what geography has to contribute to questions of Biblical criticism—above all, to discern between what physical nature contributed to the religious development of Israel, and what was the product of purely moral and spiritual forces (G.A. Smith 1910: ix).

Smith (1910: 420-22) sees similar parallels between the landscape of Galilee and its inhabitants. In speaking of the luxurious vegetation of Upper Galilee he finds a relationship of cause and effect: 'To so generous a land the inhabitants, during that part of her history which concerns us, responded with energy.' In other instances he sees parallels, as when he describes 'one another national feature of Galilee', viz. its volcanic extrusions into the limestone massive of mountains, sulphur springs and a history of earthquakes. Smith proceeds: 'The nature of the people was also volcanic. Josephus describes them as "ever fond of innovations, and by nature disposed to changes, and delighting in seditions." They had an ill name for quarrelling.' Smith adds a whole range of examples from the Gospels, the First Testament and the Talmud to bring home his point, how human nature corresponds to nature. The Galileans showed real manhood; they were 'a chivalrous and gallant race', they were sincere, anxious for honor more than for money, and so on. We may find in this list more a reflection of Victorian masculine ideals than of Galilean nature, but Smith confidently draws the conclusion: 'For this cause also our Lord chose His friends from the people, and it was not a Galilean who betrayed him.'

Thus, the idea of a causal relationship between geography and the psychological character of the inhabitants was typical of the nineteenth century. This idea was shared by Joseph Klausner (1989: 229-38) in the first part of the twentieth century in one of the earliest Jewish studies of the historical Jesus. For him, it was particularly the view from Nazareth that was important, with a range of mountains that was awe-inspiring. At the

same time they cut Nazareth off from the world and formed a perfect setting for dreams and visions, so that Jesus became a dreamer and a visionary.
In modern time the relation between geography and identity is found in a
modified way in Sean Freyne (1980a), based on relations between geography and the nature of communities.

Galilee and Nationality
When Renan and Smith drew their pictures of the nature of Galilee and the
character of the Galileans, they were implicitly or explicitly contrasting
them with their images of Jerusalem and Judea. It is important, therefore,
to consider how they conceived of this larger area at the time of Jesus.
What were the categories that nineteenth-century scholars used to describe
Galilee? I shall look at two different nineteenth-century approaches to the
question of the uniqueness of Galilee. Friedrich Schleiermacher gave his
lectures on the life of Jesus in the first part of this century, while David
Friedrich Strauss wrote his later work on Jesus 'for the German people'
in 1864.

Schleiermacher gave his lectures on Jesus in the aftermath of the Napo-
leonic wars in Europe. His remarks on Galilee should be read against his
own endeavors at the time to develop democratic ideas of a German nation
and a German people amid a situation of conservative, autocratic rule by
kings and princes (Dawson 1966). Schleiermacher denies any special relationship between Galilee and Jesus. This is partly because he follows the
chronology and outline of John's Gospel, but I think there are also other
presuppositions that have to do with his notions about country, people and
nation. It is in the context of Jesus' mission to proclaim the Kingdom of God
that he discusses his relations to various localities:

> If we now take a look at all the local relationships and ask how the public
> life of Jesus was related to the totality of the Jewish country, since he
> himself considered his vocation as limited to Palestine, this is the way
> things appear: Judea was a Roman province and other parts of the country
> were sometimes under various members of the Herodian family and some-
> times united, but the terms that were in common use were Judea, Galilee,
> Samaria and Perea. If we now have to say that Christ thought of himself
> as called to proclaim the kingdom of God and to establish it among his
> people [*Volk*] by that proclamation, this fact explains why he put himself
> as much as possible into contact with them.

After describing how Jesus chose two strategies, of remaining in Jerusalem where people from all over the country could come and meet him, and
of visiting other parts of the country, he concludes: 'We see, then, that Christ
neglected no part of the Jewish land [*das jüdische Land*], and excluded no
part of it from the scene of his personal ministry' (Schleiermacher 1975:
172, 173).

Schleiermacher shows that he is aware of the forms of rule that existed in Palestine at the time of Jesus. They were Roman provinces and personal princedoms over shifting areas (like Germany), but these are not important to him. He recognizes various regions, according to 'common use', but what was most important to him was 'the totality of the Jewish land' and 'his people'. These are entities that are difficult to define clearly: there are no fixed borders, and there are also Jews outside the land, but it is the idea of a Jewish people in a Jewish land, regardless of political divisions, that is introduced. Moreover, Schleiermacher also speaks highly of national interests. This subject is so important to him that he portrays Jesus as avoiding conflicts with the Pharisees and the Sadducees because he shared with these groups a common concern for the nation. I think that we can read here reflections of Schleiermacher's attempts to argue for the existence of a '*Volk*' as the basis for the nation and for the state, instead of an ideology built around a sovereign monarch who ruled over the people. In this structure, with Jesus as a teacher for the totality of the Jewish land, there is no room for a special relationship between Jesus and Galilee. Galilee is part of the Jewish land and Jewish '*Volk*.'

In Schleiermacher's construction of national unity there is no room for a uniqueness of Galilee. That, however, we find in D.F. Strauss and his revision of his *Life of Jesus* (1835). The English title, A *New Life of Jesus* (1879), does not convey the double meaning of the German original: *Das Leben Jesu für das deutsche Volk bearbeitet* (1864), that is, a Life of Jesus 'revised for the German people'. The introduction shows that Strauss did not intend this merely as a popular version; he meant explicitly 'the German people'. The critical spirit of the life of Jesus research was in direct continuation with the spirit of the Reformation, which was a characteristic representation of the identity of the German people. Strauss saw himself therefore in opposition both to Catholic southern Germany and to state and church bureaucracy. In consequence, his description of Palestine is different from that of Schleiermacher, not only because he uses the Synoptic Gospels for his outline of the life of Jesus, with a focus on his Galilean ministry. Strauss does not use terms such as 'Jewish land', but a vocabulary of political geography. The regions of Palestine are described explicitly in their relations to Rome, with Jerusalem and Judea under direct Roman administration. Galilee is the main scene for Jesus' ministry, while he avoids Judea and Jerusalem, which are under Roman administration. Strauss presents the scene not as one of national unity but as one of contrast between Galilee and Jerusalem, and with the presence of the Roman Empire always in view (Strauss 1879: 334).

Strauss presents Jerusalem as a picture of the 'Other', in utterly negative terms: 'There the Pharisaic party ruled over a population readily excitable to fanaticism, there the spirit of formalism in religion, the attachment to sacrifices and purifications, had its hold in the numerous priesthood, the splendid temple and its solemn sacrifices' (Strauss 1879: 345). Strauss here employs stereotypes that were prevalent in contemporary Christian studies of the Pharisees and Jewish religion. These stereotypes were employed also in inter-Christian conflicts, particularly in Protestant accusations against the Catholic church. Galilee, of course, represented the opposite of this; it was above all characterized by an open mind. To explain this, Strauss points to three elements: the population was mixed with Gentiles, Galilee was far away from Judea, and the Galileans, despised by the Judeans, were not granted full privileges as Jews. Here enters the idea of uniqueness ascribed to Galilee. The uniqueness of Jesus' speech is ascribed to his background in Galilee, very different from the dry school traditions of the Pharisees. Strauss lists most of the characteristics of the uniqueness of Galilee that are found also in later scholarship: the negative attitude of the Jerusalem elite (and maybe also the non-elite), their remote location and, above all the mixed ethnic composition of the population. Since this last aspect has come to play a significant role, it is time to look more closely at the role that ethnicity and race played in discussions of identity in the nineteenth century.

Race and Ethnicity
With the argument that a mixed population was a positive sign of uniqueness, Strauss shows how important issues of ethnicity and race were for identity and character in the nineteenth century. It may seem strange that a 'mixed race' should be regarded as more positive than a pure race, but this widely held notion frequently appears in discussions of nationality. It appears to be an argument from biology that has been transferred to humans. Especially in his last work, *The Old Faith and the New* (originally published in German in 1872), in which he returns to the question of 'mixed races', Strauss is influenced by Charles Darwin. Darwin argued that it was 'hybrid vigour', not racial purity, that was the key to success. Darwin held this as an explanation of the European colonial expansion (Christie 1998: 37). Strauss explains the success of the large European nations in the same way. In the English, French and German nations, old Celtic, Teutonic and other elements have blended into a new formation, the present nationality. This proves that purity of race is no advantage.

The question of ethnic and racial identity was raised in particular in the context of German 'Volks-ideology', which prepared the way for the later Nazi ideology. Of particular relevance were Paul de Lagarde and H.S. Chamberlain. Lagarde, an ardent critic of his contemporary German Protestant church, argued for a Germanized religion, with ideas that later inspired *Deutsche Christen*. He was especially concerned to divorce Christianity from Judaism, as he held that Christianity was distorted by Jewish ideas, introduced from the start by the apostle Paul. Therefore, part of the solution was a return to Jesus, whom Lagarde distanced from Judaism: Jesus grew up in the mountain country of Galilee, distant from the center of Judaism, and his 'inner being' was formed in conflict with the Judaism of his time (Lagarde 1878: 229-30). A central piece in this argument was the contention that Galilee in fact was not Jewish—that it distinguished itself not only by geographical and religious distance from Jerusalem but also by a different ethnic composition. This last proposition was part of a discussion of what happened after the capture of Galilee in 732 BCE when the region became an Assyrian province. Did the Assyrians settle other ethnic groups in Galilee at that time? This discussion was well known among historians and biblical scholars, but it assumed a new importance when the question of the ethnic composition of Galilee was made into a matter of Jewish identity and the identity of Jesus. The argument from Strauss about mixed population re-enters, but the consequences that Lagarde draws are more drastic.

Houston S. Chamberlain, the English-born son-in-law of Richard Wagner, was influenced by Lagarde. For Chamberlain (1899: 189-260), too, it was the historical Jesus in contrast to the developments of the later church that was his main interest. And more than Lagarde, he explicitly discussed the character of Galilee and its people. History had shown that the population of Galilee was a mixture. Even if the people of Galilee might be observant Jews, that does not give proof of their descent; religion is not the same as race. Moreover, Galileans had a different national character from other Palestinians, they were energetic, idealistic 'men of action' who stood up against the Romans, not like the Jews who accommodated to Roman rule. However, the determining factor was race according to biology. Chamberlain here relied on the new science of anatomical anthropology and on racial theories that were now becoming popular, incorporating social Darwinism and 'survival of the fittest' (Mosse 1964: 92-93).

The ultimate purpose of the discussion of Galilee is of course to distance Jesus from Judaism of his day: Chamberlain holds that Jesus as a Galilean did not have a drop of Jewish blood—he did not belong to the Jewish race, characterized by purity, whereas Galilee was a mixed area. Moreover, although Jesus was a Jew by education, he did not have anything in common with Judaism.

The ideological presupposition in asking about 'blood', that is, the emphasis on the ethnic aspect of identity, is thrown into relief by a comparison with Ernest Renan's discussion of Jesus and Galilee. In terms of his observations, there are many similarities between the discussions in Strauss, Lagarde, Chamberlain and Renan. Renan, too, remarks that the population of Galilee was very mixed, and that the province had many inhabitants who were not Jews, but Phoenicians, Syrians, Arabs and even Greeks. He likewise remarks that conversions to Judaism were not rare. But the inference he draws seems almost designed to counter the growing interest in race and ethnicity in the nineteenth century: 'It is therefore impossible to raise here any question of race, and to seek to ascertain what blood flowed in the veins of him who has contributed most to efface the distinction of blood in humanity' (Renan 1927: 83). Before we eulogize Renan too enthusiastically however we should notice that he too spoke about Jews as a race, and that was not a positive characterization. But especially in his famous 1884 lecture 'What Is a Nation?' (Christie 1998: 39-47) we should notice two very different concepts of 'nation' within Europe, most markedly contrasted in France and Germany. The German concept was based on ethnicity, race and language, while the French was based on democratic participation.

The Heritage of the Nineteenth Century
What was the heritage of the nineteenth century so far as the description of Galilee was concerned? In terms of Galilee as part of the Holy land, we notice how the very concept of 'Holy Land' was part of a colonizing attitude from Western—that is, European—powers, especially England and France. Described and disguised as a religious right to the land of Jesus, a Holy land as a special privilege for Christians, it was part of a political attempt by European powers to establish a sphere of influence in the Middle East when the Ottoman empire was in decline. Pious pilgrimage and political power thus belonged together and continued to be so even more in the twentieth century.

Likewise, the explanatory force of geography that was established in the nineteenth century continued to play a role. To nineteenth-century historians and geographers the geographical characteristics as well as the location of Galilee influenced human factors such as beliefs, language and disposition towards 'others'. For Strauss and Renan it was important that Galilee was a border area between a predominantly Jewish area and areas with Gentile populations. This made for easy contacts with non-Jews and created an openness towards others, or, in Strauss's term, an open mind in religious matters as well. This view was based on the presupposition of the mimetic role of geography that was common until the last part of the twentieth century. This 'mimetic role' suggested that it was possible to reach a description of geography that gave a true representation of the essence of the place.

When nationality and the nation-state emerged in nineteenth-century Europe as references for identity, they became important for images of the Holy Land and Galilee as well. In this regard, Schleiermacher and Strauss represent two different descriptions of Galilee. For Schleiermacher, Jewish 'people', 'land' and 'nation' are the important categories of identity. Political and regional differences are not so important, and Galilee remains part of this larger entity. It seems as if national and religious identity are so similar that they cannot be distinguished. Since Jesus' ministry is directed to the people as a totality, there is no special relation to Galilee. From Schleiermacher's work we may draw the conclusion that if the main concern is to argue for the unity of a Jewish nation, the special character of Galilee will be downplayed.

Schleiermacher's concern with 'country', 'people' and 'nation' is characteristic of the nineteenth century. The nation as state was one of the most common assumptions of nineteenth-century Europe (Mosse 1988: 65-100; Woolf 1996: 1-39), but with different configurations in different regions or countries. It took on a special significance in Germany (with the association with '*Volk*') and later for the ideology of Nazi Germany (Mosse 1964). Of special importance for Palestine was the role that the idea of the nation had for Zionism, which was strongly influenced by European nationalism in the nineteenth century (Christie 1998: 165-94). The engagement of European powers in the Near East was also part of their own national endeavors, and it happened in a period when the idea of the nation-state became stronger.

For Strauss, on the other hand, the picture was one not of unity but of conflict and contrasts not only between Jesus and the leadership in Jerusalem but also between Jerusalem and Galilee and their respective inhabitants. Strauss saw the contrast explicitly as one of religious attitudes—in short, between fanaticism and liberal openness. It is this picture of the Jewish milieu that has dominated Christian scholarship on the historical Jesus for more than a hundred years after Strauss. Moreover, it has become a paradigm within which to interpret many other conflicts, not only between Jews and Christians but also between Roman Catholic and Protestants. Thus, there has been a mutually reinforcing relationship between historical studies of Jesus and contemporary religious and cultural conflicts. Both are based on descriptions characterized by dichotomies that have been regarded as 'natural' or 'given', and therefore not questioned.

Towards the latter part of the nineteenth century, ethnicity and race made up a very popular area of research in human biology, anthropology, and so on. Great explanatory power was ascribed to it regarding both animal and human characteristics. This added a new twist to the question of nationality: it could be used to make divisions within a population. Strauss and Renan, for instance, used the 'mixed' ethnic character of Galilee to explain characteristics of the population, something that set them apart and made them superior to others, viz. the Judeans and Jerusalemites. However, they did not focus so strongly on race as Chamberlain did. He used race as a category in a study of Galilee, to distinguish privileged people (Aryans) from degenerate ones (Jews). Obviously, this was a distinction with clear implications for debates in contemporary Germany.

Thus, we can say that the descriptions of Galilee in the nineteenth century were formed by the major cultural paradigms of European societies of the time. It is time to ask what happened to these paradigms in the twentieth century. What changes took place in descriptions of Galilee, and thereby also in the relations between Jesus and Galilee?

Galilee in Twentieth-Century Interpretation

Extreme Nationalism

In the first part of the twentieth century, there was less interest in the historical Jesus, and consequently less interest in Galilee as well. But there was one question that received intense, if limited, interest. Specifically in Nazi Germany, special attention was paid to the question of the race and identity of the Galileans, which had been raised by Lagarde and Chamberlain. German Second Testament scholars elaborated the non-Jewish character of Galilee in a number of studies in the 1930s and 1940s. Walter Grundmann's book *Jesus der Galiläer und das Judentum* (1941) was introduced as a response to the question of the relationship of Jesus to Judaism that, according to the author, was of burning concern for the German people. Grundmann argued that the 'Jewish danger' was so great that the need to defend oneself against Judaism in all aspects of life became vital. Grundmann struggled with the facts of the historical origin of Jesus. It was the Jewishness of Jesus that caused the problem. Grundmann therefore reformulated the question of the relationship of the German church to the historical origin of Jesus in terms of place: the loyalty of Christians is not to Judaism but to the historical space of Jesus, to Palestine as his place of origin.

Given Grundmann's ideological warfare against Judaism, it became imperative to find a part of Palestine that was *not* identified with Judaism. Galilee provided the answer. Grundmann's first point was to establish the religious identity of Galilee (1941: 81-90). It had two major components: a small, radical Judaism represented by the Zealots, and the larger group, the *am-haaretz*, the 'common people', whose syncretistic beliefs were represented in the Enoch literature. Second, and more important, was the question of the ethnic identity of the Galileans and of Jesus (Grundmann 1941: 165-74). Grundmann argued that Galilee at the time of the Maccabean revolt had a mixed population. The judaization that followed under the Maccabeans was a forced measure, with the result that the Galileans might belong to the Jewish confession, without being ethnically Jewish.

Grundmann concludes that Jesus' Galilean origin was secure, but most likely he was not an ethnic Jew. Rather, he belonged to some of the other ethnic groups in Galilee. Like most Galileans, he belonged to the Jewish confession, but he had utterly broken with Judaism. Grundmann holds that the structure of Jesus' thoughts brought him closer to the Greeks than to the Jews. He ends his discussion of the ethnic background of Jesus by saying that it is not possible to reach a positive conclusion as to Jesus' identity, since we find traces of both 'non-Aryan and Aryan peoples' in the population of Galilee (Grundmann 1941: 200). Since Jesus could not have been a Jew in terms of his spirituality, most likely he was not a Jew 'by blood' either (Grundmann 1941: 205).

Here surfaces once more the nineteenth-century concern with 'blood' as the basis for ethnic identity. In addition to 'blood', culture was regarded as an important aspect of identity. Grundmann emphasizes the heavy Hellenistic influence in Galilee, for example, in terms of Hellenistic philosophy, architecture and art. This influence was partly conveyed through the Decapolis cities, but also by the Hellenistic inhabitants of Sepphoris and Tiberias. The ideological context of Grundmann's discussion is obvious. Ethnic identity is expressed in terms of 'Blut und Boden' ('blood and soil'), and Galilee is characterized by an ethnically non-Jewish diversity that corresponds to a Hellenistic cultural identity. The Jewish confession is only a layer that was superimposed by oppressors. Thus, Galilee is viewed primarily in terms of the ethnic composition of its inhabitants. It is also seen in terms of its cultural diversity, represented by Hellenistic dominance, in contrast to Jewish legalism and Jewish ethnicity.

Obviously, it was the political situation in Nazi Germany that governed this construction of Galilee. Galilee became a part of Palestine with which Germans could identify. It became, if not quite a 'little Germany', at least a place where there were enough Aryans to make Jesus a plausible non-Jew. This attempt by Grundmann represented the end of the construction of Jesus' Galilean identity in terms of race. That question was totally discredited after the Second World War, and Jesus' relation to Galilee became a taboo in German biblical scholarship. Even if there is still a discussion of whether there was a continuity of (Jewish) population in Galilee or an influx of new settlers (see, e.g., Freyne 1997: 53), the question (and its relevance for the identity of Jesus) is no longer phrased in terms of race or ethnicity.

In contrast to its extreme anti-Jewish attitude, but in a certain way also parallel to the nationalism of German scholars, the first major monograph on Jesus by a Jewish scholar in the twentieth century presented a Zionist nationalism. It was written by Joseph Klausner, who was born in Lithuania but became an eager Zionist and moved to Palestine, which was at the time a British protectorate. The book was written in Hebrew in 1922 and translated into several languages; the English translation, published in 1925, is entitled *Jesus of Nazareth: His Life, Times and Teaching*. Klausner claims that Jesus was fully part of Judaism of his time and has a description of his background in Galilee that is totally different from that of Chamberlain and Grundmann. Granting that there were many non-Jews in Galilee, Klausner claims that they did not in the least influence Jesus. Galilee was a center of Jewish observance of the Law, and Jesus represented the Pharisaic Judaism of his time that was loyal to the Holy Scriptures. Klausner claimed that Jesus obeyed the Torah as well as the ritual laws until the end of his life. Thus, Klausner found Galilee to be a center of Pharisaic piety. This is probably a result of Klausner's view of 'normative' Judaism, which seems to have been strongly influenced by his Zionist ideology. As a result, he saw Judaism above all as a religion for a people, a nation, and the scribes and Pharisees were carriers of the idea of a Jewish state. On the basis of this picture of Judaism, Klausner found Jesus wanting: his individualism represented an absolute break with the collectivism of Klausner's Judaism. Thus, Klausner's evaluation of Jesus as a Jew is extremely ambivalent: he is a Jew, but he does not conform to a Zionist ideology. Klausner's Jesus, moreover, also represents a reading of him with a consciously nationalistic ideology. Many of the positions that Klausner held became standard among later Jewish studies of Jesus, especially his emphasis on the 'Jewishness' of Jesus. His negative reading of Jesus within a Zionist version of Judaism does not seem to have been followed up in the same way. Another influential Jewish study of Jesus, Geza Vermes's *Jesus the Jew* (1973) explicitly reads the Judaism of Jesus much more in individualistic categories.

Jesus against Judaism: The Disappearance
of Galilee in the Second Quest
The New Quest continued the trend of distancing Jesus from Judaism, but the distancing was done now in ideological rather than in ethnic terms. Therefore, there was little interest in specific social, cultural or regional aspects of Judaism in Palestine. It was quite exceptional that Nils A. Dahl, in his 1953 argument for a new quest, said that more knowledge about Judaism in Palestine at the time was one of the most important sources for the history of Jesus (Dahl 1953: 96). This suggestion anticipated the contribution of Qumran studies to a picture of a much more multiform Judaism than had been known before. But the picture of Judaism in this period remained above all the religious system and the various religious groups, such as Pharisees, Sadducees and Essenes. The interest in 'Jesus the Jew' was more directed toward the general traits of Judaism, attitudes toward the Law, the temple, and so on, than etc., than toward specific locations.

A typical example is Günther Bornkamm's *Jesus von Nazareth*. In a discussion of 'Period and Environment', Bornkamm writes about the Jewish people, Jewish religion and groups and movements, but not regions, locations or social issues. Galilee is presented as an area with a mixed race. Rejecting the Aryan hypothesis (Bornkamm 1960: 53), Bornkamm places Jesus in the Jewish part of the community, and it is only this Jewish community that comes into view. Moreover, Bornkamm places Galilee squarely within the bounds of Judaism. Galilee had no religious peculiarities; it was only the distance from the temple that made synagogues into the religious centers, and this distance also made it easier for religious movements to develop (Bornkamm 1960: 42). In cultural terms, Bornkamm holds that Jesus showed no trace of Greek influence, nor were any of his activities located in Hellenistic towns. Thus, Jesus is identified as a Jew, fully part of a Jewish community in Galilee, which itself was an integral part of Judaism at the time.

Between the Quests: Is there a Galilean Judaism?
Geza Vermes and E.P. Sanders
The division of studies of the historical Jesus into various quests is only provisional and does not create absolute boundaries or categories. For instance, Jewish studies of Jesus are not easily put within the framework of the three quests. They do not share the specific presuppositions, often of a Christian and theological type, that underlie these quests and that aim at placing Jesus within a specifically Christian trajectory. On the contrary, as is to be expected, these studies emphasize those elements that place Jesus within a Jewish context. That is true of the first major study of Jesus by an Israeli scholar in this period, David Flusser's 1968 work *Jesus*. Flusser is primarily concerned with Judaism as a religious system. He gives a picture of Galilee that is close to Klausner's, but without his aggressive Zionism. Flusser emphasizes that Galilee is the main geographical setting for Jesus' activities, but the region does not enter with distinctive religious character-istics in his discussion of Jesus' relations to, for example, John the Baptist, the Law or ethics.

The works of Geza Vermes, who consciously locates Jesus in Galilee as a region with specific characteristics, thus represent a new beginning of interest in Galilee. Vermes's goal in *Jesus the Jew* is 'to fit Jesus and his movement into the greater context of first century Palestine'. When he poses the question of which aspects of Palestinian history and religion are most relevant, he focuses on the need to fill in Jesus' 'natural background, first century Galilee', and he speaks specifically of a 'Galilean Judaism of his day' (Vermes 1973: 43). Vermes builds his picture of Galilee primarily on the descriptions in Josephus and in the Gospels. He finds in Galilee a special religious identity based partly on the fact that the province was an autonomous, self-contained politico-ethnic unit, different from Judea. Gali-lee was also wealthy, but at the same time people led simple lives, more concerned with honor and pride than wealth. Vermes finds that the picture of Jesus in the Gospels conforms to the specifically Galilean type: Jesus was 'at home among the simple people of rural Galilee', where he had a following. Vermes does not see Jesus as a revolutionary, concluding instead that his popular following made him look like a potential rebel to the politi-cal authorities. He also represented a challenge to the established religious order. Vermes emphasizes Jesus' role as an exorcist and healer and places him in a charismatic Judaism that he associates with Galilee, in contrast to halakhic Judaism that became the cornerstone of rabbinic Judaism. Combining socioeconomic and religious factors in his picture of Jesus' Galilean background, Vermes therefore finds a specific Galilean regional identity.

Vermes continues a perspective that was launched by Klausner in 1925, and at the same time in a study of Jesus and Galilee by the German scholar Walter Bauer. The conclusions are, however, quite different: whereas Bauer and later Grundmann drew the conclusion that since Jesus was a Galilean, he was not a Jew, Klausner and later Vermes used the Galilean context to explain what sort of a Jew Jesus was. In contrast to Bauer and Grundmann, Vermes has a much broader concept of Judaism. His more recent picture of the complexity and plurality of Judaism makes it easier to defend the assertion that Jesus was a Jew.

Vermes's focus on Galilee and a specifically Galilean Judaism was not followed up by E.P. Sanders. More than any other Christian First Testament scholar in the present generation, Sanders has contributed to a new understanding of ancient Judaism. Protesting strongly against the negative picture of Judaism and the dichotomy that characterized many of the second-quest studies, Sanders has successfully established a much more positive picture with his *Jesus and Judaism* (1985). In contrast to the 'second questers', he understands himself as a historian, not a theologian. However, in many ways he continues the tendency in the second quest to focus on Judaism primarily as 'religion'. In consequence, he does not pay much attention to Jesus' Galilean context. Sanders mentions that Jesus was 'a Galilean who preached and healed' as one of the 'facts' about him (Sanders 1985: 11), but he does not have a section on Galilee, and not even a reference in the index. Thus, for Sanders, it is possible to write a book about the historical Jesus and his relations to Judaism without broaching the question of whether his Galilean background contributes to our understanding of who Jesus was as a preacher and healer.

Sanders concludes his book by saying, 'We have also situated Jesus believably in first-century Judaism' (Sanders 1985: 335). But 'situated' refers not to place but rather to Judaism as a system of religious beliefs. Important aspects of this system are Jewish restoration eschatology and covenantal nomism (a central category in Sanders's major reconstruction of Jewish beliefs in *Paul and Palestinian Judaism*), which Sanders regards as the common denominator underlying all varieties of Judaism. So, 'place' in the geographic sense does not play an important part in Sanders's description of Jewish identity. Parallel to Sanders's contextualization of Paul in a Palestinian Judaism, Jesus is situated in Judaism not as a geographical context but as a theological one. Thus, it is not surprising that Galilee blends into Judaism. The peasants of Galilean villages are law-abiding Jews, and Galilee is an example of 'the same' in terms of Jewishness.

In some later studies, notably in the more popular book *The Histori-cal Figure of Jesus* (1993a), Sanders has discussed the situation in Galilee, prompted by the positions of scholars such as Burton L. Mack (1988), John Dominic Crossan (1991), Howard Clark Kee (1992) and Richard A. Hors-ley (1997), all of which he rejects. Sanders minimizes the presence and influence of Gentiles in Galilee; he says that 'Antipas' Galilee was mostly Jewish' and that Jesus probably had little contact with the cities of Galilee, so that 'the world Jesus knew was that of the small towns and villages of Galilee' (1993a: 76-77). He rejects the idea that there was a strong influ-ence of Hellenistic culture and Roman politics in Galilee, as well as an economic oppression of the peasant population by the elite. Thus, Sanders does consider the social, cultural, and economic situation of Galilee, but mostly in criticism of other positions in which they play an integral part (1993a: 20-22, 101-107; 1993b). Although he does recognize some differ-ences between Galilee and Judea, they appear to be of little consequence for the historical reconstruction of Judaism and of Jesus. Thus, it is Jesus' relationship to the temple that is Sanders's starting point for his description of Jesus.

In terms of the heritage from the nineteenth century, Sanders has decid-edly broken with the tradition from Strauss, with its dichotomy between Judaism and Christianity, between 'law' and 'faith', and so on. This dichot-omy often implied that there was also a split within Judaism, a contrast between Galilee and Jerusalem, and between the Galilean Jesus and the leadership in Jerusalem. In some ways Sanders's position shows similarities to that of Schleiermacher: national unity was more important than regional differences. In Sanders's conception, the national characteristic is expressed as 'religion', Judaism is the common factor, and the regions, like Galilee, are not important in this regard.

THE ROAD TO REIMARUS: ORIGINS OF THE QUEST FOR THE HISTORICAL JESUS

Jonathan C.P. Birch

Introduction

As the essays in this collection show, modern scholars attempting to illuminate the historical Jesus and primitive Christianity have often sought to reconstruct both the physical space and social contexts of first-century Palestine, particularly Galilee, in order to situate Jesus within what historians have taken to be his most appropriate cultural setting. The project of reconstructing the land and the social dynamics of first-century Palestine flourished in the nineteenth-century study of Jesus and Christian origins, and it is once again central to research in the field. But what was the catalyst for the historical study of Jesus himself?

The classic account of the origins and first phase of historical Jesus studies is Albert Schweitzer's *Quest of the Historical Jesus*,[1] in which the German philosopher and expert in Oriental languages Herman Samuel Reimarus (1694–1768) emerges, out of nowhere, as the great innovator in this research tradition. On Schweitzer's account, before Reimarus 'there had been nothing to indicate to the world what a masterstroke the spirit of the time was preparing. . . Before Reimarus, no one had attempted to form a historical conception of the life of Jesus' (Schweitzer 1911: 13). Reimarus's then shocking thesis that Jesus was a failed political claimant whose defeat was turned into a spiritual victory by the apostles after his appalling death, provided sustenance for the formidable tradition of German New Testament criticism emerging in the late eighteenth century, and it continues to be

---

1. The 'quest for the historical Jesus', as used in the title of this essay, is one of a number of similar phrases, all inspired by the title of the English edition of Albert Schweitzer's *Von Reimarus zu Wrede: Eine Geschichte der Leben-Jesu-Forschung* (1906). This is a wonderful illustration of the creative force of translation: a more literal rendering of the German title would read, 'From Reimarus to Wrede: A History of the Life of Jesus Research'—not nearly as suggestive as the actual translation: *The Quest of the Historical Jesus: A Critical Study of its Progress from Reimarus to Wrede.*

cited as an intellectual landmark.[2] But as beguiling as Schweitzer's account remains, he was mistaken in both his claims about the origins of the quest for the historical Jesus (hereafter 'the quest'): the emergence of the historical study of Jesus and Christian origins, as a vital research tradition, was entirely consistent with the intellectual climate of seventeenth- and eighteenth-century Europe; moreover, while Reimarus may have produced the most comprehensive historical study of Jesus during the Enlightenment, there were notable contributions to this historical enterprise prior to his posthumous intervention.

In an essay that has helped to shape contemporary perceptions of the quest, N.T. Wright identifies 'six commonly held but erroneous views' about the tradition. First among these allegedly faulty opinions is that 'Reimarus began it' (Wright 1992: 796). This is a refreshingly bold statement considering the persistence elsewhere (Funk *et al.* 1997: 2) of the account of origins first advanced by Schweitzer in 1906. Despite laying down the gauntlet in the opening paragraph of his essay, however, Wright continues to work within the old periodic format and does not name a single author of note before Reimarus. The only corrective he provides is to say that 'Reimarus drew on the work of earlier writers, particularly the English Deists' and that 'the first phase of the quest fell historically within a wider movement in which orthodox Christianity came under attack from rationalism' (Wright 1992: 796). The first of these claims is more or less true: not all of the so called 'English deists' were English, some were of Irish and Welsh descent, but England was the intellectual centre for this loosely connected constellation of radical writers, and their influence on Reimarus is well established (Talbert 1971: 14-18; C. Brown 2008: 29-55). Wright's second claim requires more substantive qualification.

Even if we could extract all genuine examples of rational theological disputation from the ubiquitous rhetoric of reason in the seventeenth and eighteenth centuries, 'rationalism' as a broad philosophical or theological category is still of limited use as an indicator of any ideological or methodological stance in religious polemic during the period, unless it is used in a circumscribed way, say, to designate a particular hermeneutical approach to the problem of miracles,[3] or if it is understood as a commitment to natural

---

2. See, for instance, Theissen and Merz (1998: 1-2); Dawes (2000: 54-86); and C. Brown (2008: 1-56). The publication of Reimarus's work was a seminal moment in German intellectual history, and Schweitzer has helped to ensure that Reimarus remains a point of reference in New Testament studies, but the fame (or infamy) of Reimarus's polemical reconstruction has led to some inflated estimations of its significance, such as Amy Hollywood's impression that 'Reimarus's work . . . is routinely take to be the point of origin for critical readings of the Bible' (Hollywood 2004: 40).

3. In New Testament studies, rationalism is sometimes indicative of a particular stance on the question of miracles: rationalism proposes a historical core for stories of

religion over against revealed religion.[4] Just as some historians now insist that it always makes sense to ask which strand of the Enlightenment we are discussing, say, mainstream or radical,[5] it also makes sense to ask which type of rationalism we are discussing during the same period.[6] And it would be more accurate to say that the quest emerged in an era when orthodox Christianity, widely understood in Protestant circles as assent to a set of theological propositions justified by the Bible, was under attack from a whole range of intellectual positions: empiricists, skeptics, fideists and even mystics were contributors to this counterblast to Protestant scholasticism.[7] The advantage of locating the origins of the quest within religious polemic is that it brings us into direct contact with figures of the period who were reading and responding to each other's work directly: intellectual exchanges that might be regarded as the proximate cause of new developments in New Testament criticism and new conceptions of Jesus. The weakness of this approach is that it can ignore the development of wider intellectual frame-

the miraculous and explains away the fantastical elements in the accounts we now have as the result of elaboration or the misunderstanding of natural causes. The most famous (or infamous) attempt to rationalize the miracles was the 'fully developed rationalism' (Schweitzer 1906: 48) of Heinrich E.G. Paulus.

4. Specialist dictionary definitions of deism (see Blackburn 1994: 97) that emphasize natural religion and universalism are of little use when trying to understand the historical phenomenon of deism during the Enlightenment. If, as the standard accounts suggest, deism is understood as the belief in a creator God, founded on natural theological discourse, coupled with a denial of revelation, then Reimarus was a thoroughgoing deist in a way that most of his 'deistic' predecessors from the British Isles were not. Indeed, it seems to me that the scarcity of major Anglophone writers who took a consistently negative position on the truth value of revelation, and the fact that such religious labels were often forced on writers in the course of fierce polemic, makes the very use of the term 'deist' problematic. For the purposes of this piece however I will occasionally identify as 'deists' those heterodox writers who, for better or worse, are commonly known as such in intellectual histories of the period.

5. This is a shared contention of two of the most influential recent works of the period: Jacob (1981) and Israel (2001).

6. If it is doubted that there are problems with the use of 'rationalism' as a category of positions hostile to orthodoxy, consider the following conflict of Enlightenment perspectives: in the canon of modern rationalists, few rank higher than Gottfried Leibniz, yet it was Leibniz who helped to bring the work of the British and Irish deists to the attention of many German readers through his polemical reviews of their work. This quintessential rationalist at the dawn of the eighteenth century was a defender of Protestant orthodoxy against the rationalism of the Anglophone deists (Talbert 1971: 15).

7. For a seminal account of the history of modernity's attempt to render the systems of religion into propositional form, see W.C. Smith 1978; on the empirically inclined religious scepticism of David Hume, see Orr 1903; on the challenge of scepticism and fideism (the two have often been intellectual bedfellows) to orthodoxy, see Popkin 2003; on the relationship between Leibnizian rationalism, mysticism and their relationship to orthodoxy, see Coudert *et al.* 1998.

works within which those confrontations took place. What is required is an account that does justice both to large-scale conceptual and theoretical developments and to the work of particular writers engaged with specific projects. It is such an account I will attempt to provide when considering the historical dimension of the origins of the quest.

It may seem counterintuitive to suggest that there are significant dimensions to the quest apart from the historical, but that would be to misunderstand the nature of a research tradition that has rarely, if ever, constituted a purely historical enterprise. The key texts by Reimarus on the historical Jesus and Christian origins are the posthumously published *Aims of Jesus and his Disciples* (1778) and the *Resurrection Narratives* (1777);[8] but they were just two of seven controversial fragments from Reimarus's *magnum opus, Apologie oder Schutzschrift für die vernünftigen Verehrer Gottes*, issued by his literary executor Gotthold Ephraim Lessing.[9] To understand the fragments controversy in its entirety, which would certainly deepen our understanding of the intellectual origins of the quest, we would need to take into account large-scale trends in European intellectual life during the Enlightenment, not least in theology, ethics and politics.[10] This essay takes a self-consciously narrower approach, considering important historiographical precursors to the fragments controversy, considerations that fall more directly within the histories of New Testament criticism and the study of Christian origins. As we shall see, however, it will not be possible completely to separate historical criticism from its theological context, since, contrary to certain popular perceptions, intellectuals in the Enlightenment were invariably preoccupied with theological questions.

I will begin with some general observations about historiography in the Enlightenment, focusing in particular on the historical criticism of Pierre

8. These two works are collected together as 'Concerning the Intention of Jesus and His Teaching' in Talbert 1971: 59-269. The treatise on the resurrection is sometimes marginalized in discussions of Reimarus, which is a mistake: much of this sixth fragment focuses on events *after* the death of the historical Jesus, but it is central to Reimarus's conception of Christian origins, and, as we will see, the two are closely related.

9. Although the great German man of letters did not endorse the views of Reimarus, he used the debate to articulate his own controversial views on the relationship between faith and history. For an excellent account of the fragments controversy as a whole see C. Brown 2008: 1-29.

10. Reimarus engaged with all three themes, and his radical vision of Jesus and Christian origins was actually part of an attempt to defend a particular theological viewpoint, namely a strict deism which he wanted to see tolerated alongside other minority religious traditions: the title of the manuscript Reimarus left behind may be rendered into English as *Apology for the Rational Worshippers of God* (from the German *Apologie oder Schutzschrift für die vernünftigen Verehrer Gottes*). A critical edition of the work was not published until Gerhard Alexander (Reimarus 1972).

Bayle. I will then consider three of the concrete achievements that have been attributed to Reimarus: (1) separating the aims of Jesus from the aims of his disciples; (2) discovering the eschatological context of Jesus' mission; and (3) formulating an alternative account of Christian origins in the aftermath of Jesus' death. In all three cases, I will demonstrate the large extent to which Reimarus was anticipated by writers who tend to receive only nominal recognition in the history of the quest, including Thomas Chubb, Matthew Tindal, Anthony Collins and John Toland; in the third and final case, I will situate Reimarus's conspiracy-laden reconstruction of Christian origins within the context of seventeenth- and eighteenth-century theories about the probable historical causes of positive religion.

Historiography in the Enlightenment

When reflecting on Schweitzer's account of origins in *Quest of the Historical Jesus*, a number of critics have taken the German polymath to task for his implausible assertion that Reimarus was a thinker without predecessors (C. Brown 2008: 29), but few if any have tried to make sense of Schweitzer's sins of omission. When one reflects on the inadequacies in Schweitzer's account, it is worth remembering that studies of the Enlightenment at the turn of the twentieth century, particularly sympathetic ones, were not in the rude health that we find them today. Schweitzer was writing decades before intellectual historians such as Ernst Cassirer and Peter Gay attempted to capture the philosophical sweep and grandeur of the Enlightenment (Cassirer 1955 [German original 1932]; Gay 1967–70): conceptualizing the era as a more or less coherent movement in the history of ideas and celebrating its achievements. Few epochs manage to completely escape the patricidal tendencies of their immediate offspring, and the age of reason was no different. With this in mind, one charitable explanation for Schweitzer's insistence on the work of a single visionary is the influence of a common nineteenth-century judgment that intellectuals in the previous century had little interest in or conception of the historical world. One famous contributor to the nineteenth-century quest, Ernest Renan, argued that Voltaire alone 'has done more damage to historical studies than an invasion by the barbarians' (Kelly 1998: 242). Renan was writing less than a hundred years after the death of his illustrious compatriot, but more nuanced judgments in the same vein persisted well into the twentieth century.[11] Was the judgment a sound one?

---

11. One notable example is the American historian Carl Becker's celebrated polemic *The Heavenly City of the Eighteenth Century Philosophers* (1932). Becker argues that the thought forms of the leading thinkers of the eighteenth century were closer to the

It is true that philosophers became a major force in eighteenth-century historiography, and some were contemptuous of truffle-hunting antiquarians. By contrast, the nineteenth century was concerned with assembling masses of facts,[12] and such an age was unlikely to forgive or have the patience to understand Jean-Jacques Rousseau's infamous call to begin our enquiries by 'setting aside all the facts, because they do not affect the question' (1984: 78 [original 1755]). But the values of history transcend the collection of facts. In his survey of over two millennia of historical writing, Donald Kelly identifies a consistent body of values that preserve at least some of their meanings beyond particular historical contexts: 'truth, accuracy, relevance, explanatory power, literary skill, political or philosophical utility, and scholarly or popular acceptance' (1998: ix). These values were all on display in the Enlightenment, although practitioners had a tendency to indulge some at the expense of others. Edward Gibbon may have possessed the greatest balance of those values and produced the most celebrated work of the era (Gibbon 1994 [original 1787–89]), but the priority he gave to wit and literary style in his *History of the Decline and Fall of the Roman Empire* has conditioned his reputation ever since.[13] Writers like Voltaire did ransack the past to affirm a common eighteenth-century vision of a rational, benevolent human nature, while correcting the follies of their own age by appeal to those few beacons of rationality before them.[14] Lord Bolingbroke's mantra that 'history is philosophy teaching by example' (Bolingbroke 1752: I, letter 2) was a cornerstone of eighteenth-century wisdom, but the lessons of history were often drawn from superb scholarship using advanced modes of investigation.

The irony of how the historical criticism that engulfed Christianity in the eighteenth century was fostered has been recognized by even the most sympathetic chroniclers of the Enlightenment's challenge to Christian hegem-

medieval period than to the twentieth century, a truth disguised only by their employment of more familiar idioms.

12. The preoccupation with facts in nineteenth-century English thought was satirized by Charles Dickens in his 1854 novel *Hard Times*. Dickens was particularly concerned about the way statistics could be used by public intellectuals to legitimize social inequality and frustrate radical change. For an approving account of the transition to the fact-based world of the nineteenth century and beyond, see Becker 1932: 1-31, 119-68.

13. When Simon Schama nominated Gibbon's *Decline and Fall* as one of the greatest works of history ever written, he qualified his judgment with the admission that he was not actually choosing it for historical truth 'but for the jokes and fantastic footnotes' (Simon Schama, 'Simon Schama's Top Ten History Books', http://www.guardian.co.uk/books/1999/dec/10/top10s.history.books (last accessed 3 April 2010).

14. Usually Greco-Roman philosophers and statesmen whose light flickered briefly before the forces of superstition reasserted themselves: see the discussion of Voltaire in Kelly 1998: 241-44.

ony: Christian intellectual culture was not just the passive victim of developments in historical science born of an emerging secular mentality; critical history was turned against Christian orthodoxy, having first been developed and deployed for apologetic purposes. As Gay reminds us:

> Of all the Christian spoils the ones most consistently useful to the philosophes were the methods and the results of Christian erudition. In the latter half of the seventeenth century and early in the eighteenth an army of scholarly theologians employed the delicate and potent critical instruments developed in the Renaissance to advance the historical study and demonstrate the historical truth of the Christian religion. Learned Benedictines, Jesuits and Anglicans refined the canons of criticism, radically improved paleography, developed numismatics, gathered vast collections of documents. These historians confronted their task with absolute honesty and devout industry—an industry never surpassed and rarely matched by the philosophes (Gay 1967: 359).

Reimarus's radical reading of the gospels did not require much paleography or numismatics, but the fragments controversy erupted after more than a century of pathbreaking historical criticism. Gay does not devote much space to discussing major figures in the erudite apologetic tradition he describes, but they are not hard to find. Richard Simon (1638–1712), perhaps the greatest historical critic of Scripture of the seventeenth century, combined monumental historical studies of the origin and transmission of the texts of the Old and New Testaments with apologetic work that sought to demonstrate the truth of Christianity on the basis of central revelations contained in Scripture (Simon 1689).[15] Earlier that century, Hugo Grotius (1583–1645), the Dutch philosopher best known today as one of the pioneers of modern political thought and the father of international law, published *The Truth of the Christian Religion* (1689) before his annotated edition of the books of the New Testament with copious notes on authorship and historical setting.[16] But the tendency of both of these great scholars to link the truth of Christianity to fulfilled prophecy and miracle created an opportunity for the enemies of orthodoxy in future generations of biblical

---

15. Simon's historical studies of the Old and New Testament canons were published in 1678 and 1689–93 (3 vols.) respectively. Reimarus was certainly familiar with Simon's biblical criticism (Reimarus 1972: I, 828).

16. This date refers to an English translation. The original Latin edition of Grotius's apologetic work was published in 1627, while his annotated treatments of the New Testament were issued between 1641 and 1650. Reimarus's debts to Grotius are scattered throughout the *Apologie* (Reimarus 1972: I, 56, 96, 314, 742, 803, 890, 905; II, 78, 81, 170, 217, 537, 658).

critics, who would hoist these pioneering scholars with their own apologetic petard. Reimarus was one such critic.[17]

A more theologically subversive and wide-ranging historical critic to emerge in the late seventeenth century was the French-born Pierre Bayle (1647–1706), whose turbulent relationship with his homeland meant that he spent many of his most productive days in the Netherlands, where he earned the moniker 'the *philosophe* of Rotterdam'.[18] It is ironic that Bayle, a philosopher with deep-rooted Cartesian sympathies (Ryan 2009), should emerge as such a significant figure for modern historiography: the axioms that most Cartesians considered paradigmatic of knowledge were such that, by comparison, the historical world, with all its vagaries, was all but excluded from the realm of accessible truth.[19] But Bayle was dissatisfied with a rationalism that remained aloof from the historical world and reconciled himself to the existence of different orders of knowledge. While widening the scope of philosophically respectable pursuits so as to include the historical domain, Bayle carried the spirit of Cartesian doubt into his examination of the historical record.[20] Indeed, it seems to have been Bayle's preoccupation with repudiating the false and exposing the doubtful that propelled his scholarly career.

In 1697 Bayle published the first edition of the *Historical and Critical Dictionary*,[21] which delivered a compilation of all the errors he detected in other historical writings, along with his own comprehensive amendments. Bayle's *Dictionary* is significant for the intellectual background of the quest for at least two reasons. First, the work is a biographical dictionary: factual and evaluative sketches of historical characters, based whenever possible on primary sources, including biblical figures. Bayle's *Dictionary* has been called a Who's Who? of intellectual and religious history (Popkin 1991: viii). A more likely response from anyone reading Bayle's vast work today

17. Reimarus attacked the apologetic value of both miracles and prophecy; see Talbert 1971: 235-39.

18. For an overview of Bayle's life and work see Popkin's introduction to Bayle (1991: viii-xl). I am aware that Spinoza was an earlier and more direct influence in the rise of the historical-critical study of the Bible, but his contribution is already well known in the discipline. Moreover, Bayle is a more significant figure for general historiography, which is the subject of this section: Spinoza showed significant interest only in biblical history.

19. On the a-historical nature of Cartesian thought and the irony surrounding Spinoza's contribution to biblical studies, given the largely a-historical character of his own philosophy, see Cassirer 1955: 184-86, 201-209).

20. On Bayle's scepticism and its influence on his historical enquiries, see Popkin 2003: 283-302.

21. A wide-ranging selection of articles from all the editions is collected in Popkin 1991.

would be to ask, 'Who is *that*?', since Bayle eschews such obvious figures as Plato, Aristotle, Jesus and St Paul, in favour of a catalogue of relatively obscure sages, clerics, saints and heretics. Nevertheless, it was in his
investigation of these marginal figures that he displayed his ruthless pursuit
of errors, contradictions and omissions in the historical record. The lack
of popular interest that a profiled individual held, a lack of interest Bayle
almost certainly shared in some cases, only served to bludgeon the reader
with his methodological agenda, which was to put the historian and his
interests in the background, all the while sifting the sources and forming
hypotheses with apparently disinterested dedication.[22] The second point of
interest for chroniclers of the quest is the anti-metaphysical dimension of
Bayle's historical method.

The astronomical legacies of Copernicus and Galileo were vital factors
in bringing about what Hans Frei called the 'great reversal' (1974: 130):[23]
when the Bible began to be understood in the context of a larger reality—
terrestrial, cosmic and historical—rather than reality being understood in
terms dictated by a biblical metanarrative into which all additional knowledge was supposed to fit. While Bayle showed little interest in challenging the historical truth of specific biblical stories, his general method of
criticism is evidence of the great reversal being carried into the historical
domain. Cassirer offers a clear illustration of the significance of Bayle's
work for the direction of historical writing by comparing his *modus operandi* with the theological histories that were still prevalent during the age of
Enlightenment; specifically, he contrasts the *Dictionary* with the *Universal
History* by the French bishop and theologian Jacques Bossuet:[24]

> Here once more is a sublime plan of history, a religious interpretation of
> the universe. But this bold structure rests on feet of clay so far as its empir-
> ical foundations are concerned. For the truth of the facts on which Bossuet
> builds can only be assured by a logically vicious circle. The authority of all
> historical facts . . . is based on the authority of the Bible. The authority of
> the Bible in turn rests on that of the Church, whose authority rests on tradi-
> tion. Thus tradition becomes the foundation of all historical certainty—but
> the content and value of tradition can only be proved on the basis of his-
> torical evidence. Bayle is the first modern thinker to reveal this circle with
> ruthless critical subtlety Cassirer 1955: 207).

22. For an excellent account of Bayle's historical method, see Whelan 1989.

23. Another important factor was the discovery of the New World during the great
voyages of discovery in the early modern period. For a wider appreciation of the social
and intellectual conditions that created the historical context for this radical shift in biblical hermeneutics, see Dawes 2000: 1-23.

24. Bossuet was a brilliant orator and prose stylist; his most famous theological history is available in many English editions: see, e.g., Bossuet 1785.

Bayle's critique of tradition was nearly always a critique of Catholicism, with which he had a youthful dalliance (Popkin 1991: xi-xii);[25] but he could be as unforgiving of Protestant crimes against historical veracity. His article on the myth of Pope Joan is one of the most famous examples of Bayle taking Protestant thinkers to task for betraying the Christian humanist and Reformation values of textual discrimination.[26] Bayle was among the first historians in Christian Europe to absorb the Cartesian and Spinozist attack on final causes[27] and to seek explanations through proximate causes, namely the aims and motives of historical actors, within their cultural context, as they carry out their projects, replete with the moral and intellectual virtues and vices that aid or frustrate their progress. Like Spinoza before him, Bayle does not question the historicity of Old Testament characters or major narratives;[28] what he does do is to tear these characters out of the grand theological dramas of cosmic history of the kind produced by Bossuet, and subject them to a close analysis in the confines of the immanent narratives in which they exist. In Bayle's *Dictionary,* local cultural conditions and chance shape the projects that his subjects pursue, and so it would be with Reimarus: when the aims of Jesus and the aims of his disciples are asserted and contrasted in the seventh fragment, they are shaped by cultural inheritance and contingent circumstance. The moralizing tone of some of Bayle's criticism suggests a lack of tolerance for historical difference that would not find favour with later historians, but this was standard practice during the Enlightenment, and it is certainly a trait we find in Reimarus. Nevertheless, Bayle (Popkin 1991: 56) insists on going beyond the typically disapproving comments about the sexual deviances of biblical characters: after making due note of King David's adultery, he proceeds to offer a concise and systematic analysis of David's political and military career: his judgments, his strategies, his successes, and his excesses (Popkin 1991: 56-63). This is recognizable as a modern critical estimate of leadership and the uses and abuses of power. We should not underestimate the significance of this: in Christian Europe at the time, David was not considered fair game for this kind of clinical analysis because he was a hero of the Old Testament; on

---

25. A conversion to Catholicism followed by a swift rejection of the Church of Rome is something Bayle shared with Gibbon, and there is a consistently anti-Catholic dimension to the mature work of both writers.

26. For an analysis of this article, see Whelan 1989: 122, 134-36, 139.

27. Descartes is justly celebrated for his seminal contribution to the removal of teleological explanation from scientific models of the universe in such classics as *Discourse on the Method* and *Meditations on First Philosophy* (Descartes 1985a). Spinoza applied the anti-teleological stance directly to the Bible in his *Theological-Political Treatise* (1998).

28. For an excellent study of Spinoza's contribution to biblical studies, see Popkin 1996.

the contrary, the negative reaction to the article in the publication of 1697 was so strong that Bayle removed several sections of his evaluation for the second edition (Popkin 1991: 45). Reimarus was similarly critical of David in a book he devoted to the biblical king in his posthumously published *Apologie* (Reimarus 1972: I, 586-623), and, although Reimarus does not acknowledge any debt to Bayle for his evaluation of David, Bayle is cited elsewhere in the manuscript (Reimarus 1972: I, 233).

So the connection between Bayle and Reimarus is not circumstantial: Reimarus showed a direct acquaintance with Bayle's work, and the unsparing moral judgments made of Old Testament figures by Bayle are evident throughout much of the *Apologie*. There are major differences, however. Reimarus was a more metaphysically engaged historian than Bayle, in so far as his deism conditioned what he considered to be possible with respect to the history of religion and God's relationship with creation: not just methodologically but in principle.[29] Reimarus's theological interests were anything but in the background of his work as a historian, but he adopted the same kind of naturalistic analysis of biblical narratives that we find in the *philosophe* of Rotterdam. The reason Bayle never wrote in similar detail about key figures from the New Testament is still contested by historians, as is the nature of his own religious agenda.[30] Reimarus certainly did write about them, but what is his distinctive contribution to the historical study of Jesus and Christian origins?

The Achievements of Reimarus Considered

Distinguishing the Teachings of Jesus from the Teachings of his Disciples

Reimarus's great achievement in New Testament studies is often boiled down to a paraphrase of the very project he outlined for himself in the opening passages of *The Aims of Jesus and his Disciples* (Talbert 1971: 64). In the following example, his project is crystallized by Robert Funk and his colleagues at the American Jesus Seminar:

29. The third of Reimarus's fragments (1777) argued against the possibility that special revelation could provide secure grounds for rational religious conviction: *Unmöglichkeit einer Offenbarung, die alle Menschen auf eine gegründete Art glauben können* (Lachmann and Muncker 1897).

30. Bayle's religious position divides scholarly opinion: he has been characterized as a covert atheist, a rationalist critic of traditional Christianity, a Christian sceptic, a radical Calvinist, and even a Judaizing Christian; some have sought to explain his relative lack of critical interest in the New Testament by an alleged fear of persecution; others insist that he had no such fears once safely ensconced in the Dutch Republic (Popkin 1991: xix-xxix).

> The search for the Jesus of history began with Herman Samuel Reimarus
> . . . A close study of the . . . gospels convinced Reimarus that what the gos-
> pels said about Jesus could be distinguished from what Jesus himself said.
> It was with this basic distinction between the man Jesus and the Christ of
> the creeds that the quest of the historical Jesus began (Funk *et al.* 1997: 2).

The *basic* distinction between the man Jesus and the Christ of the creeds
certainly did not begin with Reimarus. Reimarus stands in a long tradition of theological dissent in the modern period, sometimes ending in the
flaying of the flesh of those who proposed such a distinction. The Spanish theologian Michael Servetus was anything but a covert sceptic in the
style of Reimarus.[31] Servetus was burnt at the stake for heresy in 1553, with
the approval of John Calvin, for his contrast between the human Jesus and
his heavenly father.[32] But these early modern dissidents were of a different order. Servetus did not seriously question the historicity of the Gospels
or try to drive a wedge between Jesus and the early church, but, radical
reformer that he was, he argued that an anti-trinitarian Christology represented a more accurate reading of the Gospels (C. Brown 2008: 29-31). The
argument for a radical discontinuity between Jesus and his disciples found
its most erudite eighteenth-century form in Reimarus, a professor of Oriental languages at the Hamburg Gymnasium, but he was by no means the first
to draw the distinction on textual or historical-critical grounds.

In 1738, Thomas Chubb (1679–1747), a glove maker and lens grinder
by training, a philosopher, biblical critic and political pamphleteer by incli-
nation and reputation,[33] published a book with an inelegant but wonder-
fully transparent title: *The True Gospel of Jesus Christ Asserted: Wherein
Is Shown What Is and What Is Not That Gospel*. Chubb's project, like
Reimarus's, is intended to separate Jesus' teachings from later doctrinal
interpolations,[34] but, whereas Reimarus understood Christianity as assent to
doctrines about Jesus—atonement, resurrection, parousia, etc.—and sought
to undermine Christianity by destroying the historical credibility of those

31. Reimarus's public persona was that of a Christian rationalist, and he was a life-
long member of the Lutheran Church, but he developed a secret loathing for Christianity,
and, in his later years, committed his wildly impious views to paper, which he communicated to trusted friends via a clandestine manuscript. These anti-Christian views became
public only after Reimarus's death, but even then their author remained anonymous until
1814 (Talbert 1971: 7).

32. For an account of the background of the execution of Servetus, see Friedman
1978.

33. One of the best recent biographical sketches of Chubb is in Bushell 1967: 3-18.

34. The earliest example I have found of a scholar arguing for parallels between Reimarus and Chubb is Lechler 1841: 343-58. A.C. Lundsteen later argued that Reimarus
had access to the writings of all the major Anglophone deists and made liberal use of
their ideas (1939: 110-46).

doctrines (Talbert 1971: 229-30), Chubb anticipated many modern theologians and New Testament scholars by offering an account of Christianity whereby membership is guaranteed by adherence to Christ's teachings properly understood: 'to submit to be governed by the laws of Christ, is what and what alone constitutes a Christian' (Chubb 1738: 5). 'The Gospel of Jesus Christ', he continues,

> is not *an historical account of matters of fact*. As thus, Christ suffered, died, rose from the dead, ascended into heaven, &c. These are *historical facts* the credibility of which arises from the strength of those evidences which are, or can be offered in their favour: but then those facts are not the *gospel of Jesus Christ*, neither in whole, nor in part (Chubb 1738: 43).

Chubb proceeds to consign an array of New Testament passages, particularly large sections from John's Gospel and the letters of St Paul, to the categories of the historically suspect and the theologically irrelevant: John's *logos* theology and Paul's discussion of the relationship between Israel and the gospel in Romans 11 both receive extensive criticism.[35] So what is the true gospel of Jesus Christ? The true gospel is to be found, most of all, in the Synoptic Gospels,[36] and, anticipating Reimarus, Chubb sees Jesus' essential mission as one of calling men to repentance and directing them to eternal salvation. According to Reimarus (Talbert 1971: 64), 'there can be no doubt that Jesus in his teaching referred man to the true great goal of religion, namely, eternal salvation'. He continues,

> we immediately find the entire content and intention of Jesus' teaching in his own words: 'Repent and believe the Gospel' [Mk 1.15], Repent for the Kingdom of heaven is at hand [Mt. 4.17] . . . Both these things, the kingdom of heaven and repentance, are so connected that the kingdom is the goal, while repentance is the means or preparation for this kingdom (Talbert 1971: 65-66).

Forty years before the publication of the seventh fragment, Chubb argued, 'The *great end* and *professed design* of our Lord Jesus Christ as to his coming into the world . . . is manifestly and apparently this, *viz, to save men's souls*; that is, it is to prepare men for, and to insure to them the

---

35. On John's Gospel, see Chubb 1738: 46-48; on Paul, see Chubb 1738: 48-49.

36. It has been suggested by some commentators that Chubb judged Mark to be the oldest and most historically reliable Gospel (Bushell 1967: 121), but I can find no compelling evidence in the text cited (Chubb 1748: 73-74). This judgment seems to depend on an unwarranted interpretation of Chubb's reflections on the authority of the Gospels, where he simply takes the author of Mark as an example of a source of information, about Jesus' life and work, whose identity and trustworthiness we ought to investigate, and whose book needs to be examined for corruptions in the course of its transmission and translation. He then makes the same point about the other three Gospels: 'they all are upon a foot in these respects' (1748: 75).

favour of *God*, and their *happiness* in another world' (1738: 1) According to Chubb, this 'great end' of Jesus' mission was intimately related to his call for repentance: 'Christ not only called upon sinners to repent and turn to God . . . but he also plainly and expressly declared this was the very purpose of his coming, *viz.* to call sinners to repentance and to assure them that except they did repent they would all perish' (1738: 33-34). Some of the scriptural passages Chubb offers as evidence are different,[37] but the message is basically the same: 'That Christ requires and recommends [of his followers] *repentance* and *reformation* of their *evil* ways as the *only*, and the *sure ground* of the divine *mercy* and *forgiveness*' (1738: 18). On the question of Jesus' originality, in substance there is none:

> I would also desire my reader to observe, that our Lord Christ did not propose or point out any *new way* to God's favour and eternal life, but on the contrary he recommended that good old way which always was, and always will be the true way to life eternal; *viz.* the keeping the commandments, or the loving God and our neighbour which is the same thing, and is the sum and substance of the moral law (Chubb 1738: 30).

Reimarus later echoed these sentiments when he wrote, 'He [Jesus] urged nothing more than purely moral duties, a true love of God and of one's neighbor; on these points he based the whole content of the law and the prophets and commanded that the hope of gaining his kingdom and salvation be constructed on them' (Talbert 1971: 71).

Neither Chubb nor Reimarus wanted to attribute that which they considered valuable in Jesus' teaching to the fertile cultural soil of Second Temple Judaism; on the contrary, Jesus' moral commands are universally true, but they have been obscured by the mutations that inevitably occurred when the gospel message was encountered by different audiences: for instance, Chubb tried to sketch a historical trajectory whereby the doctrine of atonement grew out of a need to link Jesus' gospel with the themes of sacrifice in the Old Testament, in order to appeal to a traditional Jewish audience, while he reads the incarnation as growing out of the need to bind Jesus' gospel to pagan notions of deity, when confronted by a Graeco-Roman audience (Chubb 1738: 47). In Reimarus's study, Jesus' gospel is thought to be obscured by something else: eschatology.

Eschatology
One of the main differences between the analyses of Chubb and Reimarus is that Chubb does not recognize the eschatological context of Jesus' teaching; more precisely, he does not take seriously the possibility that

---

37. Chubb draws from Mt. 18.11, Lk. 9.10, Jn 3.16-17; 6.40; 10.10; and 12.47 (1738: 1-2); and from Lk. 24.46-47 (1738: 34).

Jesus was either working towards a new political age or in preparation for an apocalyptic intervention by God. Schweitzer (1911: 22-23) attributed to Reimarus 'perhaps the most splendid achievement in the whole course of the historical investigation of the life of Jesus' because 'he was the first to grasp the fact that the world of thought in which Jesus moved was essentially eschatological.' Reimarus identified two strands of eschatology in the gospel tradition: one issuing in a new political age in the history of Israel (Talbert 1971: 123-27), the other in a redemptive act of salvation for all humanity (Talbert 1971: 240-42). He assigned the first form of eschatology to Jesus and his disciples during Jesus' own lifetime, and the second to the disciples when the first failed to materialize. In Reimarus's acutely cynical account, because Jesus had not delivered the earthly kingdom that the disciples saw as their destiny, they moved to cement their own religio-political power through a transformation of the eschatological meaning of his life:

> The Apostles were chiefly men of the lower class and of small means, who gained their livelihood by fishing and other trades . . . Now when they resolved upon following Jesus, they entirely forsook their trade . . . Here we do not require deductions or inferences as to what may have induced the apostles to forsake all . . . because the evangelists distinctly inform us that they entertained hopes that the Messiah would establish a kingdom . . . But this weary waiting only lasted until the execution of Jesus, which at once dashed all their idle hopes, and then they complain, 'But we had hoped that he was the one to redeem Israel!' (Luke 24:21). . . . we cannot believe otherwise than that the apostles of Jesus retained their previous aims and purposes, and sought to bring about their fulfilment . . . although in a different manner (Talbert 1971: 240-42).

Whereas Reimarus ultimately regards Jesus as deluded with respect to his own political destiny, and his disciples initially deluded and then mendacious, Chubb, anticipating Johann S. Semler (1780: 254), insists that the urgency of Jesus' message and his talk of a kingdom of God were best understood morally: an ethical kingdom of God without concrete political or supernatural form. Chubb argues that both Jews and Romans assumed that Christ was claiming

> such *temporal* power and jurisdiction over the *persons* and *properties* of men as the *princes* and *potentates* of the earth exercise over their *subjects*, and in this view of the case they considered him as an enemy to *Cesar*: but he assured them . . . that . . . his *temporal kingdom* was not of *this age* . . . What I observe is that as Christ, *as yet*, has not assumed nor exercised *temporal* dominion over his people, but only a dominion over their *consciences*, resulting from, and founded on only *argument* and *persuasion*: so neither has he *communicated* any *such temporal* power or dominion to *others* . . . (Chubb 1738: 13-14).

When Chubb writes about Christ exercising 'a dominion over their consciences', he is talking about more than the adoption of a set of moral instructions by his followers. He seems to be thinking about some kind of existential transformation in a person's whole outlook. As Chubb's biographer, T.L. Bushell put it:

> Chubb abhors hearing the religious individual speak of 'Christ's kingdom', as if this were either now, or should later come to be, something co-terminus with an earthly realm . . . To be 'created anew in or according to Jesus', means that one has gone beyond simply apprising oneself of the ethical aspects of the gospels; it bespeaks that a man has undergone a liberation of the heart and has acquired an inner freedom allowing him truly to love his fellow men (1967: 139).

This kind of interpretation became a mainstay of nineteenth-century scholarship,[38] and moral paradigms remain central to many reconstructions of early Christianity, some of which are favoured by readers dissatisfied with orthodox Christian theology and with New Testament scholarship that insists on the apocalyptic dimension of Jesus' teachings: one thinks, for instance, of John Dominic Crossan's 'ethical eschatology' (1999: 278). Chubb did not fail to recognize the eschatological character of Jesus' mission, but, I would contend, he was one of the first modern writers to insist on a sapiential reading of its meaning.[39]

One writer prior to Reimarus who did not moralize or spiritualize early Christian eschatology is another of the so called English deists, the lawyer and fellow of All Souls College, Oxford, Matthew Tindal (c. 1657–1733). In his *Christianity as Old as Creation* (1730), Tindal emphasized the apocalyptic lens through which the primitive Christian community viewed the world:

> And as those prophecies, if they be so called, in the New Testament, relating to the *Second Coming of Christ*, and the *End of the World*, the best Interpreters and Commentators own, the Apostles themselves were grossly mistaken; there scarce being an Epistle, but where they fortell that those Times they wrote in, were *Tempora novissima*; and the then Age the last Age, and those Days the last Days; and that the End of the World was nigh, and *the Coming of Christ at hand*, as is plain, among other Texts, from I *Cor.* 10. 11. *Rom.* 13. 11, 12. *Heb.* 9.26. *Jam.* 5. 7, 8. I *John* 2. 18. II *Pet.* 3, 12, 13. And they do not assert this as mere Matter of Speculation, but build Motives and Arguments upon it, to excite People to the Practise of Piety . . . And tho' they do not pretend to tell the very Day and Hour, when these Things must happen; yet they thought it wou'd be during their Time

---

38. This was a common characteristic of the so-called 'liberal lives' tradition of scholarship, famously lambasted by Schweitzer (1911: Chs. 4, 12, 14, 16).

39. Crossan (1991: 227-28) takes Schweitzer's survey as the point of departure for his distinction between the apocalyptic model and his own sapiential reading.

...And I think, 'tis plain *Paul* himself expected to be alive at the Coming of the Lord, and that he had the Word of God for it (Tindal 1730: 233).

Nowhere in this passage does Tindal attribute this apocalyptic mind-set to Jesus himself, but neither did Reimarus, for whom Jesus was a political-eschatological prophet. Moreover, to push apocalyptic notions back to the apostles themselves, and especially to Paul,[40] is to bring the eschatological thought world into sufficiently close proximity to Jesus to warrant some kind of mention in a history of the quest, yet Schweitzer seems to have been oblivious to Tindal. Moreover, in maintaining that the apostles were simply misguided in their apocalyptic mentality, rather than consciously fraudulent, Tindal is in some respects closer than Reimarus to Schweitzer's own understanding of early Christian apocalyptic.[41]

Reimagining Christian Origins
In one of the finest sketches of the intellectual background to the fragments controversy, Colin Brown (2008: 53) credits Reimarus with going beyond earlier writers by 'developing a comprehensive alternative account of the origin of Christianity'. According to Brown, 'The Deists had contented themselves with raising specific objections. Reimarus put forward an alternative explanation that introduced eschatology as the key to understanding the mistaken and fraudulent character of Christianity' (2008: 53). As we have seen, Tindal did cite apocalypticism as key to understanding the mistaken (though not fraudulent) character of early Christianity. It might reasonably be argued that Tindal's critique falls into the category of 'raising specific objections', but the originality of Reimarus's contribution to reimagining the birth of Christianity must be qualified and contextualized. There was at least one eighteenth-century precedent for producing an alternative historical reconstruction of Christian origins, from an author we know Reimarus admired,[42] and there were many precedents for citing fraud as an essential component of early Christianity. The fraud hypothesis and the project of remodelling early Christianity through reasoned historical conjecture are closely connected in Reimarus's own work, but I will discuss the two separately.

1. *Imposture*. Reimarus's view that the early Christian proclamation was born of conscious duplicity is consistent with one of the dominant theories about the historical causes of positive religion during the Enlightenment: the theory of religious imposture. During the seventeenth and eighteenth

---

40. Schweitzer (1931) also used an apocalyptic model to interpret Paul.
41. See Schweitzer (1911: Chs. 2; 15–16; 19–20).
42. John Toland was one of two Anglophone deists mentioned specifically by Reimarus in the *Apologie* (Reimarus 1972: I, 434); the other was Anthony Collins (Reimarus 1972: I, 728, 742).

centuries, natural explanations for the origin and development of religion
were almost all taken from the ancient world. This was part of what Peter
Gay (1967–70: I, 29) called the Enlightenment's 'appeal to antiquity'. Time
and again writers in the Enlightenment found parallels between the intellectual traumas of their own time and those experienced by the ancients, and it
was to the ancients that they often turned for solutions.

In the fourth century BCE, Cynics and other wandering intellectuals
returned to their native Athens with stories of breathtaking religious diversity (Harrison 1990: 14-18). This diversity troubled the intellectual and
political elites of Athenian society, who were scandalized by the suggestion
of relativism and, even worse, by the materialist theories offered by some
philosophers as explanations for this diversity. Four popular theories at
that time were fear, projection, euhemerism and imposture (Harrison 1990:
14-18). All four explanations were rehashed during the Enlightenment, but
the last one had the most enduring appeal.

The resurgence of these antique theories was occasioned by the disquiet-
ing variety of religious belief and practice discovered by explorers in the
New World. Walter Raleigh—one of the explorers whose reports brought
the problem of religious pluralism into sharp focus—appealed to demonic
influences on the human mind as a supplement to the standard early modern appeals to the fateful consequences of the fall (Harrison 1990: 102).
For many Christian writers of this period, the biblical tragedy of the fall,
supplemented by the doctrine of original sin, was central to any reasonable
response to theologically problematic observations concerning the diversity
of religious and moral values across cultures (Harrison 1990: 101-12). But,
as the great reversal began to take effect on European thought, explanations
drawn from a spirit world understood within a biblical framework were
superseded by universal explanations: causes that transcended particular
sacred histories. The ancient theory of imposture—the view that individuals self consciously pose as religious leaders, mediating between the human
and divine, for reasons of personal advancement and group domination—
found expression in early-seventeenth-century anti-Catholic polemic,[43] but
it quickly became the century's most frequently cited natural explanation
for the rise of all reputedly deviant forms of religion. When the republi-
can writer and deist Charles Blount sought patterns of religious thought in
antiquity, he concluded:

> Before Religion, that is to say, Sacrifices, Rites, Ceremonies, pretended
> Revelations, and the like, were invented amongst the heathens, there was
> no worship of God but in a rational way. Whereof the Philosophers pre-
> tending to be Masters, did to this end, not only teach Virtue and Piety
> but were also themselves great examples of it . . . [and] whom the people
> chiefly follow'd 'till they were seduced by their crafty and covetous Sac-

43. One notable example is Harsnet 1603.

erdotal Order who, instead of the said Virtue and Piety; introduced Fables
and Fictions of their own (Harrison 1990: 73).

In the background of Blount's speculations about religious history is
the then widespread assumption, explicitly articulated by Matthew Hale
(1677: 168), that 'truth is more ancient than error', and that pure ancient
theology, which taught appropriate worship of the one true God (primitive monotheism), had been corrupted by nefarious human intervention.[44]
This would still be evident, to some degree, in Reimarus during the high
Enlightenment: Reimarus considered the universal truth of Jesus' teaching
to be obscured by eschatological delusion on the part of Jesus and eschatological manipulation on the part of his followers. For Blount, writing in
much more general terms than Reimarus, manipulation was the only serious
candidate to explain religious diversity: 'The general decay of Piety hath
in most religions whatsoever proceeded from the exemplary viciousness
of their Clergy' (Harrison 1990: 74). When Blount (1695: 123) considered
the collective followers of Judaism, Christianity and Islam, he reckoned
that either all three religions are false and all their followers deceived, or
only one is true and the majority of their followers deceived. This glaring
non sequitur, that deception could be inferred from plurality, was surpris-
ingly pervasive among the self-styled rational worshippers of God at the
turn of the eighteenth century; indeed, it was repeated *ad nauseam* in publication after publication (Harrison 1990: 73-85). This intellectual error was
compounded by retrograde appeals to biblical history as the probable site
of spiritual degeneration. Despite the warnings of those, including Richard
Simon, who took the great reversal seriously and held that the Bible was
insufficient as a basis for universal history, the Welsh writer and self-styled
Christian deist Thomas Morgan proceeded to locate the genesis of global
religious corruption in Egypt, taking as primary evidence the fateful turn of
the Jews during their Egyptian captivity: 'This great Degeneracy, Inversion
of nature, and gross corruption of Religion, happened . . . in Egypt, when
Joseph had established an hereditary Priesthood there, endow'd with vast
Revenues in Lands, and made independent of the Crown' (1738–40: III,
93). Morgan speculated that it was in Egypt that Moses had learnt magic
and, together with Aaron, manipulated the people of Israel in the pursuit
of power. It is no coincidence that this kind of attack on historical priestly
imposture coincided with rising anticlericalism in modern Europe. Imposture was not just a theory of religious origins; it was frequently expanded
into a theory of how diverse religious traditions were sustained, namely
through a form of priest craft whereby clerical elites would conspire with,
and adapt to, the monarchies of Europe in order to retain their influence.

---

44. On the commitment to ancient theology (primitive monotheism), see Harrison
1990: 131-38.

For generations of British and Irish writers, it was common to find a three-fold commitment to an imposture theory of religious degeneration, contemporary anticlericalism and militant republicanism (Harrison 1990: 73-85). These three preoccupations were rarely presented together in one overarching critique of the monarchy and established church, but this was not necessary: readers were more than capable of joining the dots. The satirist Jonathan Swift, who had a finely tuned disdain for the Whigish republicans who tended to propagate these subversive views, regarded any silence on the part of imposture advocates as to the exact relationship between ancient imposture and the modern priesthood to be an implicit attack on the Church of England, and he targeted a number of their leading lights for vituperative literary treatment.[45] This polemic was effective: the implicit attack on the moral character of the Anglican clergy was met with explicit *ad hominem* arguments against their detractors, and when the rowdy populism of the deists was confronted in print by the best prose writers and most erudite men in England—Swift, Richard Bentley, Edward Stillingfleet *et al.*—the deists found it very difficult to maintain the moral and intellectual high ground (Harrison 1990: 77-85). Even if the imposture theory did explain the rise of positive religions, there was little evidence that the modern clergy were engaged in some far-reaching religious conspiracy against the populace, and the currency of imposture theory withered away in the face of *prima facie* implausibility. But anticlerical sentiment remained strong enough for the imposture/priest craft theory to morph initially into an attack on the institutional vices endemic in education, and on social prejudice generally, which was said to produce an ignorant and intolerant clergy (Harrison 1990: 81-85), and then later still into a theory of twofold philosophy. On this model religions were characterized by (1) a theology of the mind and spirit held by social and intellectual elites, and (2) a superstitious, ritualistic theology of the masses (Harrison 1990: 85-92). This was considered a better fit for historical and contemporary data, since there had always been cultivated minds and ignorant minds, and it avoided the problematic and potentially dangerous practice of impugning the integrity of leading ecclesiastical and intellectual figures of the day. Moreover, there was even a precedent within Christianity for conceiving of the tradition in this two-fold manner: Origen and Basil the Great both suggested that this structure might be characteristic of Christianity (Harrison 1990: 86).

By the time Reimarus came to the problem of Christian origins, he made no attempt to identify any bearers of an esoteric philosophy: a higher Christianity against which to define a superstitious populism. Although he did

---

45. Perhaps the most significant was Swift's *Mr C---s's Discourse of Free-Thinking, put into plain English, by way of abstract for use of the Poor* (1713). This was written in response to Anthony Collin, *A Discourse of Free-Thinking* (1713): a *cause célèbre* in the early-eighteenth-century European republic of letters.

recognize in Jesus' teaching the reflection of that natural religion of which he approved—which had very clear echoes of Blunt's ancient theology—the Christ cult itself was born of deception, plain and simple:

> It is clear, by their own account . . . that the apostles and all the disciples were induced by ambitious motives, by hopes of future wealth and power, land and worldly goods, to follow Jesus . . . Jesus himself gave them his promise that they should sit upon twelve thrones and judge the twelve tribes of Israel (Talbert 1971: 241).

And when the promises of exaltation failed to materialize, the apostles 'built up a new doctrine' of 'Jesus as a spiritual, suffering Savior', a doctrine 'which has every appearance of fictitious invention' (Talbert 1971: 242). This kind of conspiratorial take on positive religion generally, and Christianity in particular, may have lost ground to the twofold philosophy in the English-speaking world by the middle of the eighteenth century, but it continued to flourish in mainland Europe. Reimarus's reconstruction constitutes a particularly sustained and detailed application of a form of explanation that was advanced with monotonous regularity in European intellectual circles (Berti 1998: 19-36).

As early as 1512, Herman van Rijswijck was burnt alive for holding that 'Christ was a confused spirit, a seducer of other confused spirits, that he was not the son of God, and that he had condemned everyone and saved no one' (Berti 1998: 26-27). This was not a worked-out historical reconstruction, but it is worth noting that there were writers before Reimarus, also working in a Christian culture, who were prepared to go even further than he did in the *Apologie* and propose that Christianity's fraudulent character had its origins in Jesus himself. The seventeenth century witnessed the scandalous theories of Giulio Cesare Vanini, another martyr to theological heterodoxy, who suggested that Jesus was not only an impostor, but that he had invented the concept of the Antichrist as a bulwark against all future impostors who threatened his pre-eminence (Berti 1998: 30)! But perhaps the most notorious piece of imposture literature—of uncertain origin, but possibly predating the Enlightenment—made its greatest impact in the eighteenth century.

Like the fragments, the *Le traité des trois imposteurs* was an anonymous work;[46] unlike the fragments, the author remains unknown.[47] Like the fragments, *Le traité* claimed that Christianity was fraudulent from its very begin-

---

46. The three alleged impostors in this notorious tract are none other than Moses, Jesus and Muhammad. The most influential version during the Enlightenment (the French), and the earlier Latin version *De Tribus Impostoribus* are both available in English (Nasier 2003). For a book-length study of the tract and its place in the period, see Anderson 1997.

47. The text was first published at The Hague in 1719 under the title *La vie et l'esprit de Spinoza*, and a number of reputed Spinozist thinkers have been suggested in con-

nings, but it sought also to indict Judaism and Islam with the same charge. To place all three religions on an equal footing would be considered outrageous in Christian Europe, but to suggest that their commonality was located in deception made *Le traité* the most seductive and reviled underground document of the eighteenth century. *Le traité* is a piece of political and religious propaganda, not a strong historical argument, but it shows once again that there was little especially groundbreaking in the radicalism of Reimarus's basic contention.[48] Further, while Reimarus did, in the course of articulating his imposture theory, make a serious attempt to distinguish between different forms of eschatological expectation in first-century Judaism, his thesis that an apparent shift in conception, from worldly to spiritual, could be explained only by fraud has not fared well: David Strauss's high estimation of Reimarus is qualified by a repudiation of the theory that conscious deceit constitutes a credible historical cause for the rise of Christianity.[49]

2. *Remodelling Early Christianity*: Almost everything Reimarus wrote about Christian origins after the death of Jesus flows from the imposture hypothesis. Reimarus the religious polemicist was concerned to refute the central doctrines of Christianity, so Reimarus the conjectural historian was largely focussed on refuting the historical basis for those doctrines. On the historicity of the resurrection, Reimarus raises three main objections: (1) A theological intuition that authentic divine revelations, such as Jesus' alleged messiahship, should be convincing to all men, in and of themselves, without the need for some supernatural confirmation to a select few (Talbert 1971: 232-35). (2) There are implausibilities and contradictions within and between the resurrection narratives themselves (Talbert 1971: 153-200). (3) Following in the wake of English criticism of the apologetic value of prophecy, especially that of Anthony Collins, Reimarus rejects appeals to Old Testament prophecy as evidence that Jesus' resurrection was foretold in Jewish sacred history (Talbert 1971: 202-11).[50] This challenge to the cen-

---

nection with authorship, including John Toland (Champion 1996), a figure discussed in greater detail below.

48. I have been unable to establish whether Reimarus had read *Le traité* in any of its incarnations, but he was certainly acquainted with imposture literature on Islam, citing Humphrey Prideaux's 1697 tract *The True Nature of Imposture Fully Display'd in the Life of Mahomet* (Reimarus 1972: II, 667).

49. David Friedrich Strauss, 'Herman Samuel Reimarus and His Apology' (Talbert 1971: 44-57).

50. In the *Apologie* Reimarus refers to two English authors, Anthony Collins and Samuel Clarke, who were noted for, among other things, their controversial work on the difficulty of taking events in the New Testament as literal fulfilments of prophecies in the Old Testament, and he cites both men on this very subject: on Collins see Reimarus 1972: I, 728, 742; II, 271; on Clarke see Reimarus 1972: II, 271.

trepiece of the Christian revelation may have scandalized sections of the German-speaking public and intelligentsia, but only those who were not aware of the New Testament criticism produced in the English language throughout the eighteenth century, much of which had been translated into German (Talbert 1971: 15-16). The question of the historicity of the resurrection narratives had been the most heated subject during the deist controversy in England, where the reading public had been captivated by the pitiless, mocking deconstruction of the resurrection by the uproarious Thomas Woolston in his *Sixth Discourse on the Miracles of our Saviour* (1729),[51] and the mighty counteroffensive that followed, the high point of which was Thomas Sherlock's *Tryal of the Witnesses of the Resurrection of Jesus* (1729).[52] Once again, Reimarus was revisiting, in a particularly detailed way, arguments that had raged elsewhere in Europe throughout the Enlightenment.

Having rejected the resurrection, Reimarus redoubles his attack on trinitarian theology by deconstructing the story in Acts of the Apostles that underpins the Christian feast of Pentecost.[53] Reimarus offers some qualification to his imposture hypothesis when he acknowledges that by the time the author relates the story of the descent of the Holy Spirit, at least some Christians were sincere believers in the risen Lord (Talbert 1971: 260), the original deception having done its work. Nevertheless, the miracle of Pentecost, with wind, fire and the speaking in tongues, is rejected on three counts: (1) the aforementioned philosophical/theological judgment that any genuine divine revelation, in this case Jesus' supposed resurrection, should not require a subsequent miracle to make it more credible (Talbert 1971: 261-62); (2) internal contradictions and implausibilities in the account (Talbert 1971: 260-69); and (3) an alleged repudiation of at least elements of the miracle within the early Christian community itself (Talbert 1971: 263-64). 'The whole description', writes Reimarus,

> is more that of a prophetic vision to represent the prompting of foreign languages by the Holy Spirit. The mighty wind represents the Holy Spirit blowing into the apostles and kindling a blazing fire which shoots forth in forked flames from their mouths, signifying the gift of many languages. It is a good picture of the imaginary vision of the prophetic writer, but we

51. Woolston, who served time in prison for his blasphemous works, proposed an allegorical interpretation of all the miracles, which some scholars have seen as a precursor to the mythological model employed by David Strauss in the nineteenth century (Herrick 1997: 100).

52. It was Woolston, the accuser, who would end up on trial—in the law courts, not just the court of pamphleteers' opinion. On the rise and fall of this turbulent priest, see Herrick 1997: 78-101.

53. Reimarus had already attacked the Christian concept of the Holy Spirit as a divine person (Talbert 1971: 88-98).

cannot by any possible means make it rhyme with a true history. And why should some of those present have mocked at the apostles, and supposed them to be drunken with wine if these miraculous tongues were indeed visible to the spectators? The thing contradicts itself (Talbert 1971: 262-63).

The most authoritative Christian opposition that Reimarus detects to the miracle of Pentecost is found in Paul's First Letter to the Corinthians:

[H]e has not the courage to utterly forbid the speaking with tongues, as such a command would have been equivalent to accusing the apostles—with all their miraculous Corinthian gifts—of juggling and imposition, but, nevertheless he gives them to understanding, that he deems it advisable to refrain from speaking in unknown tongues which no man understands, and which, unless they be interpreted, are not edifying to the Church (Talbert 1971: 264).

Reimarus does attempt to draw attention to possible tensions in the early church, in this case over the question of appropriate modes of religious practice and evangelization, but they are all put to the service of undermining key Christian doctrines, so the scope of his reconstruction is narrow and theologically determined. One earlier scholar began his publishing career with a definite concern with Christian doctrines, but he moved quickly onto more advanced questions (in terms of the history of New Testament studies), including the question of how different early Christian communities defined themselves and their relationship to the Jewish law—the radical Irish-born writer John Toland (1670–1722).

Toland rose to infamy with the publication of *Christianity Not Mysterious* (1696), which already has a place in the canon of modern New Testament scholarship (Baird 1992: I, 39-41). Unlike Reimarus, Toland does not attack Christian revelation per se; indeed, with his exclusive focus on the Gospels, Toland's *modus operandi* looks like a modified version of *sola scriptura*. He consistently questions what doctrines can legitimately be constructed on the basis of recorded revelation without recourse to ineffable mystery and the supposed higher wisdom of ecclesiastical elites. But in the clandestine *Christianisme judaique et mahometan* and the subsequently published English version *Nazarenus, or Jewish, Gentile and Mahometan Christianity,*[54] Toland rewrites the history of Christianity in Ireland, rejecting Catholicism as an imposition, and, more significant for our enquiry, he proposes the *Gospel of Barnabas* as a source that illuminates the close historic relationship between elements in primitive Christian thought and Islamic views of Jesus (Champion 1996: 139-48).[55] The comparison between Islam and

54. French and English versions of the work are collected in Champion 1996.
55. The oldest known texts of this Gospel are an Italian manuscript dating from approximately the end of the sixteenth century and a Spanish manuscript from the eigh-

primitive Christianity was a dangerous one, even more so when made in connection with an alternative gospel. It was typical at the time to equate primitive Christianity with true Christianity, which Protestants generally assumed to be consistent with the contents of the New Testament, so any comparison with Islam supported by a noncanonical text would simultaneously challenge theological orthodoxy and the historical monopoly of the New Testament canon, opening the way for new sources to be used for the reconstruction of Christian origins. Why should this relatively obscure text, the apocryphal *Barnabas*, have captured the interest of radical writers in the early Enlightenment?

Amid the mass of anti-Islamic literature in the seventeenth century, Henry Stubbe circulated a sympathetic account of the prophet Muhammad and the rise of Islam.[56] One of Stubbe's arguments concerned a connection between the Ebionite Christian heresy and some aspects of Islamic theology, including the Islamic conception of Jesus: a messenger of God, but not divine. Toland appears to have accepted this argument (Champion 1996: 152-53), and, armed with *Barnabas*, he sets out to show that this Gospel reflected the belief and practice of the Ebionite community (which he equated with an early Christian movement he called 'the Nazarens'). Perhaps the most controversial twist in Toland's theorizing was his argument that, contrary to the judgment of the church fathers, not to mention almost every Christian historian in early modern Europe, Toland proposed that the Ebionites were closest in their religious practice to the intentions of Jesus, whose aims were continuous with, not a break from, Mosaic law (Reimarus made the same claim about half a century later):

> JESUS did not, as tis universally believed, abolish the law of Moses, neither in whole nor in part, not in the letter no more than in the spirit: with other uncommon particulars, concerning The True And Original Christianity. Finally, you'll discover some of the fundamental doctrines of Mohometanism to have their rise . . . from the earliest monuments of the Christian religion (Champion 1996: 135).

teenth century, although there is some dispute over the original language of composition (Joosten 2002: 73-74). Toland had access to the Italian version, then kept in Amsterdam, and later sold to Prince Eugène de Savoy; today it resides in the Austrian National Library in Vienna (Joosten 2010: 201-202). The dates suggested by scholars for the original composition of *Barnabas* range from antiquity to the seventeenth century, but most scholars prefer a late medieval or early modern date (Joosten 2002: 73-74). For an English translation, see Ragg and Ragg 1907.

56. Stubbe (1632–1676) was a librarian at the University of Oxford, a medical doctor and political controversialist; for a text of his work on the prophet Muhammad, Islam and what he took to be their misrepresentation in the Christian world, see Stubbe 1911. On the connections between the work of Stubbe and Toland, see Champion 1996: 333-56.

Toland's account of the derivation of the name Nazarens is the obvious one: 'these Jewish converts were term'd Nazarens from JESUS of Nazareth' (Champion 1996: 151). More interesting is the assumption that those from Nazareth, in Galilee, were closely bound to the Jewish law and resisted the influence of Hellenistic culture. Whether this is a safe assumption to make is among the most contested issues in the reconstruction of the Holy Land in the time of Jesus.[57] Toland thought that it was safe, and, in so far as *Barnabas* could have emanated from this community and impacted upon the Islamic world, Toland (Champion 1996: 135) also considers it safe to conclude that Islam is a 'sort of sect of Christianity, as Christianity was first esteem'd a branch of Judaism'.[58] Although Toland offered a radically antagonistic challenge to his contemporaries' notions about the historical relationship between Judaism, Christianity and Islam, his motives and results cannot be considered wholly destructive. On the contrary, Toland seizes on the diversity in early Christianity and, instead of trying either to impose absolute unity or to suggest that such plurality undermines revelation, Toland argues that this diversity was 'design'd in The Original Plan of Christianity' (Champion 1996: 117); he continues:

> From the history of the Nazarens, and more particularly from the evident words of Scripture, I infer in this discourse a distinction of two sorts of Christianity, viz., those from among the Jews, and those from among the Gentiles: not only that in fact there was such a distinction (which no body denies) but likewise that of right it ought to have been so (which everybody denies) . . . I mean that the Jews, tho associating with the converted Gentiles, and acknowledging them for brethren, were still to observe their own Law . . . and that the Gentile who became so far Jews as to acknowledge ONE GOD, were not however to observe the Jewish law . . . This fellowship in Piety and Virtue is the Mystery that PAUL rightly says was hid from all other ages, till the manifestation of it by Jesus; and this Union

---

57. Mark Chancey (2002) recounts and critiques a substantial tradition of twentieth-century scholarship that insisted on a large Gentile presence and influence in Galilee.

58. Toland tried to prove his case by comparing the picture in *Barnabas* with Islamic notions about Jesus (presumably drawn from the Qur'an, although there is no substantial engagement with the text) and references to the Ebionites in patristic sources (Champion 1996: 136-52). There does seem to have been an early Jewish Christian sect sometimes know as the Ebionites (meaning 'poor ones'), but they were probably a second-century phenomenon (Ehrman 2008: 3) which Toland conflated with the oldest Jewish Christian movement. More recent scholarship has also indicated that the Ebionites and the Nazoraeans (possibly Toland's Nazarens) were distinct Jewish Christian groups, possibly with their own gospels: see Petersen 1992a: 261-62; 1992b: 1051-52. Contemporary scholars generally hold that *Barnabas* contains material *from* Islamic sources, not, as Toland seemed to suggest, from early Jewish Christian sources that later informed or corresponded to Islamic thinking. *Barnabas* is actually thought to contain material from all three religious traditions (Joosten 2010: 200).

without Uniformity, between Jew and Gentile, is the admirable Economy of the Gospel (Champion 1996: 117).

According to Toland, the explanatory power of his reconstruction is vast:

> I judge it to be most right and true, the genuine primary Christianity; and therefore producing the promis'd effects of the Gospel, GLORY TO GOD ON HIGH, PEACE ON EARTH, GOODWILL TOWARDS MEN . . . I have moreover prov'd, that the distinction of Jewish and Gentile Christians . . . reconciles PETER and PAUL about Circumcision and the other Legal ceremonies, as it does PAUL and JAMES about Justification by Faith, or . . . by Works; it makes the Gospels to agree with the Acts and the Epistles . . . but, what is more than all, it shows a perfect accord between the Old Testament and the New; and proves that God did not give two Laws, whereof the one was to cancel the other, which is no small stumbling block to the opposers of Christianity, as the resolving of this difficulty is no sign, I hope, of my want of Religion (Champion 1996: 119).

Toland's acceptance of the heretical Ebionites as those closest in spirit to the religion of the historical Jesus, along with his acceptance of pluralism as inherent in primitive Christianity, provided little comfort for systematic theologians seeking a single, consistent and coherent doctrinal picture supported by Scripture. But theology was not Toland's primary concern. Justin Champion writes in his editorial introduction to the French and English versions of Toland's account of primitive Christianity:

> Having reconstructed the historical Milieu of early Judaeo-Christianity, Toland then proceeded to reinterpret the scriptural accounts of disputes between Peter, Paul and James about the relationship between Jewish ceremony and the soteriological efficiency of faith, not as theological systems, but as practical injunctions about how different types of believer, (Jewish, Nazarene, Gentile) could co-exist in civil society. Toland in effect used New Testament and patristic sources, not as material for authorising a 'system' of theological doctrine, but as an historical record of religious practice . . . Any distinctions in scriptural language and meaning do not translate into doctrinal conflict, nor indeed (for Toland) undermine its integrity, because all scripture has only historical rather than synchronical meaning. Just as Moses spoke to the Jewish nation, so Christ and Mahomet addressed their own historical communities. This was part of the reasoning behind advancing the *Gospel of Barnabas* as a Scriptural text that was used by Jewish-Christians and Muslims: Scripture was effective not for its doctrinal content (foisted by priests) but because it enables communities to live a virtuous life (1996: 75, 77).

Toland's insistence that the earliest Christians were, at least in their own minds, located within Judaism, has become common currency in the academic study of Christian origins, and Toland should be considered a pioneer in confronting diversity of belief and practice in early Christianity. In terms of methodology, Toland confronted this diversity historically, however inadequately—and it was inadequate. Toland's scholarship—apparently intended to legitimize *Barnabas*,[59] vindicate the Ebionites and show that Islamic teachings about Jesus have their origins in primitive Christianity— was soon subjected to massive and ultimately decisive criticism in England (Champion 1996: 89-96). Nevertheless, Toland's willingness to use noncanonical documents to try to establish the history of early Christian communities is now established practice in the study of Christian origins. In his monumental history of modern New Testament criticism, Werner Georg Kümmel (1973: 35-6) praises Hugo Grotius's 'bold conjectures concerning the historical situation of some New Testament letters . . . What is important in this connection is not whether Grotius's hypotheses are convincing (they are hardly that!), but that Grotius makes any use at all of historical conjecture as a tool of New Testament interpretation.' I hope that Toland's importance will be more widely recognized in this regard.

Conclusion

Like many intellectual monuments, Reimarus's writings on the historical Jesus and Christian origins are works of synthesis. The sixth and seventh fragments of Reimarus's *magnum opus*, issued by Lessing during the high Enlightenment, followed established lines of argument that had already made critical inroads into the orthodox picture: the attack on miracles, including the resurrection (Woolston); the denial of historically realized prophecy (Collins); the distinction between the teachings of Jesus and the teachings of his followers (Chubb); recognition of the central importance of eschatology (Tindal); and the use of conjectural historical hypotheses to understand the communities behind the literature of early Christianity (Toland). The road to Reimarus is paved with writers who sometimes went beyond the more scholarly German critic, pointing towards later developments in the discipline: Tindal confronted apocalyptic eschatology; Woolston tried to reconceptualize the miracles as allegory; and Toland was prepared to consider noncanonical accounts of Jesus in conjectural historical reconstruction. All these writers worked in the traumatic early phase of the great reversal: an intellectual reorientation that would change the way Christian history was written forever. In biography, those changes were most evident in the work of Bayle, as he ranged over a bewildering number of historical figures, debunking the myths that had grown around these subjects and isolating the historical core. The seventeenth- and eighteenth-century writers profiled in this essay, of whom Reimarus was the latest and the most celebrated in the history of the quest, broke new ground by daring

---

59. Toland later denied that he had ever promoted *Barnabas* as an authentic ancient source (Champion 1996: 95).

to take the most iconic figure in Western culture and Christian piety as one of those historical subjects. Whether Jesus was wholly and only human or, as Christian orthodoxy insists, wholly human and wholly divine, his human story and his human legacy could now be studied like any other person of his time.

But however great the methodological continuities are between modern historical disciplines, it would be unrealistic to expect studies of Jesus to be conducted or received with the same levels of disinterestedness that are characteristic of histories of other figures of the ancient world. During the European Enlightenment, Jesus was a vital cultural figure in a way that Julius Caesar and Alexander the Great were not, and this remains true in the present century. The production and reception of historical studies of Jesus have always functioned within wider discussions about religious, cultural and political identity,[60] and the historical dimension of this interplay is not restricted to the study of Jesus as an individual. At the start of this essay, I noted the close relationship between the quest for the Jesus of history and what we might call the quest for the Jesus of place. Other essays in this volume demonstrate how the construction of historical landscapes for Jesus, and for ancient Christianity and Judaism, has often been inseparable from contemporary questions concerning religious, cultural and political identity.[61]

60. In his famous survey of historical Jesus research, Schweitzer argued that the scholarship he encountered often reflected the imperatives of European liberalism and the kind of Christian identity that thinkers of this orientation thought appropriate in the modern world (1911: Chs. 4; 12; 14; 16). Arguments about the role of religious and cultural self definition in scholarship continue in contemporary analysis, although North America has replaced Europe as the dominant focus: see, for instance, the central argument running throughout Arnal 2005.

61. I would like to thank Samuel Tongue, of the University of Glasgow, for his valuable comments on this essay.

LANDSCAPES OF DEMOCRACY[*]

Burke O. Long

The American School of Oriental Research in Jerusalem began mod-
estly in 1900 with little financial backing. However, a dedicated few gar-
nered much in the way of institutional good will, for they hoped that such
a research venture would stir national pride, stimulate scholarly study and
strengthen religious faith. Some thought it might even compensate for
the embarrassing failure in 1884 of a research organization modeled after
the very successful, and British, Palestine Exploration Fund (King 1983:
27-53).

For better than a half century, most scholars associated with the new
initiative would follow the general approach to Holy Land exploration that
Edward Robinson had established in the 1840s. They would help develop
a community of seminary and university scholars who, deploying specific
skills and theoretical perspectives, would define the 'ancient Near East' as
a new field of professional study (Kuklick 1996). Despite increasing secu-
larization of knowledge during these years, many would continue habits of
imagining Near Eastern Palestine as ancient, but vestigially present, biblical
space, a mostly Christianized heritage awaiting reclamation.

However, the years spanning two world wars brought stressful changes
to the United States—and newly intense configurations of Holy Land infatuations. Encoded in scholarly activities would be holy lands constructed of
the familiar elements of geopiety, now supported by increasingly technical
bodies of knowledge and given voice in strident political debates of the
1920s–1940s.

One of the prime movers of the American School in Jerusalem was
J. Henry Thayer, professor of New Testament at Harvard University and
president of the Society of Biblical Literature and Exegesis. In an 1895
meeting of the Society, Thayer put the case for Americans to explore Pal-

*This essay was first published as Chapter 4 in *Imagining the Holy Land: Maps,
Models and Fantasy Travels* (Bloomington and Indianapolis: Indiana University Press,
2003), pp. 131-63. It is reprinted with permission of Indiana University Press.

estine. Consider, he said, that the French had already started a school with its own scholarly journal, all to advance 'Biblical learning and missionary work'. Could the Americans do any less? Warming to his task, Thayer summoned up a genealogy of ancestral pioneers—rough and ready explorers, meticulous scientists, and soldiers of the faith—to arouse slumbering colleagues to their patriotic duty.

> Shall the countrymen of Robinson and Thomson, Lynch and Merrill, Eli Smith and Van Dyck, look on unconcerned? Shall a Society, organized for the express purpose of stimulating and diffusing a scholarly knowledge of the Sacred Word, remain seated with folded hands, taking no part or lot in the matter? (Thayer 1895: 16).

Thayer's call to activism drew some of its political urgency from an explosive growth in Holy Land tourism, the public's infatuation with discovering holy lands that confirmed the Bible, and governments that, in growing nationalistic competition, saw strategic value in Holy Land exploration (Silberman 1982). While perhaps implicitly acknowledging the power of these factors, Thayer chose his own heroes from a roster of popular Christian explorers who combined more or less technical learning with lives as churchmen and public intellectuals. Like Chautauqua's leaders and other promoters of surrogate study tours to the Holy Land, these pioneers accepted the Bible as inerrant Scripture, unfurled American flags in the promised land and searched out geographical facts to defend biblical truth against its detractors.[1]

For many of Thayer's colleagues in 1895, the pedigree he cited was both cultural heritage and fresh memory. They had witnessed the founding of the American Palestine Exploration Society in 1870 and its early demise fourteen years later. Most had sanctioned its chartering documents that encouraged on-the-ground research to illustrate the Bible and refute new literary and historical theories that challenged traditional notions of biblical authorship and divine inspiration. The Society's second president, Roswell D. Hitchcock, was friend, colleague, and biographer of the greatly revered Edward Robinson, the most gifted explorer-hero Thayer summoned up in his call to action (King 1983: 8-9).[2]

Robinson was well known to academics for his distinguished philological studies, but he achieved public stardom, nineteenth-century style, from his accounts of travels to Syria and Palestine in 1838 and 1852.[3] Robinson produced the first truly rigorous study of Palestine's surface features for the

---

1. For the larger picture, see Queen 1996: 209-28; Vogel, 1993: 185-211.
2. For a history of the American Palestine Exploration Society, see Moulton 1926–27: 55-78.
3. Compatriot Eli Smith, also cited in Thayer's clarion call, accompanied Robinson on his first journey. Smith had been Robinson's student, was fluent in Arabic and local

Edward Robinson. Portrait by Daniel Huntington. Photo by
David A. Tewksbury. Courtesy of Hamilton College, Clinton,
New York

English-speaking world. Notably, he evaluated modern Arabic place-names
to establish linguistic and geographic connections with ancient biblical peoples. Joining this evidence with careful evaluations of other sources and
fresh geographical observations, Robinson identified genuine, as opposed
to legendary, biblical sites and strengthened belief in the Bible's historical reliability.[4] In the process, he advanced quasi-political claims to the
land itself. Refined maps of biblical geography imposed emotional affinity,

custom and was a leading missionary to Beirut and explorer in his own right (Smith
1833).

    4. Robinson's ideological conviction was evident when he became a moving force
behind the *American Biblical Repository*, a journal of conservative biblical apologetics.
Contributing authors, including Robinson, frequently opposed European historical criticism and its few New England proponents, mostly Unitarians, who were undertaking
biblical study with a decidedly nontraditional bent. The *Repository* provided conservative readings of the Bible and reports from missionary travelers and explorers as con-
firming evidence of the Bible's historical accuracy and orthodox theology.

personal kinship to biblical presence, on what to many Americans were uninspiring and foreign-held provinces of the Ottoman Empire.

Robinson's reports took form as a travel diary that, along with numerous excerpts published in newspapers and journals, achieved surprising popularity. [5] On the advice of friends, Robinson abandoned his original plan for a technical work and wrote more in the vernacular style of Holy Land discovery narratives filled with personal comments and religious devotion. He relieved long stretches of scientific tedium with vignettes of local people and customs, scriptural illustration and digressions to recall narratives of Old and New Testament events.

Robinson was as dedicated to Christ as he was submissive to scientific method and Mistress Holy Land herself. The Holy Land, like science, demanded meticulous devotion, and she revealed herself to reverent seeker and scientist alike who, like the ancient Israelites, stood poised to know thoroughly what God had provided. Robinson wove personal narrative with scientific research, he told his readers, so as 'exhibit the manner in which the Promised Land unfolded itself before our eyes, and the processes by which we were led to the conclusions and opinions advanced in this work' (Robinson 1841: I, vii).

Moreover, particular aspects of American experience offered special access to Holy Land truth. From earliest New England childhood, Robinson wrote, scenes from the Bible had made a deep impression. As an adult with sensibilities formed by uniquely American experience, youthful impression became a strong desire to visit the places where formative events had occurred.

> Indeed in no country of the world, perhaps, is such a feeling more widely diffused than in New England; in no country are the Scriptures better known, or more highly prized. From his earliest years the child is there accustomed not only to read the Bible for himself; but he also reads or listens to it in the morning and evening devotions of the family, in the daily village-school, in the Sunday-school and Bible-class, and in the weekly ministrations of the sanctuary (Robinson 1841: I, 31-32)

Quickly setting an international standard for critical work in biblical geography, Robinson's harmonious blend of American exceptionalism, piety, and rigorous scholarship would characterize the short-lived American Palestine Exploration Society as well as much subsequent Holy Land research. He also began a process by which American politicians and diplo-

---

5. Robinson and Smith 1841 (published concurrently in England and in Germany). An account of his second journey appeared as Edward Robinson, *Later Research in Palestine and in the Adjacent Regions: A Journal of Travels in the Year 1852. Drawn up from the Original Diaries with Historical Illustrations, with New Maps and Plans* (1856). Subsequent editions removed some of the technical material and compressed the diaries into more manageable proportions.

mats would soon compete with their more experienced European counterparts in sending scholarly explorers to lay claim to Ottoman Palestine in the
name of science, fatherland and the Bible (Silberman 1982: 46-47). A colleague's eulogy for Robinson eloquently caught that nationalist sentiment:

> Resolved, that his departure takes from our country the patriarch of sacred
> scholarship, an untiring student, a careful, learned and sagacious author
> whose works have enriched our own libraries, done honor to the American
> name abroad and written his own name with that of our Nation upon the
> land and language of the Bible.[6]

To claim the Holy Land for one's own nation—the naturalness of that
colonialist metaphor reflected deep connections between nineteenth-century Protestant religion and the United State's emerging imperial policies
(Smylie 1963: 297-311). It could easily have been applied to another of
Thayer's explorer-heroes, William M. Thomson. A missionary in Palestine
for more than forty years, Thomson had provided local assistance on Robinson's journey of 1852. Shortly thereafter, it will be recalled, he achieved
unusual literary fame with the lavishly illustrated *The Land and the Book*,
a report of travels that popularized the notion that the Holy Land's physical
characteristics directly spoke of Christ.[7]

For Thomson, Protestants held a particular right to this land, just as
their version of Christianity, by divine promise, supplanted practices of
non-Christian religions. Because Abraham, traveler through Canaan, had
been justified by his belief in God, so latter-day Christians, heirs to Abraham through faith, should explore the Promised Land unhindered, whether
equipped with scholarly training, an adventurer's pious courage, or both,
which was Robinson's mien. 'To walk through the land is the exact purport
of my visit,' Thomson told his readers. 'And I mean to make it mine from
Dan to Beersheba before I leave it' (Thomson 1859: I, 24).[8]

6. *Minutes of the New-York Historical Society*, 8 February 1863, cited in Williams
1999: 332. The main nineteenth-century biographical sources for Robinson are the eulo-
gizing addresses of H.B. Smith and Hitchcock (1863). See also Silberman 1982: 37-47;
American National Biography, vol. 18 (1999), pp. 647-49.

7. See Long 2003: 39-40. Outselling Robinson and Smith (1841) by far, Thomson's
book eventually appeared in over thirty editions.

8. Some twenty years earlier, the Archbishop of York had marked the founding of
the Palestine Exploration Fund with similar fanfares of British imperial, Christian rule.
'This country of Palestine belongs to you and to me, it is essentially ours', he said. 'It
was given to the father of Israel in the words, "Walk through the land in the length of it
and in the breadth of it, for I will give it unto ye." We mean to walk through Palestine,
in the length and breadth of it, because that land has been given to us. It is the land from
which comes news of our redemption. . . It is the land to which we look with as true a
patriotism as we do to this dear old England' (*Palestine Exploration Fund Proceedings
and Notes* [London, 1865–69], cited in Silberman 1982: 86).

Thomson's readers probably needed no convincing. Many likely felt dispossessed, given the widely accepted opinion that the medieval Crusaders' aim to restore the Holy Land to Christian influence was finally being realized in Anglo-European explorations and, after World War I, in political control by Great Britain. [9] Others undoubtedly had encountered reports of righteous invaders recapitulating the biblical conquest of Canaan with cameras, paintbrushes, notebooks, sextants and evangelical zeal. American travelers, like their counterparts from European nations, ardently displayed their national flag at sacred spots, over their tents, on their backs, or streaming from parasols, as one diarist complained huffily about a prim Victorian lady who took 'possession of each place she passed thru'.[10]

William Francis Lynch, cited among Professor Thayer's heroic explorers, fit this mold of imperious crusade, if a little incongruously. Described as an 'earnest Christian and lover of adventure',[11] Lynch embodied the very ideas of science-authorized Christian piety and staking-a-claim adventures. In 1848, bearing the requisite permission from Turkish authorities, he led, in his words, 'young, muscular, native born Americans of sober habits' on a somewhat preposterous flag-planting expedition down the Jordan River into the Dead Sea. Afterwards, Lynch quickly popularized his exploits with a report illustrated with wood engravings claimed to be 'true to nature' but drawn with conventional romantic drama (1849: 13-14).[12] His circumnavigation of the Dead Sea and geographical survey of the Jordan Rift, firsts among American explorers, was truly epoch making, even as his bra-

9. Lyman Abbott, a nineteenth-century cleric and prolific writer, was typical of many who presumed that the privilege accorded to scientific rationality also justified uninhibited exploration of Palestine. 'We trust that the science of the nineteenth century', Abbott wrote of British excavations in Jerusalem, 'may accomplish what the armed piety of the twelfth century essayed in vain—the recovery of Jerusalem' (1871: 206). Nearly a half century later, newspapers, magazines, stereographs, postcards, not to mention some biblical scholars, routinely celebrated the military capture of Jerusalem near the end of the war as an entirely justifiable restoration of the Holy Land to Christian rule. See, for example, an essay by prominent biblical archaeologist John P. Peters (1918a: 47-580; 1918b: 31-32; 1919: 1229-36), a photo essay that portrayed long-suffering biblical peoples witnessing 'a dawn of promise' brought by British victory and its prospect of liberal governance. See further Finley 1919; Whitehair 1918: 325-44.

10. 'Middle East Diary of Isabel M.C. Church,' 28 March 1868. Typescript, Olana State Historic Site, Hudson, New York. Cited by J. Davis 1996: 33.

11. *Dictionary of American Biography* (New York: Scribner, 1946–58), XI, pp. 524-25. See also *National Cyclopaedia of American Biography* (New York: James T. White, 1906), XIII, pp. 172-73.

12. A competing account of the expedition, also seeking public fame for its author, appeared the same year under the editorship of Montague (1849). Lynch and other early explorers receive colorful treatment in Finnie 1967. See also Silberman 1982: 51-62.

ENCAMPMENT ON THE RIVER BELUS.

"Encampment on the River Belus," from Lynch, *Expedition to the River Jordan and the Dead Sea*

zen conquest in the name of science, the American Navy and 'native born' Americans earned him a place in the litany of Professor Thayer's heroes.

Another was Selah Merrill, Congregational clergyman, theological seminary professor and American Consul to Jerusalem during the years 1882–85, 1891–93 and 1898–1907. In 1875–77, he had been staff archaeologist, then leader, of a rather unsuccessful expedition east of the Jordan River on behalf of the short-lived American Palestine Exploration Society. The final reports were incomplete, but the undertrained Merrill (1881a) trumpeted his work anyway in a highly romanticized account of his travels.[13]

Merrill avidly fed the public's appetite for pious heroics. Saying he had sought appointments as consul to enable his exploration of the Holy Land, Merrill amassed a huge collection of antiquities and natural history specimens that eventually found its way to the Harvard Semitic Museum. He wrote discovery books on Jerusalem, a sentimental idyll on Jesus' Galilee and numerous popular essays dealing with local curiosities and archaeological findings. He also promoted Holy Land infatuations of others and

13. Further biographical material in *Dictionary of American Biography* (New York: Charles Scribner's Sons, 1928–36), XII, pp. 564-65; *Appleton's Cyclopaedia of American Biography* (New York: D. Appleton & Co., 1887–89), IV, p. 307; *National Cyclopaedia of American Biography* (New York: J.T. White, 1893–1984), XIII, p. 218. Thayer mentioned a little-known Henry L. Van Dyck, who served as travel assistant and interpreter for Merrill's explorations.

collaborated in producing *Picturesque Palestine*, a consummate example of armchair journeys into the manufactured spaces of the Holy Land (Merrill 1908; 1881a; 1881b: 287-358).[14]

Not one to discourage private enterprise either, Merrill once enthusiastically endorsed a scheme to boil, cool and ship some thirty-four tons of purified Jordan River water to the United States. Merrill was considerably less generous toward Jews and the Protestant residents of the American colony in Jerusalem, whom he publicly disparaged, even vilified (Goldman 1997: 151-72; Vogel 1993: 157-69, 181-83). As both a highly visible government representative, Bible student and Holy Land explorer, Selah Merrill embodied, perhaps more than any other American figure at the time, the entangled strains of adventure expeditions, *Realpolitik*, Christian triumphalism and scholarly possession of a biblically signposted Holy Land. One alarmed critic, the consul general of Beirut, complained that Merrill 'considered the whole of Palestine and its works to be his special bailiwick' (Kark 1990: 138).

J. Henry Thayer's rhetorical praise of famous men had quick effect. Within five years a formal proposal gained financial pledges from twenty institutions and thirteen individuals. With governing resolutions voted, the school's doors could open and American biblical scholars could set about (re)claiming the Holy Land for science, America, and God. As much as they could, that is, with limited funds and a rented room in the New Grand Hotel, just inside the walled city of Jerusalem. About a kilometer away was the American Consulate and the good offices of Selah Merrill. The effort at concerted scholarly exploration looked something like an American protectorate. At the least, it had claims on official and personal assistance, which Merrill gladly supplied (King 1983: 30).)

By this time, around 1900, Thayer's stirring address had been reduced to the necessary tedium of resolution and constitution that would govern the school. Religiously nonsectarian and forward-looking in admitting both men and women, the school's stated purpose was to 'enable properly qualified persons to prosecute Biblical, linguistic, archaeological, historical, and other kindred studies and researches under more favorable conditions than can be secured at a distance from the Holy Land'.[15]

Invisible in this formulation of nonsectarian academic purpose, however, were two important factors. First, study of the Bible and the Holy Land as envisioned by the School's founders was largely a Protestant affair. It would be two to three decades before significant numbers of Jewish and Roman

14. Merrill wrote introductions to a children's book (Knight 1888) and a collection of flower specimens (Greene 1880).

15. Official policy statements may be found in *Journal of Biblical Literature* 20 (1901), pp. iv-v.

AMERICAN CONSULATE AND TOWER OF DAVID, JERUSALEM.

American Consulate, from DeHass, *Buried Cities*.

Catholic scholars would participate (Fogarty 1989; Sperling 1992). Second, the animating piety and spirit of Edward Robinson would in effect define a culture of the 'properly qualified' and their main activities at the school. Indeed, from the beginning well into mid-century, Robinson's harmonious blend of scientific rationalism, geopiety, patriotism, and Protestant devotion to the Bible were strongly in evidence. George Barton, for example, the distinguished Quaker scholar of Assyriology, Bible and archaeology, and the School's third annual director, retraced some of Robinson's explorations and tried to fill remaining gaps and tried to pinpoint as-yet-unlocated biblical events. Barton's published account of those journeys conformed to the popular type: a scholar-pilgrim's diary of discovery in a Christianized Holy Land. Like Jesse Lyman Hurlbut's and Charles Foster Kent's parlor tours, Barton sought refuge in biblical memory, listening for 'echoes of the footsteps of the religious heroes of both Testaments'. Decrying modernization, he found unmediated encounters with biblical reality hard to come by, but no less desirable or attainable on that account. Muslim residents, whom he often dismissed as 'fanatics', got in the way, as did those non-Quakerish 'ecclesiastical trappings [that] would overlay so thoroughly the reality of the past as to rob it of all significance' (Barton 1904: 141, 97, 233, 185-86).[16]

16. See also Barton 1916, which was published in many editions into the 1930s. Barton's letters, the basis for his book, may be consulted among the Barton Papers,

William Foxwell Albright, the American School's director from 1920 to 1929 and the major influence on the School's development, was more circumspect but no less at home in this Protestant ethos. Despite his success at encouraging scholarly cooperation across sectarian and national divisions, Albright's first field studies as well as typical programs for resident students and scholars followed Robinson's lead. Geography and archaeology went hand in hand to build confidence in the Bible and to establish background and precise locations for biblical events. Like Robinson, Albright fed the public's hunger for Bible-centered romance, partly because the School's financial solvency depended on it. 'These unassuming mounds among the hills of Ephraim and Benjamin are of the greatest interest to us', Albright once wrote for readers of the School's nontechnical *Bulletin*,

> They represent authentic monuments of the Israelite past. Every stone and potsherd they conceal is hallowed by us by association with the great names of the Bible. Who can think of the tells which mark ancient Mizpah and Gibeah without a thrill as memory calls up the shade of Samuel, and the heroic figure of Saul? (Albright 1922: 9).[17]

James Montgomery, chair of the School's executive committee and editor of the *Bulletin* for thirty years, drew on such sentiments more explicitly to help secure financial support of the fledgling School. 'If America is to maintain an honorable place in the international plan for archaeological work in Palestine', he said after World War I, 'increased income must be

---

Archives, the Library of Bryn Mawr College, Bryn Mawr, Pennsylvania. For additional material, see George Aaron Barton, Papers, 1903–1942, University of Pennsylvania Archives, Philadelphia, Pennsylvania. Biographical sketches may be found in *National Cyclopaedia of American Biography* (New York: James T. White, 1934), current vol. D, pp.441-42; *Bulletin of the American School of Oriental Research* 87 (October, 1942), pp. 2-6; *Bryn Mawr Alumni Quarterly* 13, no. 3 (November 1919), pp. 5-17; *American National Biography* (New York: Oxford University, 1999), II, 291-92.

17. In 1911, David Lyon, an accomplished biblical scholar, Assyriologist and archaeologist-curator of Harvard's Semitic Museum, explicitly acknowledged a common bond between tourist and scholar, both of whom sought 'religious quickening' or 'confirmation and elucidation of the Scriptures' (Lyon 1911: 4). See also Lyon's undated illustrated lectures 'Palestine and the Bible'. These handwritten notes, like Hurlbut's and Kent's parlor tours, constructed memories of glorious biblical days in the light of, as a press release noted, 'Palestine of today that is a living commentary on the Bible' (David Lyon Papers, Harvard University Archives, box 1, folder: 'Palestine and the Bible'). See also David Lyon, 'Palestine, the Bible, and Archaeology', a handwritten manuscript later published in the *Boston Evening Transcript* (February 26, 1910; Lyon Papers, Box 2). For biographical information, see *Dictionary of American Biography*(New York: Charles Scribner's Sons, 1958), XXI, supplement 1, pp. 518-19; 'David Gordon Lyon: In Memoriam', *Bulletin of the American School of Oriental Research* 62 (April, 1936), pp. 2-4.

obtained at once . . . and all lovers of the Bible are earnestly urged to come to our aid' (1919: 4; see also 1920: 9). It was, after all, a matter of civic honor and duty, especially for Americans, to respond to this new opportunity. The 'preeminently Bible-studying land'—Montgomery echoed Robinson here—should play its part 'now that Palestine has fallen into Christian and civilized hands'(Montgomery 1918: 173).[18]

Montgomery had some success and the Jerusalem school grew. But radical changes were in the air at home. Finding cultural benchmarks in classical antiquity, such as were embodied in the St. Louis World's Fair, was losing its popular appeal. At the same time, increasingly vigorous study of the ancient Near East was pushing the limits of antiquity far beyond Greece and Rome. Moreover, social turmoil was intensifying in the United States. Waves of European immigrants, socialist philosophies, excesses of capitalist enterprise, racial conflict and two world wars—all posed challenges to the easy optimism of turn-of-the-century America and the unquestioned presumption that Protestant America was heir to the promises of Holy Land.

These were also the years, it will be recalled, of inventive entrepreneurial responses to fever-pitch interest in the Holy Land. Models, World's Fair spectacles, exhibits of landscape paintings, photographs and postcards, diaries and travelogues, parlor music, cabinets of Bible land artifacts—these were some of items of Holy Land consciousness that were becoming mass marketed commodities. Many were apt to show up in homes, churches and local libraries, along with sensationalized reports of archaeological discoveries, Bible dictionaries and atlases purposefully coordinated with the expanding curricula of the American Sunday School movement.

In the early days of the American School, William Foxwell Albright, Chester Charlton McCown and Max Leopold Margolis developed their professional careers in relation to this flowing stream of cultural imagination. They also responded to changing political circumstances. Deeply committed to harmonized ideologies of science and Protestant Christianity, Albright and McCown imagined the Holy Land primarily as biblical space fraught with declarations of God's purposes and events to be recovered, revered and relived in historical knowledge. Margolis, an ardent Zionist, joined the same canons of scientific and historical inquiry to a quite different ideational space, an ancient Holy Land of national independence reenacted as cultural and religious renaissance for Jews and Judaism.

---

18. Albright shared Montgomery's desire to assert American primacy in Palestine research, to judge from comments in *Bulletin of the American School of Oriental Research* 11(October 1923), p. 4; *Bulletin of the American School of Oriental Research* 12 (December 1923), pp. 11-12. For biographical material on Montgomery, see Speiser 1949: 4-8; *Dictionary of American Biography* (New York: Charles Scribner's Sons, 1974), XXIV, supplement 4, pp. 594-96.

All three men deployed technical scholarship to imagine divinely sanctioned truths rooted in the Holy Land that helped them negotiate the political crosswinds blowing across the America of their day. While reinscribing
many vernacular representations of the Holy Land onto the body of biblical
scholarship, each invented a holy land nuanced for his own time. And all
three men advanced programs at the American School of Oriental Research,
that mighty propagator of scholarly knowledge and spaces of Holy Land
consciousness.

Albright's Holy Land: A Fountainhead

Seeing himself as distinctly removed from those untrained, adventurer-
pilgrim-travelers of an earlier century, Albright made his way through
Egypt to British Mandate Palestine in December 1919.[19] He was twenty-
eight years old and about to begin postgraduate research as the Thayer Fellow of the American School in Jerusalem. The following year he would
begin his distinguished service as Director of the School during 1920–29
and 1933–36, while pursuing an extraordinarily productive career at Johns
Hopkins University, 1929–58. Epitomizing what was then called 'Oriental
studies', Albright would preside over major efforts, especially by his many
students, to deploy linguistic, archaeological, literary and material studies
to advance scientific knowledge of the Bible and promote a theological
view of Western intellectual history.[20])

In mid-summer of 1921, flush with early successes, Albright told his
mother about the pleasures of living and working in Jerusalem. 'It is the first
place I have yet been in', he wrote, 'where I really wanted to stay. There is
not a spot in the whole world which suits me like Jerusalem, not only for its
associations, but also because of the opportunities for research at the foun-
tain head, and because of the cultivated cosmopolitan atmosphere which I
love.' Carried along by this rush of feeling, Albright extolled the wondrous

19. Albright had scant sympathy for those he viewed as driven by irrational passion
to take up impractical ventures in Palestine. About a year after his arrival in Jerusalem,
he reported that he had met a 'poor, deluded American religious fanatic', (perhaps typical of the Christian millenarian colonists of the day), who had 'sold his farm in Okla-
homa and come to Palestine to invest in a fruit-farm!' Noting that economic realties were
against the scheme, he concluded, 'And still they come, Jews and Christians, following
the same bubble which swept millions into eternity in the past.' Albright to his mother,
Zephine Viola Albright, June 3, 1921, courtesy of Leona Glidden Running.

20. See Running and Freedman 1975; King 1983: 58, 63-84. Further biographical
material may be found in Freedman 1975: 3-40; 'William Foxwell Albright', in Louis
Finkelstein (ed.), *American Spiritual Autobiographies: Fifteen Self-portraits* (New
York: Harper and Brothers, 1948), pp. 156-81; *American National Biography* (New
York: Oxford University Press, 1999), I, pp. 227-28.

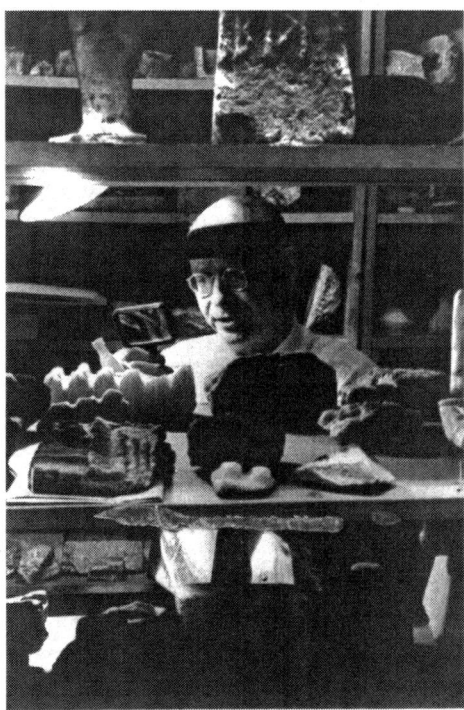

William Foxwell Albright,
c. 1950. Courtesy of the Ferdinand
Hamburger, Jr. Archives, Johns
Hopkins University.

variety of people who made their way to Jerusalem. 'It is all interesting', he said, his prose swelling with postwar optimism. Marching under the banner of 'our beautiful international science', he added, 'little bands of scholars in the various countries are again exchanging discoveries and methods, while our knowledge of the lands where human material and spiritual civilization originated increases by leaps and bounds'.[21]

When he confessed such delight in Jerusalem, Albright was already preparing an essay that would evince similar enthusiasm for the ideologies of evolutionary advancement, lionized science, and privileged origins. He wanted to help his Christian readers realize that accelerating postwar archaeological research was uncovering 'the mighty sweep and momentum

21. Albright to Zephine Viola Albright, 13 July 1921, courtesy of Leona Glidden Running. However strong the appeal of science without borders might have been, harmonious academic exchange involved national competition, too. Albright responded to that melody as well and wrote of it a year later in praising C.C. McCown's studies of Arab folk religion. McCown had followed in the line of Samuel Ives Curtis, Albright wrote, 'whose pioneering work in this field placed American scholars under an obligation to continue the studies begun by their illustrious compatriot' (1921: 4).

of the spirit of progress in man, ever striving forward and upward' toward its culmination in Christian civilization. No one could detect divine providence in history so clearly as 'the reverent archaeologist' whose one great aim was 'to know the past as it really was, and to deduce the laws which govern the development of man toward that ultimate goal which the Creator has set for him'.

In the service of such ambitions, Albright continued, archaeology in Palestine held a 'peculiar interest that no other branch of the science has'. As an enterprise carried on at the fountainhead, excavations could confirm and reinforce in Albright's reader and, just as importantly, in Albright himself, deep emotional attachment to an idealized Holy Land. It was a land of religious imagination and historical facticity, a place of beginnings etched in desert tracings and sandstone ruins, yet pregnant with ultimate value and significance. In its most revered, almost sainted application, Albright suggested, archaeology laid bare the birthplace of the Bible, the

> land where the sacredest of human possessions came into being, and [where] hardly a mile of its surface is not hallowed by Biblical associations. In the illustration, elucidation, and, if need be, confirmation of this masterpiece of world literature archaeology justifies itself finely (Albright 1922: 402, 412, 418; see also 1933: 12-15).

The following year, Albright referred to the land exposed by archaeology and imagined by piety as the 'cradle' of Christianity. Sure that the 1920s turmoil in Palestine meant 'little in comparison to the eternal verities of religion', Albright made his own claim to ownership. He dismissed the current troubles as a 'contest between Jew and Arab (for control) of the Holy Land'. It was the ancient, universally influential place, not the modern protectorate of the British Empire that was to be recovered and revered. 'To the Christian', Albright continued, recasting the fervor of his nineteenth-century predecessors, 'Palestine has a personal attraction as the cradle of his faith and the enduring witness to the genuineness of the documents upon which that faith is primarily based'. By using all available information to illuminate the Bible, every teacher and student would be able to see 'revelation as a logical, consistent whole, and to combine his data into a solid foundation for confidence in the purposes of God and the destiny of man' (Albright 1923: 7).

About a decade later, Albright observed that the results of such grand endeavors made him and his readers 'spectators at the unfolding of the greatest drama of history, the origin and early development of our own civilization and our own religion' (1932: 62). By 1940, Albright presented a compelling and comprehensive rendering of that drama by tracing, as he told the readers of *From the Stone Age to Christianity*, 'our Christian civilization of the West to its earliest sources' (1957: 32).[22] Two years later, he described his purpose in writing *Archaeology and the Religion of Israel* as 'nothing less than the ultimate reconstruction, as far as possible, of the route which our cultural ancestors traversed in order to reach Judeo-Christian heights of spiritual insight and ethical monotheism' (1967: 4).[23]

Imagining the Holy Land in a narrative of evolutionary perfection did not appeal only to Bible-centered sensibilities and traditional geopiety. It had a political bite as well. From this ancient 'fountainhead' flowed democratic values and social organization that Albright, without specifying matters too closely, accepted as being consistent with American forms of Christianity and Judaism. Thanks to the results of increasingly scientific archaeology, Albright wrote in 1922, enlightened people could now see that institutions, which had evolved over thousands of years, had 'an inherent stability and a permanent value'. Measured against such granite-hard and empirically tried foundations, 'hasty generalizations of modern speculative sociology' (by which he apparently meant Marxist/Leninist philosophy) looked quite insubstantial. In a gesture of containment, Albright declared checkmate:

> Our radical Socialist friends would do well to immerse themselves in the study of archaeology before attempting to repeat an experiment which failed a thousand times before the abortive communism of Mazdak, so like that of Lenine [*sic*], fifteen centuries later (Albright 1922: 402-403).

When Albright wrote these words, the United States was coming to terms with increased immigration from Eastern Europe. The Russian revolution of 1917 was a fresh memory, and growing numbers of socialists and Leninists clamored for a newly ordered society in Europe and North America. Turmoil swirled about big business, labor unions, and voting rights. A war had been fought and sloganeered to 'save democracy'. It was a time in the United States, as James Weinstein put it, in which 'few active intellectuals avoided the challenge of socialism' (Weinstein 1967: 74). Journals of opinion and Christian theology were filled with debate about the virtues and vices of socialism, especially its Marxist forms.[24]

Evidently, Albright believed that Near Eastern and especially biblical antiquity spoke to the anxieties of 1920s America. For him, correctly recovered history explained and justified the superior value of non-socialist (presumably democratic) institutions that had survived the winnowing tests of evolution.

---

22. Originally published in 1940. All citations follow the second edition.

23. Originally published in 1942; revised edition 1967.

24. For example, Hillquit and Ryan 1913: 482-89. The debate was continued in subsequent monthly issues of *Everybody's Magazine*: 29.5 (November 1913), pp. 629-43; 29.6 (December 1913), pp. 816-31; 30.1 (January 1914), pp. 80-101; 30.2 (February 1914), pp. 225-41; 30.3 (March 1914), pp. 369-86; 30.4 (April 1914), pp. 529-42. See G.B. Smith 1919: 3-13, 133-45, 245-58, 408-23, 493-507, 628-39.

By asserting continuities with a land and civilization rooted in the Bible's permanent values and, moreover, by presenting those connections as natural and unassailable, Albright tried to counter early-twentieth-century rumblings of revolutionary change. Palestine, the ancient biblical land constructed out of archaeology and religious memory, was the mythic place that nurtured his sense of identity as American, democrat, and Christian.

Nearly twenty years later, Albright would suggest that the waters streaming from the sacred land of the Bible had even nourished modern empirical rationalism, against which new totalitarian regimes were destined to fail. Since empirical reasoning, an evolutionary stage beyond pre-logical rationality, had developed out of the experience of biblical peoples, Albright declared, the 'Judeo-Christian tradition', which embodied true religion and the seeds of clearheaded, empirical and scientific rationality, offered the only defense against modern-day regression to raw primitivism. The political pressures of totalitarian empires, by whatever name, threatened to plunge the world into pre-logical, irrational chaos. Yet Judaism and Christianity, joined in evolutionary advance to the discovery of scientific rationality, offered common cause of resistance in a world under threat from totalitarian ambition (Albright 1967: 33).

Thus joined together in their development, scientists, Jews and Christians should now unite in defending the Bible and opposing those forces of darkness.

> In these days when the tyranny of European dictators employs every means
> to eradicate Judaism and Christianity from their empires, it is incredibly
> [*sic*] folly to attack the Bible because it was written in a day when the sun
> was still believed to revolve around the earth . . . The religious insights of
> the Bible remain unsurpassed and have sustained our western civilization
> for nearly two thousand years since the collapse of pagan culture.[25]

For all its sophisticated scholarly authority, Albright's declarations shared the tone and reductionism of wartime propaganda. Authors, artists and government agencies routinely invoked heroic images of the cross, the Holy Land or the 'Judeo-Christian tradition' as self-evident surrogates for allied European and North American resistance to fascism, and later, communist Russia (Silk 1984: 65-85).[26]

Louis Finkelstein, chancellor of the Jewish Theological Seminary in New York, did his part as well. He organized a conference to 'rally intellectual and spiritual forces' to meet the threat of totalitarianism and build

25. Albright, 'Science and Religion in a Changing World: Historical Religion and Scientific Thought', lecture delivered 3 February 1941. Albright Papers, American Philosophical Society, Philadelphia, Pennsylvania.

26. See Anthony Rhodes (1976) for a number of Bible-based Christian images.

'more secure foundations for democracy' (Finkelstein 1941). Each participant, Albright among them, addressed the Nazi and Marxist threats by showing how disciplines of science, philosophy, and religion were entirely supportive of democratic, not totalitarian, values.

It seems hardly accidental that *From the Stone Age to Christianity*, published at the beginning of World War II, concluded by offering a similarly urgent defense of a beleaguered West. 'Yet today we see Occidental civilization tottering', Albright wrote, referring to a broad recrudescence of tendencies that were sending the world back to primitive states of disorder. 'We see scientific methods and discoveries judged by Marxist and racist gauges instead of by independent scientific standards.' In such a world, Albright pleaded, we need a return to biblical faith (1957: 403). And, one may add, a return to secure historical knowledge. On that bedrock, Albright believed, he could recover and enter the spaces of the 'real' Holy Land, the salutary Holy Land, cradle of Judaism and Christianity, source of empirical rationalism and true religion, the fountainhead of waters most sweet.

McCown's Holy Land: A Democracy of God

Chester Charlton McCown never escaped the thrall of a Holy Land of Christian devotion, especially the Galilean countryside, which evoked appealing images of biblical peoples and an out-of-doors Jesus. Like Albright, he also imagined the Holy Land in the rhetoric of oppositional politics. Ancient Palestine gave birth to Jesus and, in resistance to tyrannical empires, to Jesus' ethic of egalitarian social justice. That, McCown felt, was a message still relevant to the United States as it faced urgent calls in the 1920s to 1950s for social change and reform.

Methodist minister and professor of New Testament at the Pacific School of Religion, McCown made his first trip to Palestine in the fall of 1920. Acting Director Albright welcomed the new Thayer Research Fellow. Always cautious, Albright was pleased to discover an unexpected affinity with McCown, who was older and rather austere but happily deferential toward Albright's authority. 'So far at least we have got on very well', Albright told his mother early that October.

> He is here to work and not to enjoy a vacation. He is a very good Greek scholar, trained in Germany, and tho about fifteen years older than I am is not disposed to resent our relative place on the faculty of the School. Dr. McCown and I, being both evangelicals, of Methodist antecedents and liberal theology, seem, at least so far, to agree thruout in our religious and critical views.[27]

27. Letter, Albright to Zephine Viola Albright, 3 October 1920, courtesy of Leona Glidden Running.

During that year, McCown followed his own research interests but also took field trips with Albright to study geography and archaeology. With the director's encouragement and the help of a native speaker of Arabic, he also undertook systematic studies of local Arab Christian and Muslim religious practices.[28]

During Albright's absence in 1929–31, McCown returned to direct the American School, including its expedition to biblical Jerash jointly undertaken with Yale University. He was Annual Professor and Acting Director in 1935–36. As director of the Pacific School of Religion's Palestine Institute (1936–47), though not a field archaeologist, McCown built a considerable reputation for expertise in biblical geography and archaeology as well as New Testament history and theology. He served the Pacific School of Religion as professor, and twice as dean.

On McCown's retirement in 1947, Albright celebrated their nearly three decades of association. It was McCown's 'nobility of character' and dutiful 'capacity for painstaking labor and intelligent grasp of (academic research) problems' that Albright admired, 'and his rare combination of talents for family life, personal relationships, professional life and scholarly activities' (Albright 1947).[29] The intellectual kinship that Albright had felt as a young man had remained strongly in evidence too. Both men believed that under God's direction human beings were making moral and cultural progress. Each man looked for theological payoff from the broad range of ancient Near Eastern studies, and both shared a fearless penchant for ambitious narratives of intellectual history.[30]

In British Mandate Palestine, McCown was drawn to open spaces away from the clutter and shouts of urban life, and to the night, when the clear waters of poetry ran their strongest. Like George Adam Smith, whose lyrical *Historical Geography of the Holy Land* captivated the reading public through some twenty-five editions between 1894 and 1931, McCown sought to sense the poetic 'atmosphere of antiquity'. And like Edward Robinson, he sifted pious legend, disappointing for the truly religious, from historical fact. From the gleanings, McCown described ancient Palestine of Jesus' day, the better to inform authentic Christian practice of his own day.

To understand the New Testament, McCown wrote in 1920, 'one should spend the day under the bright sunlight examining the ancient ruins of a city,

---

28. McCown had pursued this anthropological interest in local religion, as distinct from theology, during his missionary days in India. See McCown 1912: 5-7, 23; 1923.

29. For further biographical information, see Otwell 1958: 2; Hogue 1965. Note also McCown, 'Ninety Years of Faith and Freedom', typescript and audio recording of a lecture celebrating the faculty and history of the Pacific School of Religion. Special Collections, Library of the Graduate Theological Union, Berkeley, California.

30. Compare McCown 1929 with Albright 1957. See also McCown 1943.

and then, as the sun sets, climb to some point of vantage and sit and think it all over'.[31] McCown did just that, perhaps to help offset the privations he felt while living in Jerusalem, which was 'very far from being in the van of civilization'.[32] Like generations of pilgrims before him, McCown sought a glorious biblical city whose soul was at rest, beyond the daytime hubbub of grime and poverty. 'Such a panorama of white buildings!' he wrote one evening after a walk about Jerusalem's medieval walls. 'White tombstones dotting the hillsides, with occasional splotches of green trees and the long line of gray walls.' The world seemed asleep, save for

> the ravens we disturbed as we went along the city walls and which flew out, dark silhouettes against the moonlit sky. Was it on such a night almost as bright as the day, but with a mocking ghostly uncertainty in its light, that Jesus and his disciples took their way across the brook Kidron to the Mount of Olives, where in the uncertain shadows the officers from the high priest sought him with torches and swords and staves?[33]

McCown traveled everywhere that first year with camera and tripod. He took hundreds of snapshots, carefully filed the negatives, and gathered selected prints for later use. Some found their way into popular lectures, seminary classes and museum exhibits. Others McCown pasted into souvenir-like albums. He affixed a few to the typed pages of an unfinished travel guide entitled 'On Foot in the Mountains of Judea'. Decrying modern conveniences and tours that encouraged superficial visits, McCown offered a 'tramping trip' for intrepid travelers who refused too much comfort—a note, it will be recalled, that Charles Foster Kent had struck some years earlier. Like many of his fellow travelers to Palestine, McCown desired to recover the primitive originality of things biblical, and he longed to quicken

31. McCown, letter, 17 September 1920, McCown Papers, Correspondence 1920–21, Archives, Pacific School of Religion, Berkeley, California. McCown called his lightly edited letters 'annals' and 'chronicles'. He sent them from Palestine during 1920–21, 1929–31, and 1936, apparently as a record of his experiences, but they now bear no names of recipients.

32. Meat was scarce, auto transport unreliable or nonexistent; drinking water had to be transferred into old petroleum tins, carted five minutes to the American School, and then stored in a large covered jar. The city had no sewage system; food costs, he complained, were very high, and cook Frau Stahel's culinary 'German regime'—despite good breakfasts of porridge and soft boiled eggs—was 'enough to wreck any stomach' (McCown, letter, 9 October 1920, McCown Papers).

33. McCown letter, 28 September 1920, McCown Papers. See also the letters of 6 November 1920 (McCown felt repulsed by 'gaudy altars and quarreling sects' in Bethlehem and preferred the open fields 'where David drove his flocks and the shepherds watched on that "glorious night"'); 17 January 1921 (seeing Nazareth in the moonlight would 'make a poet of anyone', but the 'next morning we had to come down to Nazareth as she is').

Chester Charlton McCown dressed for explorations, c. 1920. Courtesy of the Pacific School of Religion and Badè Institute for Biblical Archaeology.

faith through fresh discovery, vivid descriptions of people and recollections of biblical history.[34]

McCown disdained the cheap sentimentalism of many popular Bible guides, but he lived and photographed a version of them too. His snapshots that are most suggestive of Christian pilgrimage, for example, recall stereographic tours, which encouraged a viewer to imagine the Holy Land as it really was, but which to us seems a fantasy enabled by the illusory realism of photographs. Other McCown photographs embody the idea of Palestine as the 'fifth gospel', a place where even barren topography is fraught with testimony.[35]

Indigenous peoples of Palestine appear in this world of Christian witness, but, as convention dictated, they mostly illustrate some feature of the Bible. In McCown's 'Tomb of Lazarus', they ornamentally frame a Chris-

34. 'On Foot in the Mountains of Judea', unfinished typescript, c. 1930, McCown Papers. Compare similar travel memoirs by McCown's University of Chicago teachers and colleagues. Mathews 1903: 493-560; Goodspeed 1900: 407-13; also Edgar Goodspeed's unpublished work, 'Abroad in the Nineties',' Edgar Goodspeed Papers, University of Chicago Archives, box 19, folder 1.

35. See Thomson 1859 and Vincent, Lee and Bain 1894. For analysis of the latter, see J. Davis 1996: 77-88.

Road to Bethany. Photo by C.C. McCown. Courtesy of the Pacific School of Religion and Badè Institute for Biblical Archaeology.

tian subject. Another snapshot blends the ornamental with McCown's ethnographical interest—in this case, a scientist's look at rural Arab shrines. The result follows the familiar aesthetic of Palestine the picturesque.[36]

McCown adopted the social position and perspectival conventions common to most mass-produced Holy Land memorabilia of the time. His was the gaze of an outsider who reinforced an unequal social relationship between photographer and posed subject. Artists and McCown—as well as commentators and viewers of photos—created an alterity of things familiar and foreign, revered and ignored. These were biblical people, yet valued mostly as ornamental frames for Christian dioramas. The land was forbidding, yet contemplating its appearance and constructing its geography opened onto transcendent universal realities of true religion.

In 1952, near the end of his life, McCown was preparing an essay that was to be his consummate portrait of early Christianity. He painted with an Orientalist's eye, a geographer's palette and a theologian's passion. Picking up the metaphor that had become vernacular commonplace, McCown wrote that the Holy Land itself constituted a 'fifth gospel'. Sandstone ruins, the 'changeless mountain, river and sea', the hills and lakes of Galilee all spoke of glorious events. Annually awakening flora recalled a rural teacher who responded to the land's 'smiling invitation to the out-of-doors. There we can follow him', McCown wrote,

36. Besides Charles William Wilson 1881, see Fulton 1891, and Edward Wilson 1895.

Tomb of Lazarus. Photo by C.C. McCown. Courtesy of the Pacific School of Religion and Badè Institute for Biblical Archaeology.

Weli Ibrahim. Photo by C.C. McCown. Courtesy of the Pacific School of Religion and Badè Institute for Biblical Archaeology.

the 'Master of the rugged hills, the desert, and the storm swept sea,' Master also of the open road, the flower-strewn plain, the sunny olive-clad valleys, and the shining blue lake.[37]

Henry van Dyke (1908) had made this out-of-doors Jesus famous in a series of popular magazine essays nearly fifty years earlier. Then, a younger McCown was not entirely happy with its soft focus. In the year America's Great Depression began, McCown depicted Jesus as a fairly astringent successor to sharp-tongued biblical prophets. Impatient with governmental restraints and formed by a desert ethos of individualism, these prophets bitterly opposed organized 'civilization' that brought 'growth of luxury, extravagance, and social injustice'. They followed a nomadic ethic, McCown wrote, and demanded 'economic justice, economic democracy . . . in the distribution of the good things with which God has blessed the earth'. They wanted to 'make the most of life in industrious and independent simplicity' (McCown 1929: 361-62, 147-48).[38]

God-empowered Jesus opposed the social institutions of his age in the name of those same nomadic ideals, McCown wrote.

> The very geography of Palestine had providentially conspired to prevent the blood of the Hebrews from ever becoming completely poisoned by the virus of a greedy agricultural-commercial conception of life . . . From the ancient nomadic ideal he [Jesus] inherited his hatred of wealth and luxury, his love for simplicity in living and for democratic brotherliness in economic and social relationships (McCown 1929: 156).

A prophet in his own time, Jesus, the child of the Holy Land's particular geography, still offered to McCown a bracing political philosophy nearly two millennia later. In the aftermath of the First World War, when issues of Bolshevist revolution, democratic survival, nationalist and internationalist politics were hotly debated in the United States, McCown reclaimed both Jesus and the Holy Land as participants in contemporary political debates.[39]

---

37. McCown, 'Things Said and Done 1900 Years Ago', section 3, 19, unpublished typescript, 1952, McCown Papers. Another manuscript, dated 1928, surveyed recent study of Palestine under the rubric, 'The Fifth Gospel Written in the Dust of the Holy Land' (McCown Papers, letter box, section R). See further, McCown 1927: 5-6, 520-39; 1947: 231-46.

38. The last reference is in a chapter entitled 'The Dawn of Democracy'. See also McCown 1921.

39. The political debates carried on in the popular press from the 1890s to the 1930s were fierce, complex, and difficult to summarize. Writers dealt variously with real and imagined threats from anarchism, socialism, Bolshevism and, after World War I, communism and fascism. The religious press was certainly not univocal. Some writers found socialism attractive, as, for example, Rosenberg (1902: 37-44) and Van Rensselaer (1905: 39-44). Others linked Christianity in origin and essence with non-collectivist democratic, not socialist, ideals. For example, Abbott (1896: 97-100) and Brewster

Jesus was, McCown wrote, in *The Genesis of the Social Gospel*, 'neither communist, Bolshevist, nor socialist'. He was instead a prophet of the heart.

Protestant ethicists and theologians had long preferred to emphasize that meaningful social change flows from an inward conversion of the will, not from imposed regulation and duty. For McCown, Jesus embodied that conviction, in effect imagined as the model for Protestant formulations of social ethics.

> The issues of life are out of the heart. Laws cannot affect the will, but only the outward conduct, and outward conduct is of importance only as expressing the will. Jesus had all the sympathy for the wrongs of the poor that any communist could ask. His purpose to do away with these wrongs was steadfast, but his method poles apart from those of the socialist, the communist, and the modern reformer-by-legislation.

In enunciating these principles, Jesus went 'far beyond the best of his immediate predecessors' (by which McCown, like many a triumphalist Christian theologian, meant beyond the best that Judaism had to offer).

> Jesus demanded a peaceable and teachable temper, a modesty and kindliness that made aggression and injustice toward anyone impossible; he demanded also the willingness to suffer for righteousness' sake, the readiness to sacrifice all that was dearest in the interest of the kingdom . . . Jesus insisted, not on passive endurance, but on sacrificial activity for the sake of the kingdom . . . If he was to save the world, he must include the oppressed poor in his salvation, and the social organization which was responsible for their oppression must be transformed (McCown 1929: 370-73).

How to cure social ills, then? Jesus answered in a way that surmounted temptations posed by both secular activism and spiritual quietism, wrote McCown. Jesus said 'No!' to spiritually empty materialism (just feed the hungry); 'No!' to nationalist revolutions (just transform the world through political revolution); and 'No!' to religious apathy (just wait patiently for God to overcome the world's suffering). There was another way. Jesus lived and proclaimed an 'oriental realism' which required acts of sacrifice in order that God's kingdom, the 'Democracy of God', might come on earth (McCown 1919: 402-407).[40]

(1910: 302-10). The First World War gave the edge to democracy in such debates, as interest in socialist philosophies gave way to a wartime posture of, as Woodrow Wilson announced, 'making the world safe for democracy'. See Weinstein 1967. After the war, some writers, celebrating recent victories and looking toward rising nationalistic forms of communism and fascism, renewed discussion about 'Americanism' and the origin of its clearly superior democratic ideals. Charles Foster Kent (1919–20: 131-42) pushed the question beyond the classic Greek and Roman worlds to the 'hilltops of Palestine.' See also Gillin 1919: 704-14, which includes the Hebrews among other 'primitive' peoples who gave birth to democratic forms of polity.

40. See further, McCown 1933: 161-85; 1940a; 1940b: 212-36; 1940c: 54.

The history that produced this Jesus was partly a function of geography, the lay of the land that, as McCown asserted, 'had providentially conspired' to keep the nomadic ideal coursing through generations of Hebraic peoples. McCown construed Jesus' homeland as a biblical landscape—the only Holy Land that mattered to him—a place whose deserts favored the ways of austere individualism within communality, but not anarchy. Its hills had received nomadic peoples, cradled the biblical prophets, and nurtured the prophets' God-directed assaults on economic injustice. Finally, this Holy Land had given birth to Jesus, an incipient economic democrat who proclaimed a self-sacrificing ethic leading to a 'Democracy of God'. And this, for McCown (1919: 402-407), was a perduring antidote to the despairing politics of disengagement and the repressive activism of revolutionaries.[41]

One sunny Friday in mid April 1949, Chester McCown brought something like this democratic Holy Land before an audience in Berkeley, California. Civic leaders had gathered at the Berkeley City Commons Club, about a block from the main campus of the university. The building's elegant stone and ironwork façade still bespeaks the comfortable demeanor of the urban elite who regularly met in those days to promote, as the club's *Bulletin* declared, 'good fellowship and community solidarity, civic pride and intelligence, national and international understanding'.[42]

A past president of the club, McCown brought a collection of photographs that day to illustrate a talk entitled 'Arab Justice, a Spring-Time Parley'. Taken during McCown's first year in Palestine, the photographs depicted a gathering of Bedouin elders who, in long night discussions over strong, sweet coffee and a feast of lamb, had settled communal obligations incurred by a private killing. The reporter for the Club's *Bulletin* noted the 'picturesque simplicity and good common sense of the Arab farmer in Palestine', whose social rituals repaired the torn fabric of wilderness society. 'No policeman or other representative of government was present to supervise', he wrote, 'and none would enforce the verdict. The settlement had been reached under public participation and no culprit dared defy unanimous public opinion.'[43]

McCown had long been attracted to these nomadic folk. They suggested biblical types and universal aspects of religion. Perhaps the 'springtime parley' that had captured McCown's imagination in 1920 offered something

---

41. Writing nearly thirty years later, McCown tenaciously held to the promise he found in the idea of a 'Democracy of God'. It was a message McCown still felt to be urgently needed to be accepted in the anxious days of post-World War II America. Jesus' embodiment of the God-commanded 'proletarian ethical tradition' (the phrase is remarkable for its delicate traversal of America's Cold War hysteria) marks the way and the truth, despite its being nearly forgotten (McCown 1958: 268, 271, 293).

42. *City Commons Club Bulletin* 21.1 (1949), p. 1, McCown Papers.

43. *City Commons Club Bulletin* 21.1 (1949), p. 1, McCown Papers.

more. Did the Bedouin live that ancient nomadic ideal, however vestigially, that McCown would later claim to have driven the biblical prophets and Jesus? Did these people born of Holy Land space, like Jesus the social gospel prophet, remain relevant as contemporary political commentary?

The idea of 'nomadic ideal' that McCown (and many others) found so appealing has long since lost its prestige among biblical scholars. It was a powerful construct that associated the ancestral and prophetic literary traditions in the Bible with European romanticism and idealized reports of Arab life.[44] Yet for McCown, 'nomadism' was a settled and uncomplicated fact of early Israel's emergence in Canaan. The 'nomadic ideal' was an objective value trait of those immigrants from the desert who were the ancestors of the prophets who preceded Jesus. For his Berkeley audience, McCown seems to have enlivened those dwellers on Palestine's steppes with similar romance. They were austere, independent people who were admirably suspicious of centralized governments, zealous for individual liberty, and careful arbiters of community consensus. Their justice would require no policeman 'to supervise [. . . or] enforce the verdict'.

As McCown had written two decades earlier, the rugged mountains of ancient Judea 'constantly invited the Bedouin from his still more barren desert' into a geographic zone of religious significance, where the 'rough hills bred a hearty, prolific, and adventurous race, given to plain living and high thinking'. These migrants might have been monetarily poor among the nations. But they 'became the world's teachers in those matters in which their gifts and their austere mountain home had made them preeminent, morals and religion'.[45] These morals and religion, I suggest, were born of a Holy Land configured for McCown in terms of Jesus and his particular vision of an inner directed, socially powerful 'Democracy of God'.

Margolis: Holy Land Homeland

When Albright and McCown first went to Jerusalem, Max Leopold Margolis, at fifty-three, was already a highly respected scholar. Since 1908 he had been professor of philology at Dropsie College in Philadelphia. He was editor of the *Journal of Biblical Literature*, a position he held from 1914 to 1922, followed by similar duties for the *Journal of the American Oriental Society* (1922–32). Author of many learned works on the Bible and rabbinics, Margolis was committed to historically oriented modes of inquiry, now increasingly linked to archaeological data.

---

44. The trajectory of 'nomadic ideal' from enthusiastic acceptance, through fundamental questioning, to abandonment is nicely reflected in successive reference works. See Wolf 1962: 559-60; Gottwald 1976: 629-31; Knauf 1992: 634-38.

45. McCown, 'On Foot in the Mountains of Judea', 26-27, McCown Papers.

Max Leopold Margolis, c. 1920. Courtesy of the Library of
the Herbert D. Katz Center for Advanced Judaic Studies,
University of Pennsylvania.

Nonetheless, Margolis recognized that Christians dominated this scholarly approach to the Bible, and that they generally ascribed ultimate religious importance to the Hebrew Bible, or Old Testament, only insofar as the
'old' witness to God's covenant had been perfected in the 'new' covenant
of Christ, or New Testament. Sometimes this scholarship, particularly in
nineteenth-century Germany, was downright hostile to Jews and Judaism.

Given this situation, Margolis urged in 1910 and again in 1915 that the
people for whom the 'language of Scriptures is in large measure a living
tongue' must claim their rightful place among modern students of the Bible,
many of whom were associated with the American School in Jerusalem.
Resisting a theologically proscribed guild while speaking from its margins,
Margolis urged Jewish scholars to defend the Hebrew Bible as fundamentally a Jewish book, even while accepting that it had been incorporated into

the Christian Scriptures and read in ways that were often antithetical to Jewish sensibilities. Moreover, Jews must rescue the Bible from neglect by a community that, under the conditions of European and North American modernity, had largely abandoned its own Book. Jews must join the guild dominated by Christians and embrace the historical and philological training required to set forth the Bible's correct relevance for Jewish, rather than Christian, practice.[46]

When he wrote those words, Margolis (1908) had already shown what was possible by writing a scholarly commentary on the book of Micah. He also carried his message to wider audiences. Margolis lectured on the Bible at the Jewish Chautauqua Society (modeled on John Heyl Vincent's Chautauqua Institution) and frequently commented on Bible study and contemporary Jewish affairs in popular magazines.[47] It is not surprising that he embraced Zionism, too, for it similarly claimed space from the margins of a European world in which Jews were persecuted, or at the very least, accorded little political and cultural relevance.

Following an ambivalent awakening in 1907, Margolis resigned from what was then a decidedly anti-Zionist faculty at the Hebrew Union College in Cincinnati and enthusiastically, if guardedly, embraced the cause. Margolis recognized the socialist, secular, and colonizing aspects of the Zionist movement, but he believed even more fervently in its promise to revitalize Jewish culture and religion for Jews who might choose not to settle a new homeland. In this regard, Margolis imagined the Holy Land not so much as a place of biblical origin (like McCown and Albright) but above all as a nationalistic destination. Writing in 1907, Margolis explained that physical return, repentance and revitalized religious life came together in the Zionist cause.

> In going back (*teshuvah*) to Jewish life and Jewish ideals and Jewish hopes lies our salvation. Its work must necessarily consist, on the one hand, in strengthening the hands of those who volunteer to build up the waste places on the hills of Palestine and, on the other, in building up the Jewish consciousness in the Diaspora Jew (Margolis 1907b: 97-99).

Holy Land then was a physical and ideational space of reclaimed national and spiritual identity. Its 'waste places' (note that the land is rhetorically emptied of its current residents) were to be populated in settlement and possessed in cultural renaissance. As Margolis would suggest after a year of travel and study in Palestine, the Holy Land could also become a place of proud, but not prideful, Jewish independence exercised through American-style democratic sensibilities.

46. Margolis 1910–11: 32-33; 1915: 10. For more details, see Greenspoon 1987: 111-33. For other biographical information, see Gordis 1952; Sperling 1992: 48-51.
47. For the scope of Margolis's less technical writings, see Reider 1987: 165-78.

Margolis first traveled to Mandate Palestine in 1924. It was an anxious and heady time for Americans at home. Post-World War I prosperity was under way for some, but for others, threatening Klansmen roamed country roads and city streets of the poor. Fears of Bolshevist revolution and labor strife—the same fears that brought forth Albright's and McCown's defenses of democracy—fed the demons of isolationism, anti-Semitism, and xenophobia. Recalling his month-long travel to Palestine, Margolis reflected on the conditions of shipboard confinement that temporarily kept these troubles at bay. Thrown together, 'traveling humanity seeks and finds its own level', he wrote. Few travelers of 'Nordic prejudice' espouse 'the doctrine that America is for Americans and Christians only', and even 'caste distinctions are for the moment discarded' (Margolis 1924–25: 8).[48]

Margolis accepted appointment as Annual Professor at the American School in Jerusalem. Albright (1924: 12), then in his fifth year as director, noted for readers of the School's *Bulletin* that Margolis's training and research fit 'extraordinarily well' his own topographical studies of the ancient biblical landscape. The gesture of welcoming inclusion, for all its truth and goodwill, sidestepped political fault lines. In those days, Albright was less friendly to the Zionist cause than he would later become, and Margolis deeply believed in the Zionist dream. One outcome was that they harnessed their scholarship to different constructions of the Holy Land.

Margolis's affection for Palestine was stirred less in retrospect, by evoking biblical associations, than in prospect, by witnessing and celebrating, as he wrote, the 'dawn of the national resurrection' (Margolis 1925: 16). Of course, he trekked through a reassembled landscape of biblical desire—this was after all a dominant feature of the American School's activities at the time. Margolis reported on land traversed, places observed and named, hills dug into and identified as this or that biblical location. He paid homage to Albright, Edward Robinson and a host of earlier scholar-pilgrim travelers by imposing an affective geography of biblical event on the hills of Palestine, always alive with biblical memory. 'We passed through Kesla, the biblical Chesalon,' he wrote for readers back home,

> and in getting to it the hoofs of our horses must have trodden the mountain which in the book of Joshua is called Seir . . . Gradually we descended, on towards the Low Lands, crossing and recrossing the scenes of mighty battles between the Israelites and the Philistines, the ground where Samson performed his feats before he was robbed of his strength by the treacherous Delilah (Margolis 1924–25: 182; see also 1925: 9-10).

48. On page 44, Margolis mentions the welcoming (and welcome) deference extended to the special needs of Jews on board the steamship. Reports of his travels appeared serially in the *B'nai B'rith Magazine*: 39.1 (October 1924), pp. 8-10 (part 1), 44-45 (part 2); 39.2 (November 1924), pp. 74, 86 (part 3); 39.3 (December 1924), pp. 106-107 (part 4); and 39.4 (February 1925), pp. 167, 182-83 (part 5).

A Holy Land reconstituted in biblical memory and sought after by countless earlier pilgrims now lay open to scientific conquest and religious awakening.

> We are after the pulsating life that ceased to be, but once was there; the
> spirit with which in bygone days it was animate; the workings of the divine
> breath in men and movements long past. Exploration of sites and excava-
> tions must needs be carried on upon the very spot, though the explorers
> and excavators come from afar (Margolis 1925: 3).

Despite occasional flights of such romantic fancy, Margolis gave sur-
prisingly little attention to biblical sites in his reports. He was far more
stirred by contemporary conditions in Palestine and their power to inspire
a Jewish future. In contrast to Albright's priorities for archaeological work,
which went to probing biblical origins, Margolis looked for inspiration in
the Jewishness of life in Tel Aviv, and in the excavation of places that could
evoke an idealized memory of Jewish nationhood in Greco-Roman times.
The Holy Land was not just biblical land, not the cradle of Western civilization, not the lightening sky of democracy's dawning. The Holy Land was
ancient homeland, and now, under the watchful gaze of British authorities,
it might even be a homeland regained, inspired by ancient images of heroic
aspirations toward national independence.

Ancient sites of home rule called for excavation too. In addressing students at the Jewish Institute of Religion in 1925, Margolis pleaded for
archaeological explorations at Beth-ther, the second-century site of Jewish
nationalist Bar Kokhba's fortifications. Then, turning to Stephen Wise, an
ardent Zionist and president of the school, he urged fundraising for such
excavations, 'I put it up to him as a sacred duty, in the name of historical
science of antiquity and by all that stirs Jewish sentiment for a most glorious
period in Jewish history' (Margolis 1925: 11).[49]

Margolis believed that a Holy Land uncovered and known would inspire
a much broader cultural and religious revival.

> We Zionists clamor for the one land where the Jews may constitute the
> majority and where alone a full national Jewish life becomes possible.
> Palestine is just now within the grasp of the Jewish people. For any Jew to
> obstruct the path to the land of the fathers is treason, treason to the cause
> of the Jewish people, treason to the cause of Judaism (Margolis 1917: 23).

On the matter of actual political sovereignty for a Jewish state, however, Margolis was circumspect, at least in his publications. The question
drew to itself an unstable mix of issues and dilemmas that still, even today,

---

49. Indeed, study of the ancient land was a *mitzvah*, a religious duty. Margolis
(1925: 4) fully agreed with an early-nineteenth-century Bavarian Jew, Joseph Schwarz,
who closely studied the land five years before Edward Robinson began his famous journeys, and felt ashamed that Jews had paid so little attention to topographical details.

inflame Zionist politics in America. What of the rights of non-Jews who had lived for generations in the region then called British Mandate Palestine? How could one counter charges of divided national allegiance leveled at Jews who supported Zionism while remaining citizens and residents of the United States? And what of the personal discomfort engendered by choosing to live as Jews in the United States while others built up a homeland for persecuted Jews abroad? As for life in America, how could support for Zionism be disentangled from 'Nordic prejudice', the host of exclusions that contributed to conflicting demands of assimilation, ethnic identification, and desire to create a safe haven for Jews?[50]

Margolis and other cultural Zionists (Mordecai Kaplan, Judah Magnes, Israel Friedlander, and Louis Finkelstein, for example) believed that a properly executed revival of Jewry in Palestine would counteract such deleterious political pressures. The solution was thought to be apolitical. 'Education, rather than politics, was the decisive Zionist act' (Goren 1996: 169).[51] One heart, beating in the breast of an ardent Zionist and loyal American, could safely support cultural renaissance for all Jews and argue the necessity of a politically sanctioned safe haven for the persecuted. The new Zion should be created, Margolis wrote in 1917,

> not only for the oppressed Jewish people, but in particular for the suppressed Jewish soul, to the end that, released from her prison, she may, like the dove sent out by Noah, find a rest for the sole of her foot (1917: 227).

As early as 1907, Margolis wrote an essay that brought the weight of his authority and technical scholarship to bear on this particular conception of the Zionist imperative. The patriarch Joseph, he claimed, was both a historical figure and a timeless exemplar of something repeatedly experienced in Jewish history. Joseph was an admired Egyptian Jew of 'dual allegiance' (Margolis's phrase ennobled a demeaning accusation frequently leveled at Jews). He was also a 'type of the Diaspora Jew who, through rigid discipline and self-control, rises to the position of a court-favorite'. Other Jews, other 'types', lived in ancient Palestine, fully at home and devoted to 'the God of promises, not yet the God of fulfilment; the God of a nation in the making, not yet the God of a nation consummated'.

Moses, the great teacher and giver of Torah, is a timeless exhortation to all the Josephs who continue to live outside of the promised land. On the one hand, Moses was of the Diaspora, and knew that for 'Israel to realize itself to the full of its capacity, it must have a soil under its feet, a home wherein it may dwell securely, free to develop its powers'. On the other hand, Moses looked to 'a home for the suppressed Jewish soul' (Margolis 1907a: 41-46).

---

50. See Halpern 1979: 15-33; also Goren 1996: 165-92.
51. See Bloch 1952: 53-57.

Both Moses and Joseph, Margolis implied, are instructive for American Jews. Like Joseph, Jews could be successful (and loyal) in any Diaspora homeland. And like Moses, they could look to what the 'God of promises' demands—attention to spiritual vitality and settling a land where Israel, the people of God, might freely develop to its fullest capacity. With safe haven in Jewish Palestine, the Zionist movement could be fully sacralized, overcoming the limits of its secular origins. With the Holy Land fully materialized, Zion could become more than a centuries-old pious hope. Cultural, spiritual and secular energies could be concentrated in a renewed world center, that ultimate point of sacredness from which human beings derive their highest moral and religious principles.

This Holy Land of Jewish renewal would not rise up, alive, merely in mental constructs of biblical origins. It would be both spirit and material, a vital contemporary reality and dawning future rooted in ethnicity and soil, but without compromising the demands of fatherland patriotism. 'From redeemed Zion,' Margolis wrote in 1918,

> there will be shed luster upon scattered Jewry, who in their various abodes will continue loyal citizens, and while loving their many fatherlands will cherish the mother country, the seat of Jewish culture in the land of the fathers.[52]

After his year in Jerusalem, Margolis linked the newly founded Hebrew University to this vision of material, cultural and spiritual revitalization. 'In the dawn of national resurrection', he wrote, the truths of Judaism would be distilled in the 'laboratories and institutes on Mount Scopus, the place from which in ancient days men could see the Temple.' The university would serve as a 'lesser Sanctuary, that out of Zion once more may go forth the Torah, and the word of the Lord from Jerusalem'.[53]

With similar enthusiasm, Margolis noted reassuring scenes of revitalized Jewish life as he traveled through Palestine. He marveled at economic miracles and vernacular Hebrew; the normalcy of self-determined Jewish life; the shuttered public face of Shabbat in 'wholly Jewish' Tel Aviv.[54] He was greatly moved in observing *Tisha B'av*, where

> not an eye remains dry. It is gripping, overwhelming. It is an event hallowed by centuries, from the time when Roman soldiers guarded the approaches and the Jews had to buy the privilege of weeping for the departed glories. Today a Jewish policeman keeps order.[55]

---

52. Margolis, *B'nai B'rith News* (September-October, 1918), p. 17, cited in Gordis 1952: 53.
53. Margolis, 'Oriental Researches', 16-17.
54. Margolis, 'A Year in the Holy Land', part 3, p. 74.
55. Margolis, "A Year in the Holy Land', part 4, p. 106.

The note of pride in that reversal of governance (even while recogniz-
ing the fact of British rule) suggests the delicate positioning of a desired
Jewish majority in this Holy Land of Zion. The Palestinian Jew is 'free
politically', Margolis wrote, suggesting an Americanized vision of Zionist
social order. 'Free to speak his own language, free to bring up his children
in Jewish schools', and moreover, free 'to walk with head erect', Margolis
wrote. Yet a Jew in Palestine 'need not become provocative' and the rights
of others could be guarded. Therein lay political wisdom and future well
being.[56] And, one might add, the installation of values prized in America,
now imagined as a better rule for the hearts of settlers creating a Holy Land
of Zionist imagination.

Retrospective

In looking forward to a Holy Land of Jewish renewal, Max Margolis was
no less scholarly and no less romantic than Albright and McCown. Albright
imagined Bible times and the 'cradle' of Western civilization as a scholarly defense of democracy under threat. In similar circumstances, McCown
constructed a place whose uniqueness nurtured Jesus' enduring hope for the
'Democracy of God'. Margolis negotiated the perils of minority politics at
home by plotting an affective geography of a Jewish homeland shaped by
American ideals of democratic rights.

Three American scholars, three 'holy lands'. Images of the Holy Land
entangled with shared ideologies of scientific discovery and privileged American values, embedded in the exegesis of text and artifact. Each man gave
voice to learned discourse about the Holy Land and constructed spaces of
moral and political imperative. Each lived his own version of a Holy Land
myth, American-style, inspired in part by the American School in Jerusalem,
the great nurturer of Holy Land travels and enabler of fantasy realism.

Travelers required real maps, however, something more than those metaphorical charts of romanticized Holy Land prose and scholarly discourse.
Even surrogate travelers, whether joining parlor tours or wandering through
Chautauqua's Palestine, demanded the assurance of cartography that their
holy lands were anchored in real territory, on the ground, so to speak. Yet,
what if Holy Land maps were special cases of conjuration too? In a basic
Euclidian sense, of course, maps could be true or false. But suppose that
even the most scientifically and historically accurate maps of the Holy Land
were themselves vehicles of Holy Land myth and articulators of holy lands
at home?

---

56. Margolis, "A Year in the Holy Land', part 5, pp. 167, 182-83. The reference to
freedom of choice in schooling comes from Margolis and Marx 1927: 737.

NATION MAKING: MAPPING PALESTINE IN THE NINETEENTH CENTURY

Keith W. Whitelam

Introduction

The nineteenth century, Walter Bagehot famously claimed, was the period of 'nation-making', when 'the best nations conquered the worst; by the possession of one advantage or another the best competitor overcame the inferior competitor' (1905: 81). He added:

> And it explains why Western Europe was early in advance of other countries, because there the contest of races was exceedingly severe. Unlike most regions, it was a tempting part of the world, and yet not a corrupting part; those who did not possess it wanted it, and those who had it, not being enervated, could struggle hard to keep it. The conflict of nations is at first a main force in the improvement of nations (Bagehot 1905: 82-83).

Just as Albright (1957: 280-81) was later to say that it was only natural that the inferior Canaanite culture should be replaced by the superior Israelite, so Bagehot saw the contest between emergent European nation-states as a 'tendency toward progress'. Our histories of Israel, Judah, Yehud and Judaea are often narrated in similar terms as a struggle for political, religious and cultural supremacy—and ultimately survival. The alignment of the biblical presentation of the history of Israel, including the so-called Second Temple period and beyond, as a working out of the theological judgment on disobedient nations, along with assumptions about the nature of political progress built into Western historiography from the time of Bagehot onwards has meant that this narrative has become so natural as to be self-evident and virtually immune from challenge. Such a presentation of history, common in biblical studies, is comforting and reassuring. It offers a landscape that looks familiar since it resembles modern European history. It is an expression of the inevitable march of a divinely controlled history imbued with the theological lessons of obedience and disobedience so familiar in Deuteronomy–2 Kings.

A glance at nineteenth-century maps illustrates the power of Bagehot's characterization of the period. This was a world of nation-states, clearly demarcated by defined boundaries that outlined their sovereignty, often defined by different colours. It is as if the earth's surface is composed of a set of interlocking jigsaw pieces. Just how deeply ingrained this notion of the nation-state with its well-defined borders, expressing difference and separation, had become can be seen in Thomas Spurrs map of matrimony from Sheffield in 1840 (figure 1). The mythical map uses this image of clearly demarcated states to get over its moral message about the importance of marriage and the dangers of remaining single. The 'Land of Spinsters and the "Bachelors" Tract' are adjoining territories in the north with 'Honeymoon' and the temple of Hymen in the centre. This is surrounded by the 'Unsettled States of Hopes and Fears'. 'Empire of Encouragement', 'Empire of Engagements', 'States of Distraction', Region of Repentance' and 'Kingdom of Happiness', among others. A typical set of playing cards from the same year shows the individual pieces of this global jigsaw as a clear hierarchy of states, as defined by the number of the playing card. The six of diamonds is entitled 'Turkey in Asia' and contains Palestine (figure 2). Interestingly, it does not have well defined boundaries, is not set off clearly from Syria, for instance and, by implication, has not scaled the pinnacle of political evolution like European nation-states. This notion of hierarchy, or superiority in Bagehot's terms, highlights the other important aspect of the nineteenth century that has so influenced historiography and biblical studies in particular, the notion of empire. A map of the world, with most of the surface covered in pink, denoting the possessions of the British Empire, is typical of the kind of map that adorned my own school classrooms as late as the 1950s and 1960s.

However, Hobsbawm's (1991: 14) fundamental point that 'the basic characteristic of the modern nation and everything connected with it is its modernity' has all too often been overlooked in biblical studies and its constructions of the past. In fact, discussions of Palestine's past—from the Late Bronze Age to the Roman period—have often assumed the very opposite, that 'national identification is somehow so natural, primary and permanent as to precede history' (Hobsbawm 1991: 14).

Yet to see how very different this self-evident world of separation and boundedness is to that of previous centuries, we only need look back to the cartographic representation of Palestine in maps in the sixteenth and seventeenth centuries. These maps offer us very different images of Palestine; images of the Holy Land that have also become deeply ingrained in Western memory. Maps from this period, often composed by the greatest names in cartography at the time, are dominated by particular biblical events: five traditional subjects depicted: the wanderings of the patriarchs, the route of the exodus, the division of the land among the twelve tribes, Palestine at

Figure 1: Map of Matrimony by Thomas Spurr from A. Blaynton-Williams and M. Blaynton-Williams, eds., *New Worlds: Maps from the Age of Discovery* (London: Quercus, 2006: 205). Printed with permission of Ashley Blaynton-Williams.

the time of Christ and the spread of Christianity in Acts, particularly the journeys of Paul.[1]

What is most striking about these early European maps or maps in six-teenth-century Bibles, which reached very wide audiences, was the seem-

1. The first Bible map was of the route of the exodus in Lutheran Bibles from Zurich in 1525 and Antwerp in 1526. J.Z. Smith (1990: 68-69) deals with the history of the exodus map in various Bibles.

Figure 2: 'Turkey in Asia' (the Six of Diamonds) from
playing card maps by James Head Stopforth from A.
Blaynton-Williams and M. Blaynton-Williams, eds.,
New Worlds: Maps from the Age of Discovery (London:
Quercus, 2006: 204). Printed with permission of Ashley
Blaynton-Williams.

ing lack of interest in the notion of the state that is so dominant in later
nineteenth-century maps. There appears to be little or no interest in cartographic images of the kingdoms of David or Solomon, for instance, or
Herod's dominions. Although artwork from the period is interested in such
royal themes, the notion of state is one that is conspicuously absent from the
vast majority of maps from these earlier centuries. It appears to hold no significant interest for cartographers until sometime in the eighteenth century.
Georg Seutter's map from 1725, one of the earliest that I have found, takes
the traditional topic of the tribal divisions and superimposes the kingdoms
of Judah and Israel.[2] Seutter, the official geographer of the kaiser of the
Holy Roman Empire, produced a number of maps of German states at a time
when the demarcation of state boundaries was a critical issue in Europe.

2. For Seutter's map, see Nebenzahl (1986: 144-45).

The most explicit representation of the early monarchy, and so the bounded state, is to be found in Gilles Robert de Vaugondy's magnificent 'Map of the land of the Hebrews or Israelites' from 1745.[3] It includes an inset in the upper left corner entitled 'the Monarchy of the Hebrews,' displaying the administrative structure under Solomon. Once again, the larger map shows the divisions of the twelve tribes. The smaller inset map has twelve districts, roughly corresponding to the tribal divisions, with the names of the officials in charge. At the bottom is a small vignette showing Solomon's judgment. It would appear from the evidence of cartography and common Bibles that the monarchy was marginalized in Western memory before this time and only began to form a significant element of collective memory during the period of the triumph of the European nation-state. It was, it would appear, not only a period of 'nation making', as Bagehot termed it, but also the period when the state was put firmly on the map.[4]

Maps in the Nineteenth Century

When we turn to nineteenth-century maps of Palestine, we discover a very different world to the images that have dominated cartography of the region and so influenced collective memory through their repetition in popular Bibles. Yet it is not the clear representation of 'nation making' that we might expect to find given the proliferation of such images on general maps or other artifacts. Pierre Jacotin's map produced for the Holy Land Survey of 1799 as part of Napoleon's scientific mapping and recording of Egypt and Palestine is the first such map of the region based on triangulation pioneered by the Cassinis.[5] At first glance, it would appear that biblically inspired representations of Palestine as Holy Land had now been replaced by the scientific objectivity of modern advances in trigonometrically based cartography and the skill of contemporary engravers. Its military purpose is clear, with the route of the army and their encampments marked: towns and villages were marked only if the army passed through them. The topography is accurately depicted near roads, close to the route of the army, but less accurate the farther away from them we stray.

The plethora of details presented with such scientific detachment encouraged trust in the view that what was on display was the disinterested reflection of reality. The power of such maps, as a representation of social geography, as Harley (1992: 231) noted, is that they operate behind a mask of seemingly neutral science. The major function of the plethora of details was to provide, what Harley termed 'a mode of access to reality' (1992:

3. For Vaugondy's map, see Nebenzahl (1986: 148-49).
4. For a more detailed treatment of some of the issues, see Whitelam 2007; 2010 .
5. For Jacotin's map, see Nebenzahl (1986: 154-55).

231)—in this case, access to a supposed Oriental reality. As Edward Said notes of Napolean's larger project, 'Europe came to know the Orient more scientifically, to live in it with greater authority and discipline than ever before' (2003: 22). What we see in Jacotin's map, and the many maps of the period that are influenced by its cartographic achievement, is 'a truly scientific appropriation of one culture by another, apparently stronger one' (Said 2003: 42) or in Bagehot's terms, 'the best nations conquered the worst'.

We see this same disinterested reflection of reality mirrored in the maps of countless European travellers and scholars who followed in the wake of Napolean's appropriation of Egypt and Palestine. Although not based on the scientific principles of Cassini, so brilliantly realized by Jacotin, and in some cases relying on the eighteenth-century map of Jean-Baptiste Bourguignon d'Anville for information about particular areas, these maps in the journals and textbooks of travellers and scholars exhibit the same touch of the real. Ulrich Jasper Seetzen's detailed map or that of John Lewis Burckhardt, reproduced in his now famous *Travels in Syria and the Holy Land* (1822), being based on their own explorations, provide the reader with a confidence in the artless reflection on view. Similarly, the text of the classic *Biblical Researches in Palestine, Mount Sinai and Arabia Petraea: A Jourrnal of Travels in the Year 1838* by Eli Smith and Edward Robinson (1841) was illustrated by Heinrich Kiepert's map based on the results of survey work and information provided by Smith and Robinson. Yet what is striking about the beautifully engraved image of Jacotin's map and those by Seetzen, Burckhardt, Kiepert and many others is that despite their appeal to the real and their seeming advance on biblically inspired maps of earlier centuries, there is a conspicuous absence of the boundaries that dominate many other more general nineteenth-century maps.

The culmination of this scientific enterprise came with Claude Reignier Conder's proud announcement, in the introduction to his two volume *Tent Work in Palestine: A Record of Discovery and Adventure*, published in 1878, that the completion of the trigonometrical Survey of Western Palestine was 'an accomplished fact' (see figures 3 and 4). Despite the hardships and dangers faced by the team of Royal Engineers, Conder remarks how 'the great map now extends over 6000 square miles, from Dan to Beersheba, and from the Jordan to the Mediterranean Sea'. He goes on to add:

> The Survey is being prepared in twenty-six sheets. The plan will show towns, villages, ruins, roads, water-courses, and buildings, tombs, caves, cisterns, wells, springs, and rock-cut wine-presses. The hills will also be delineated, and the cultivation shown, olives, figs, vines, and palms being distinguished; and the wild growth, oak-trees, scrub, and principal separate trees will appear. The Roman milestones on the roads are marked, and every similar relic of antiquity; the heights of the various principal

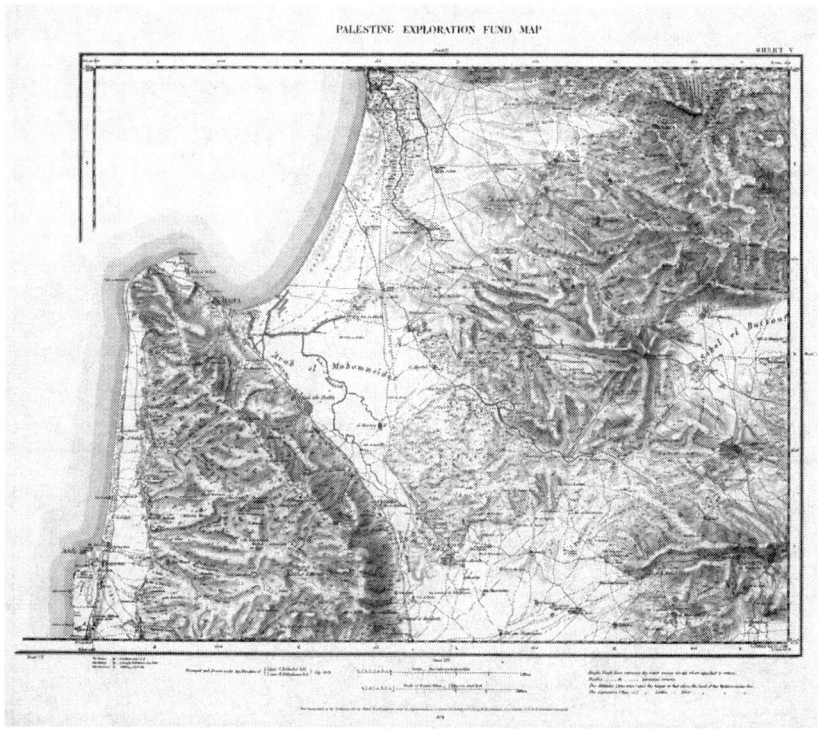

Figure 3: The Survey of Western Palestine Sheet V. Taken from Historic Views of the Holy Land in the 1870s: Survey of Western Palestine: The Maps (BiblePlaces.com). Printed by permission of Todd Bolen.

> features are given, and the levels of the Sea of Galilee and Dead Sea have been fixed within a foot (Conder 1878: I, xvi).

Yet, once again, the boundaries that characterize the period of nation making are seemingly absent.

Palestine could now be possessed, unfolded, and refolded in living rooms and studies of England. It could also be experienced as performed space, a timeless land in which the contemporary inhabitants have little or no value except as biblical extras, a land in which the biblical events are re-enacted in perpetuity, through the descriptions contained in Conder's memoirs or in Rev. William M. Thomson's *The Land and the Book: Or, Biblical Illustrations Drawn from the Manners and Customs, the Scenes and Scenery of the Holy Land* (1859).[6] The map provides the stage on which biblical events and scenes are continually renewed. Thus, Conder remarks that the

6. See Whitelam 2008 for a fuller discussion of Palestine as performed space in travellers reports and textbooks from the period.

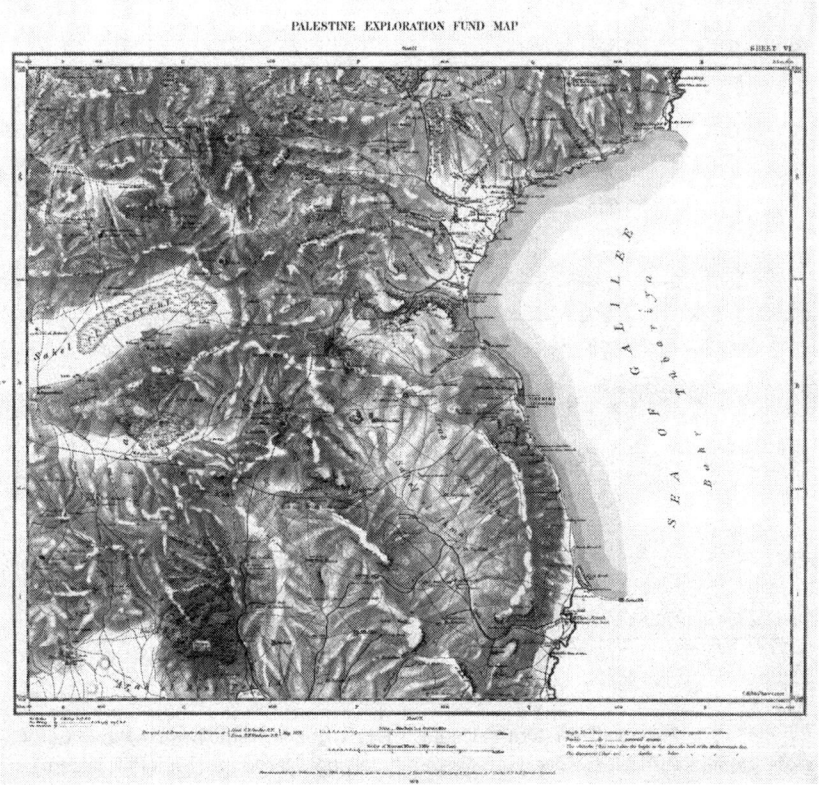

Figure 4: The Survey of Western Palestine Sheet VI.Taken from Historic Views of the Holy Land in the 1870s: Survey of Western Palestine: The Maps (BiblePlaces.com). Printed by permission of Todd Bolen.

map is only part of the material collected; 'and the map without a memoir would be a sealed book' (Conder 1878: I, xvii). In addition, it requires a general résumé to bring it within the reach of the general public, who might not read the memoir or fail to get from it a vivid idea of Palestine, or the discoveries of the survey party. 'The book is intended to give as accurate a general description as possible of Palestine' (Conder 1878: I, xx). Such a scientifically detached angle of vision, the ability to look down on the map of Palestine from an elevated position, allowed the viewer to appropriate Palestine in a way never before possible. Yet Conder then reveals what lies behind the mask of reality:

> The main object of the Survey of Palestine may be said to have been to collect materials in illustration of the Bible. Few stronger confirmations of the historic and authentic character of the Sacred Volume can be imagined than that furnished by a comparison of the Land and the Book, which

shows clearly that they tally in every respect. Mistaken ideas and precon-
ceived notions may be corrected; but the truth of the Bible is certainly
established, on a firm basis, by the criticisms of those who, familiar with
the people and the country, are able to read it, not as a dead record of a
former world or of an extinct race, which can still be studied by any who
will devote themselves to the task (Conder 1878: I, xxi).

Sir Walter Besant (1889: 127) sums up the real significance of the
survey—and by implication the many other maps of Palestine from the
period—in his *Twenty-One Years' Work in the Holy Land* by claiming of
Conder and H.H. Kitchener's Survey of Western Palestine that 'nothing has
ever been done for the illustration and right understanding of the historical
portions of the Old and New Testament, since the translation into the vulgar
tongue, as this great work.' Thus, although, the biblically inspired images—
the patriarchs, exodus, conquest, tribal divisions, Christ in the Gospels, or
the spread of Christianity—that dominate the cartographic representation
of Palestine in the sixteenth and seventeenth centuries are missing from the
surface of these maps, they are lurking behind the mask of reality.

Just as significantly, the notions of difference and boundedness that are
the prime characteristics of the nation-state underpin these influential representations of Palestine despite the absence of explicit boundaries on the
maps. George Adam Smith's classic work *The Historical Geography of the
Holy Land* (1901) provides a useful illustration (see figures 5 and 6). The
six maps that accompany the text echo the objective representation of Palestine, as we can see from the map of Esdraelon and the Lower Galilee.
Once again, the attractive relief map shows the location of major towns,
villages, rivers and roads. However, a close reading of the text begins to
reveal the models that underpin it, that are left unexpressed on the map, but
which have placed, and continue to hold, a conceptual lock on the history
of the region.

Despite the sly rhetoric of neutrality of the maps, providing the reader
with a detailed bird's-eye view of the surface of Palestine, it is the notions
of difference and separateness that dominate Smith's reading of the land and
its history. It is a land that is to be occupied: 'we are ready', he says of the
plain of Esdraelon, 'for the arrival of those armies of all nations whose almost
ceaseless contests have rendered this plain the classic battleground of Scripture' (1901: 391). His chapter on Galilee, which opens with the words, 'This
name, which binds together so many of the most holy memories of our race,
means in itself nothing more than The Ring', is a study in difference and
separation: Gentile, Jew, Christian, Samaritan, Phoenician, and so on. The
land he describes in detail is said to be 'thickly peopled' (1901: 421); the
'national characteristics', as he terms them, are fanaticism and being quarrel-
some. The difference between Galilee and Judaea is expressed in nationalist
terms: it is like the difference between England and Scotland shortly after the

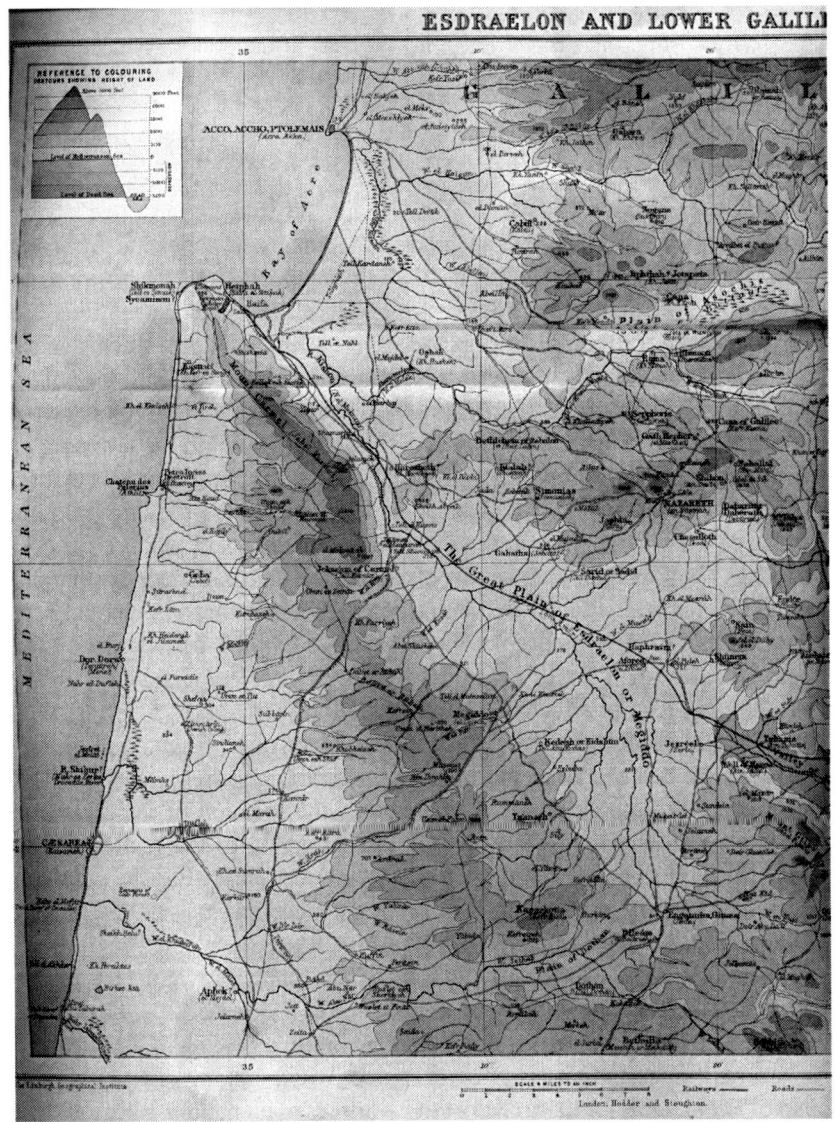

Figure 5: Esdraelon from George Adam Smith, *The Historical Geography of the Holy Land* (London: Hodder & Stoughton, 13th edn, 1907).

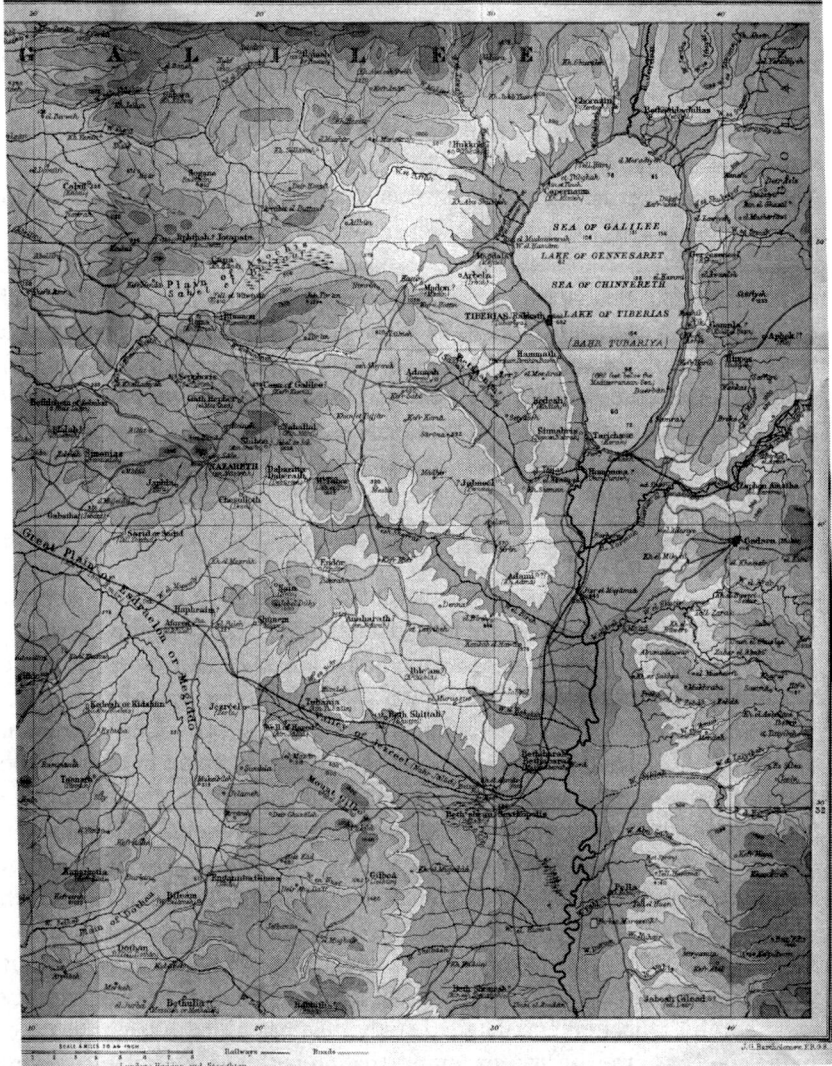

Figure 6: Lower Galilee from George Adam Smith, *The Historical Geography of the Holy Land* (London: Hodder & Stoughton, 13th edn, 1907).

Union: 'But the Galilee had as much reason to resent the scorn of Judaea', he says, 'as Scotland the haughty tolerance of England'. When he emphasizes the importance of the roads running across Galilee (1901: 425), one of the key features of the maps, it is not to stress connectivity and mobility but again the notion of difference and what separates. Such roads also allow the 'heathen provinces' close by to pour 'upon Galilee the full influence of their Greek life' (1901: 439). Galilee is threatened by the neighbouring Gentiles; 'their loose living, their sensuous worship, their absorption in business, [and] the hopelessness of the insights of their tombs' (1901: 434). He concludes his chapter with these words: 'A vision of all the kingdoms of the world was as possible from this village as from the mount of temptation. But the chief lesson which Nazareth teaches to us is the possibility of a pure home and a spotless youth in the very face of the evil world' (1901: 435). The model that underpins the representation of Palestine, despite the seeming objectivity of the maps, is that of the nation-state, its sense of boundaries, and its notion of ethnic identity. A true homeland is a nation-state.

An Integrated History of Palestine

I often point out to my students that in order to understand the history of ancient Palestine it is necessary to understand the history of the European powers, the United States of America, and modern Israel from at least the nineteenth century onwards. This is not true only of the historical moment when Europe's re-engagement with the Middle East forged the dominant discourse of biblical studies but also of the present moment in the struggle for new models and paradigms. It is not that contemporary scholars have suddenly become more or less objective than their predecessors but that the social and political perspectives have changed so radically in the wake of the break-up of the Soviet Union.[7] What has become clear is that terms such as 'nation', 'national consciousness', 'national culture' or 'nation-state' are now as problematic in our study of the ancient past as 'tribe' was in previous generations. The pervasive use of these terms in biblical studies requires more careful reflection and detailed study than has hitherto been the case. In the context of the nineteenth century, nation building 'was plainly a central fact of historical transformation' (Hobsbawm 1991: 169). History as a discipline owed its appearance to a rising concept of nationality and the

---

7. Hobsbawm (1991: 165) however points out that the situation following the Soviet break-up in 1991 is not entirely new. In fact, he goes so far as to say that the 'apparent explosion of separatism in 1988–92 is the "unfinished business of 1918–21".' This is also the context for the work of William Foxwell Albright and his followers, suggesting that the shifts we have been witnessing are part of the unfinished business from the early part of the twentieth century.

concern with national origins. These same concerns are deeply embedded in the historiographic impulse of biblical studies. Yet this imposed a notion of the nation on scholarship, and biblical scholarship in particular, in which states were seen to be ethnically and linguistically homogenous entities, the standard form of the 'nation-state' (see Hobsbawm 1991: 169). Thus, as Hobsbawm argues, the situation in which the model of the nation-state grew up is peculiar in that it emphasizes not 'the pre-nineteenth-century world of uprejudiced [*sic*] local attachments'—what might be termed 'the unruly autonomy of the local'—but states based on 'the blinkered view that what should hold people together is ethnic, religious, or linguistic sameness'.[8] We might also say that it is this blinkered view that also separates and divides Historians, particularly biblical scholars and archaeologists, have been beguiled by the surface movement of great men and empires and a sense of time reflective of the state and its demands. As Carlo Levi said of Gagliano in his evocative and moving *Christ Stopped at Eboli*:

> none of the pioneers of Western civilization brought here his sense of the passage of time, his deification of the State or that ceaseless activity which feeds upon itself. No one has come to this land except as an enemy, a conqueror, or a visitor devoid of understanding. The seasons pass today over the toil of the peasants, just as they did three thousand years before Christ (Levi 1982: 12).

The history of ancient Palestine, as told by biblical scholars and archaeologists, has all too often been a history of ethnic difference and neat chronological divisions corresponding, supposedly, to ethnic, material and cultural differences. This burden of ethnicity is seen in the dominant discussion in biblical studies over the question of Israelite identity. Rather than accepting that the weight of evidence shows that the developments are indigenous and focusing on the processes that have contributed to these changes, historians are still obsessed with the identity of the villagers and the need to impose a label in order to structure and control the past. It is the impulse of Smith, Thomson, and the many other scholars and adventurers of the nineteenth century. It is also the impulse of modern scholarship as seen in the myriad discussions of whether Galilee was Gentile or Jewish or the notion of regionalism. It is the first question asked of the archaeological materials in the work of Mark A. Chancey (2002; 2005), for example. Such labels tend to separate, to emphasize that which is different and, in many cases, to lay exclusive claims to the past. The rhythms of time, those recurrent patterns that tie together the history of the region, are ignored in the search for that

---

8. Cited by Hobsbawm 1991: 186. Both quotations are taken from 'The State of the Nation State', *Economist,* 22 December 1990–14 January 1991, p. 178.

which separates, defines, and makes exclusive.[9] But in order to be heard, it is a history that needs to be freed from what Levi termed, 'the pioneers of Western civilization, their sense of the passage of time, and their deification of the State and its hierarchy'.

The maps of the nineteenth century, freed from the texts that accompany them, offer an alternative perspective on the history of Palestine; a site of resistance, we might say. Their lack of borders and the roads that criss-cross them suggest that mobility and connectivity are key characteristics of the history of the region. The major historiographical task is to see how all periods, including the Roman, form part of an integrated history of Palestine from its ancient past to the present. If an integrated history of Palestine is to be written, it is vital that the interconnections between all periods are explored. The many threads that tie together the distant past and the recent present need to be reconnected in order to allow us to appreciate the rich tapestry of Palestine's history. If we are to challenge the standard histories of differentiation—so dangerous in our modern world, where the focus is on a supposed clash of civilizations rather than the values that unite us in our humanity—then it is important to try to write an integrated history of Palestine. Palestine as a homeland for its indigenous population, rather than a Holy Land for those outside who wish to possess it.

An integrated history of Palestine that traces the rhythms of the region in connecting past to present is not the same as nationalist histories in which ethnogenesis has been frozen in time and which assumes that the lines of descent of a group in the present can be traced back easily into the past and to a territory now controlled or coveted. An integrated history is concerned with trying to expose and understand the processes in which demographic, social, and political changes take place, tracing the fortunes of the patchwork of towns or the responses in the countryside to economic and political crises.

The sharply bounded images of our maps in many textbooks, with Philistines, Canaanites, Israelites, Jews or Gentiles separated by clear lines of demarcation only serve to reinforce this notion of difference, the clash of cultures and the architecture of enmity, as Michael Shapiro termed it.[10] The very idea of the mobility of the population of ancient Palestine and wider movements throughout the eastern Mediterranean militate against the idea of

9. The recent detailed study of ancient Israel's ethnogenesis by Faust (2006), for example, emphasizes the notions of difference and separation in attempting to identify various traits that define 'Israelite' ethnicity in the Iron Age.

10. See Whitelam 2007 for a discussion of the ways in which modern nationalism and the nation-state have influenced the construction of maps in biblical atlases and text books.

attachment to land that is at the heart of modern nationalism.[11] It is a notion of boundedness, a static view of history that does not accord with the realities of life in Palestine. Ironically, the images of nineteenth-century maps without well-defined boundaries of the state suggest a world of interconnectivity that is often missing from the pages of our histories of the region. The construction of this architecture of enmity inevitably means that the question of what were the hopes, fears or aspirations of the villagers and pastoralists who populated the landscape is rarely asked. It also means that the historian seldom, if ever, considers what are the most crucial questions faced by the villagers themselves: the struggle to survive, the harsh realities of everyday life, and the constant worry of whether there will be enough food to eat.

The journeys of Ibn Battutah in the fourteenth century CE alert us to the interconnectivity of the region as a whole. For him, Palestine was inseparable from 'Syria', just as it was for Herodotus, and just as it was for the producer of the set of playing cards from the nineteenth century. Even at the very time when the European powers were carving up the region and imposing their artificial boundaries, the Hachette *Illustrated Blue Guide to the Eastern Mediterranean and Egypt* for 1938 suggested a four-day trip setting out from Beirut to Damascus, Jerusalem and Cairo with an alternative itinerary skipping Damascus and travelling down the coastal route (Alcalay 1993: 59-60). The author of the *Blue Guide* seems to view the region as interconnected, not dissimilar to Ibn Battutah six centuries earlier. The region was what Alcalay (1993: 84) terms, 'an itinerary through an intertwined network of cities in a still accessible space'. The boundaries imposed by the era of 'nation making' have all too often been imposed on Palestine's past. Instead, it is important to recognize and accept the shifting, fluid and overlapping spheres of influence that are integral to its history.

While the different areas of Palestine bear witness to its geographical diversity—the many Palestines—we must not lose sight of the interconnections among these micro-regions. Similarly, the towns of Palestine throughout its history were hardly 'islands on dry land' or 'a little world cut off by both mountains and sea', as Fernand Braudel (2002: 260-61) referred to the Greek cities, but were integrated into their own immediate micro-environments and were the hubs on the roads that crossed the great turntable of trade. The fluidity and adaptability of its population and the permeability of any borders meant that is was constantly responding to and adjusting to the wider environment.

---

11. The attachment to the land of the indigenous population is driven not by a sense of nationalism but by a care for the land in return for its fertility and produce. Mobility and adaptability are essential for a rural population faced with the demands of a wide range of microregions and the variability of the climate.

We might ask, Is the state such a significant category in the history of Palestine? Are such structures fundamental to the rhythms and patterns of Palestinian history, as our standard histories suggest, or are they ephemeral? Is the state a helpful category in understanding the deep-seated structures of the history of the region or is it epiphenomenal? It has been elevated in our standard biblical histories to such a highly distinctive and supremely significant historical category that its history is written as if the state dominates every aspect of life for the inhabitants of the region.[12] Yet as Horden and Purcell (2000: 250) point out about Mediterranean history in general that 'many different powers may be found intervening in the life of the microlocality. They vary in scale and in kind. One is the state—in all its various manifestations. But there is no need, whatever the state's pretensions, to assign to it a special place of its own in an ecological Mediterranean history.'

A detailed analysis of the social and political context of the shifts that have engulfed our discipline, and many others, remains to be done. What is becoming increasingly evident is that the set of assumptions that were brought by European visitors to Palestine in the nineteenth century no longer have the explanatory power for many scholars that they once had. It is important to diagnose the problems accurately and understand their far-reaching implications before it is possible to offer convincing alternative constructions of the past. Rather than accepting the assumptions of the period of nation making, it is important to expose the histories of difference built on the architectures of enmity, which impose on the past the insidious clash of civilizations and fail to recognize the many interconnections that help to bind the region together. It helps to reveal Palestine and Galilee, in particular, as a homeland for its inhabitants rather than as a Holy Land to be appropriated by outside powers.

---

12. Note that Horden and Purcell (2000: 91) say all of this about the town in Mediterranean history. However, I think that it is a more important question about the nature of the 'state' within the history of ancient Palestine.

JESUS ON WATER: IN A 'DEFINITE PLACE'
CALLED THE LAKE REGION

Rene Baergen

Jesus in Capernaum but out of Place

The historical Jesus is tied increasingly to the fact of Capernaum—it is his 'centre' (Sanders 1985; 1993a) and 'headquarters' (Horsley 2003), his 'base' (Theissen and Merz 1998: 166) and 'hub' (Reed 2000: 139), emblematic of his kingdom (Crossan and Reed 2001) and constitutive of his career (Freyne 2004)—but the fact of Capernaum seems not to have required corresponding engagement with the particular geographic conditions that make it so. The geological basin that determined Capernaum's particular horizon, in other words, the routes that led in and out and the water that must surely have conditioned its material existence—these have not been found significant for the commemoration of Jesus, even Jesus (allegedly) in Capernaum. Despite its rhetorical prominence, Capernaum has been in the quest strikingly disembodied, and Jesus in and around Capernaum left strangely out of (geographical) place.

The dislocation of Capernaum anticipates the analogous fate of the Lake Region of Galilee, though if anything the effacement of the Lake Region in the quest is even more complete. It is common enough to grant the geological division (by the Meiron massif) between the Upper and the Lower Galilee; in the quest the cultural elaboration of this distinction (especially by epigraphical and iconographical indices; cf. Meyers 1976; 1979; 1985) seems now to go without saying.[1] The Lake Region is a proposition similarly geological—the Rift Valley on the eastern edge of the Galilee is as topographically pronounced as the Meiron massif (if not more so) and its agricultural effect as clearly recognized by the Mishnah[2]—but it is only

---

1. So, recently, Reed 2000; Freyne 2004; Fiensy 2007; and Craffert 2008, though Reed's caveat—that Galilee nonetheless remained 'homogenous against its neighbors' (2000: 216)—is perhaps equally representative.

2. *M. Šeb.* 9.2: 'Three regions are to be distinguished in what concerns the law of removal: Judea, beyond the Jordan and Galilee; and each of them is divided into three

rarely registered in the quest, and even then it remains without apparent
significance for the reconstruction of Jesus.[3]

Exemplary in this regard is that series of articles by Eric Meyers first
expounding archaeologically the theory of Galilaean regionalism (1976;
1979; 1985; 1997). Here Meyers is concerned primarily to elaborate the
distinction between the Upper and the Lower Galilees, but in the process he
attests repeatedly a 'Rift Valley region' (later the 'Lake Kinneret region'),
defined economically by the 'busy trade' of the Kinneret (1976: 95), icono-
graphically by 'an increasingly developed aesthetic' along the lake shore
(1976: 99) and culturally by the influence of the Hellenistic cities on the
other side (1985: 126). In what he calls 'the culture of the Lake' (1985:
126), Meyers implies significant and sustained contact between west and
east, especially in the second and third centuries but also in the first. This for
Meyers is the place of Jesus' headquarters, but the peculiar 'culture' of this
locale seems not to extend to Jesus (resolutely 'of Nazareth') or his Galilaean context (for which the character of the Lower Galilee is consistently
privileged). The progression in Meyers's argument is striking:

> Strangely enough the bulk of Jesus' career is located in Lower Galilee
> (Nazareth, Nain and Cana) and in the Rift Valley region, *with headquar-
> ters in Capernaum*. The isolation that is often associated with the Galil-
> ean personality is therefore quite inappropriate when we speak of Jesus
> of Nazareth, *who is growing up along one of the busiest trade routes of
> ancient Palestine at the very administrative centers* [*sic*] *of the Roman
> provincial government* . . . The real question is whether or not anyone *in
> Lower Galilee* who might have lived along so busy an area could have
> escaped the dominant cultural tendencies in their region? (Meyers 1979:
> 698 [emphasis added]; cf. 1976: 95; 1997: 59)

Jesus' affinity for the Lake Region is allowed (though it seems already
strange) but immediately obscured by his reputed hometown of Nazareth,
which raises to prominence by geographical association the nearby administrative centre of Sepphoris, in the end to focus the 'real question' in Meyers's construction on the dominant profile of the typical Lower Galilaean.
Jesus, whose headquarters are admittedly in Capernaum in the Rift Valley region of alleged cultural distinction on Meyers's account, is without
real argument ensconced in the 'dominant cultural tendencies' of the Lower

---

lands. [The Galilee is divided into] the Upper Galilee, the Lower Galilee and the Valley.
From Kfar Hananiah upwards, wherever sycamores do not grow, is the Upper Galilee;
from Kfar Hananiah downwards, wherever sycamores do grow, is the Lower Galilee; the
region of Tiberias is the Valley.'

3. Josephus (*War* 1.22; 3.35-39) is routinely invoked to sponsor the division of
'two Galilees'. But he also distinguishes the whole Rift Valley as a region climatically
distinct (*War* 4.455-56). See below.

Galilee. The historical Jesus is not often Meyers's explicit design but his implicit substitution of a centre 'first and foremost' and 'overwhelmingly' Jewish 'in every respect' (1997: 64) for a periphery found culturally complex sets the tone for the quest and its Galilaean (qua Jewish) Jesus.

The geological premise of the Lake Region has not been brought to bear on the historical Jesus, despite its relevance for one memorialized, as nowhere else, on water. In fact, when it comes to reconstructing Jesus, the very voices that instruct regional thinking (helpfully) seem to forget the data they produce vis-à-vis the peculiarity of the Lake Region and revert midstream to the safer shore, which is actually no (lake) shore at all. The difference of the Lake Region is not allowed to complicate by making significantly different (but no less 'Jewish') the cultural identity of Jesus; on the contrary, it seems to me that notice of the Lake Region gives way without notice to the discursive privilege of an inland Galilee culturally normative for even the 'border regions' of geographical and cultural distinction that Jesus is said repeatedly to occupy.[4]

Jesus in Capernaum seems entirely defensible: In the Q material, Capernaum is the only named location for a saying or action of Jesus (7.1-9), singled out later (10.13-15) from even Chorazin (four km to the north) and Bethsaida (four km to the east) for particularly harsh critique (Theissen 1989: 51; Reed 1995). In Mark it is the place where Jesus is 'at home', repeatedly (2.1; 9.33); in Matthew it is 'his own *polis*' (9.1) where he might be expected to pay the half-shekel tax (17.24-27); and in Luke it is the place apparently most associated with his healing activity (4.23). Even in John, where Cana vies for equal prominence (Richardson 2002), it is the place to which Jesus is expected to return (6.24). I can agree—if only for the sake of argument—that Jesus had a 'home' in Capernaum. But what happens to the reconstruction of a historical Jesus if this point is not so quickly forgotten? What happens to the discourse, more importantly, if we grant the premise that Galilee matters but include as significant—especially methodologically—the particular and particularly inhabited landscape of the lake?

'Definite Place'

Notwithstanding the geographical designation that Meyers signals and contemporary geographers endorse, unanimously to my knowledge,[5] the Lake

---

4. So especially Reed 2000: 117; and Chancey 2002: 169, 180; 2005: 20.

5. On the basis of climatic data (especially temperature and precipitation) and physiographic particularity: Orni and Efrat 1971 [1964]: 88-92; Karmon 1971: 169-73; Schattner 1973: 88-90; Baly 1974 [1957]: 196-98; Avi-Yonah 1977; Aharoni 1979: 33; the *Atlas of Israel* (1985: iv) and the Israeli Meteorological Service (Rubin, Israeli, Gat *et al.* 1992, cited in Goldreich 2003: 19-21).

Region has not often suggested itself as a discrete area of historical investigation. In the usual historical narrative, the valley appears more often as
a line of dissociation between east and west along the (sometime) lines of
Roman administration: The eastern side falls under the political jurisdic-
tion of the Decapolis, Gamla and the so-called Golan to the north excepted.
The west, now excluding the territory of Scythopolis to the south, which
belongs with the east, is variously Hasmonaean, Herodian and (nominally)
Roman. This demarcation of east from west is received largely (though not
exclusively; cf. Cappelletti 2007) on the strength of Josephus's account,
but it has been variously elaborated[6] and considered sufficiently concrete to
discourage consideration of the particular ecological identity of the valley.

Much the same applies to the region of the Mediterranean according to a
recent treatment by Peregrine Horden and Nicholas Purcell (2000: 23), and
I think the analogy is instructive:

> [T]he most disturbing feature of the Mediterranean past must be the infre-
> quency with which even a significant part of the sea and its hinterlands
> have constituted anything remotely like a political entity. The empires
> whose sphere of control or influence has embraced some Mediterranean
> shores have nearly all had centres of gravity well beyond the region . . .
> The single conspicuous example of the pan-Mediterranean empire is that
> of Rome . . . Yet not even the celebrated *pax Romana* could hope to eradi-
> cate the immense diversity of provincial loyalties and cultures . . . Rome's
> was an empire in which the precarious unity of Greek and Roman lan-
> guage and culture and an economy of extraction and coinage were totally
> dependent on communications; and for all the fame of the Roman road, the
> most basic and the most vital lines of communication lay across the sea.

What interests me in this quotation is the way in which Horden and Purcell pursue a Mediterranean region quite in contrast to the realities of political fragmentation to find it not in what Fernand Braudel might have called
l'histoire événementielle (i.e., the surface disturbances of historical events)
but in the connecting medium of the sea (the lead, already, in Braudel's
longue durée). The fracture of the Mediterranean, Horden and Purcell suggest (2000: 22-23), has been political, 'in every sense', owing more to a
paradigm that privileges the nation-state, endorses the political concerns

---

6. Mordechai Aviam (2007) has proposed a cultural distinction between Jewish
Galilee and Gentile surround on the basis of the distribution pattern of no fewer than
11 archaeological indices (Hellenistic period pottery, Hasmonaean coins, ritual baths,
stone vessels, pagan temples, synagogues, churches and monasteries, Kfar Hananiah
type pottery, statuary and figurative art, ossuaries and secret hideaways), though his
interest seems primarily a northern demarcation line. Reed (2000: 216) would make the
valley in particular a 'cultural barrier' between a 'homogenous' Jewish community and
the (Gentile) other, with the former archaeologically attested by the 'ethnicity markers'
of *miqva'ot*, stone vessels, secondary burial practices and the absence of pig bones.

of the texts on which our histories rely and embodies contemporary religious division, than it does to natural frontiers and physical environment. Horden and Purcell's Mediterranean is evidently a region on a far different scale than the Kinneret; I would not want to push the analogy too far.[7] But it serves at this point to loosen the grip of the usual narratives of political history and to anticipate in their place the (geographical) significance of water. Horden and Purcell (2000: 53-88) go on to develop the Mediterranean as a collection of 'definite places'—distinguished not by geology or topography or climate alone but by the particular interplay of multiple human productive response—and it is to these definite places that I suggest the Lake Region is more analogous. Not 'the bald facts' are most important, in other words, but the very human elaboration, on the basis of these various 'facts', of a productive landscape particular, in no small measure, because it is particularly inhabited.

A 'Definite Place' Called the Lake Region

The biblical Sea of Galilee is by any other name a lake,[8] and a rather small one, easily navigable and exceptional not for its surface area (c. 165 km²) but for its age[9] and its topographical predicament: the lake surface is 210 m below the level of the Mediterranean. In fact, the lake and its immediate basin are entirely contained in the deep and very narrow tectonic trough of the Jordan Valley, itself an element of the Great Rift Valley, bounded in the east and west by the steep basalt ridges of the Golan and the Lower Galilee. Alluvial valleys rising from the lakeshore to the northeast (Buteiha) and northwest (Gennesar) present a bridge of sorts out of the trough to the surrounding plateau 400 to 500 m above. But considerable seismic activity, numerous thermal springs (especially lacustrine) and the relative salinity of the lake—which recalls the extension from the Hula to beyond the Dead

---

7. At the same time, scale is not necessarily prohibitive of the comparison—Horden and Purcell (2005: 366-67) agree, for instance, that their approach is very clearly applicable to the Baltic world, the Indian Ocean or even the Thames Valley, without, however, becoming a universal solvent; likewise the enduring and still vital debate regarding specifically the alleged unity of the Mediterranean, on which compare Horden and Purcell 2000: 485-523 with especially Harris 2005a and Herzfeld 2005.

8. Kinneret: Num. 34.11; Josh. 12.3; 13.27. Gennesar/Gennesaret: 1 Macc. 11.67; Lk. 5.1; Josephus, *War* 2.573; 3.463, 506, 515-16; *Ant.* 5.84; 13.158; 18.28, 36; Pliny, *Nat. hist.* 5.71. Tiberias: Jn 6.1; 21.1; Josephus, *War* 3.57; 4.456. Taricheae: Pliny, *Nat. hist.* 5.71.

9. The Kinneret is considered in limnological parlance a 'relict' lake from the Tertiary period—meaning that it preserves archaic fauna and supports a larger number of endemic species than many relatively younger post-glacial lakes found elsewhere in the northern hemisphere. Compare Serruya 1978a.

Sea of a prehistoric and hypersaline Lisan sea—make the valley much more clearly participant in the geology of the Jordan Valley extending north to south than partner to the sloping plateau of the east or the highlands of the west.

The water of the Kinneret complicates this participation in so far as it moderates winter temperatures and increases relative humidity sufficiently to distinguish climatically the area immediately around the lake from the Hula valley to the north, which experiences regular winter frosts as a result of its proximity to Mount Hermon (Orni and Efrat 1971 [1964]: 155) and the lower Jordan Valley to the south, where rainfall remains usually below the minimum necessary for dryland agriculture. Tropical temperatures and the availability of water drew to the lakeshore in antiquity a dense belt of settlement: Tiberias, on the southwest shore, just to the north of the hot springs of Hammat Tiberias; Magdala/Taricheae, 6.5 km north at the southern edge of the infamous Gennesar valley (and the mouth of the Nahal Arbel); Capernaum, on the northern shore, adjacent to the most shallow point in the lake but also (because of its thermal springs) one reportedly most attractive to fish[10]; Chorazin 3 km in- (and up-)land; Bethsaida/Julias (et-Tell), on the east bank of the Jordan, some 2 km inland of the lakeshore very likely because of the accidents of erosion;[11] Gamla, further to the east, on an isolated spur 10 km inland of the lakeshore, staring directly across the water at Taricheae; Hippos (Susita), on another spur, 350m above the lake, directly across from Tiberias; and at the lake's southeast corner, at the mouth of the Yarmouk Valley, the hot springs of Hamat Gader and on the ridge overlooking the entire basin (and like Gamla 10 km inland) the city of Gadara.[12]

Indications are that the population represented by these settlements will have been growing in the first century. Jonathan Reed (2000: 84; 2008: 11) in particular has suggested that Galilee's population 'more than doubled' from 50 BCE to 50 CE, whatever its absolute numbers. The foundation of Tiberias in 18 or 19 CE and the raising of Bethsaida/Julias to the status of *polis* in 30 CE make especially plain the participation of the Lake Region in this trend. But the expansion in physical size of Capernaum and Gamla during the same period (Reed 2008: 10) and the archaeological appearance

10. So, for instance, Masterman 1908: 41; Nun 1989a: 14; and Rousseau and Arav 1995: 94. Serruya (1978b: 132) notes too the attraction of the deltaic formation at the mouth of the Buteiha valley to the northeast.

11. On the location of Bethsaida, see especially Arav 1988; 1997; 2006; Kuhn and Arav 1991; and Shroder and Inbar 1995; but see also Notley 2007.

12. Compare Rousseau and Arav 1995: 247 and now Vaage (this volume), in the opposite direction.

of new and expanded settlement on at least the western side of the valley[13] suggest that population growth around the lake was not simply an urban phenomenon.[14] Given the limited land base in the valley, it is not surprising to find at least the elite of first-century Tiberias pursuing estates beyond the bounds of the valley (Josephus, *Ant.* 18.36-38; *Life* 33; cf. Freyne 2004: 49).

Among historians, the same two factors of temperature and rainfall have tended to inspire confidence in the valley's agricultural potential bordering at times on romantic nostalgia. Josephus is predictably effusive of especially the northwest corner:

> There is not a plant which its fertile soil refuses to produce and its cultivators in fact grow every species; the air is so well-tempered [εὔκρατον] that it suits the most opposite varieties. The walnut, a tree which delights in the most wintry climate, here grows luxuriantly, beside palm-trees, which thrive on heat, and figs and olives, which require a milder atmosphere. One might say that nature had taken pride in thus assembling the most discordant species in a single spot, and that, by a happy rivalry, each of her seasons wished to claim this region for her own' (3.516-19; Loeb translation).

Josephus's account has been criticized. Most acutely, I think, Gildas Hamel (1990) has found Josephus's vision indebted to the conventional idealization of the country life, complete with the standard elements of exceptional diversity (as per Pliny, *Letters* 5.67.7-13), year-round harvest (Homer, *Odyssey* 7.112-32) and the beneficent agency of 'Nature herself' (Lucretius, *On the Nature of Things* 5.1261-78). In Hamel's opinion, the trope of the bountiful countryside is more indebted to the interests of a leisured class dependent on the extraction of an agricultural 'surplus' and committed to the imperial project than it is reflective of any particular material reality.

More often, though, it seems primarily Josephus's lyricism that is found difficult: 'Josephus doubtless exaggerates', Martin Goodman (1983: 22) begins, representatively, 'but the picture is essentially correct'.[15] It may be that soil variety in the northwest is sufficient, 'essentially', to support

13. As throughout eastern Lower Galilee according to Leibner (2006: 115): 'The number of settlements multiplied during this period [i.e. the early Roman period] in comparison with that of the previous one and so did the range of settled dunams in the entire survey area [extending roughly 15 km westward of the lakeshore], a picture pointing to a dramatic population growth.'

14. Reed (2008: 12, 23-25) argues that cities actually act as 'demographic brakes' on population growth. This is of a piece with his caution that population growth not be equated with economic prosperity, at least not without argument. The latter still needs to be brought to bear on the relatively populous region of the lake.

15. Compare Avi-Yonah 1977: 204; Aharoni 1979: 33; Freyne 1980a: 15; 2004: 49; and Reed 2000: 144; 2007: 57.

something of Josephus's vision of verticality. Arieh Singer (2007)[16] finds in the Gennesar valley a combination of soils at least potentially fertile: the association here of terra rossa, in particular, with the alluvial soils of the littoral plain is among the most productive complex in the region, though the former tends to be particularly shallow, thus susceptible to drought (Singer 2007: 94, 97), and the latter tends to be poorly aerated and drained, and so easily water-logged in the rainy season (Singer 2007: 152, 160). The basalt-derived soils predominant in the remainder of the region are allegedly prime grain (Zohary 1969; Renfrew 1973: 67; Applebaum 1976: 639) and/or vine (Applebaum 1976: 654; Reed 2007: 57) growing stock, though their productivity in the valley in particular will have depended on intensive clearing and terracing.[17] Mean annual temperatures in the northwest as immediately around the whole lake are also well above those in the Lower Galilee (Rosenan 1970a). When the Mediterranean sea breeze that daily cools the region of the Lower Galilee reaches the steep descent of the lake valley, it is compressed, and so warmed, tending rather to insulate the valley floor than rejuvenate its air mass (Karmon 1971: 170). The same temperature inversion means that annual rainfall in the valley (in the range of 350–450 mm/year) is lower than either west (500–800 mm/year in the Lower Galilee) or east (700–1000 mm/year on the Golan plateau). Precipitation in the valley is further affected (again adversely) by its distance from the Mediterranean, its elevation and its position in the rain shadow of the Lower Galilaean highlands (Rubin 1978: 69-70; Goldreich 2003: 56-62; Katsnelson 2007). But the lake still receives sufficient rainfall, on average, to sponsor an impression of agricultural fertility, at least in theory, and this has been enough for most to follow Josephus, hyperbole aside.

The practical conditions of the Lake Region and in particular the severe relief that gives to this place its distinctive topographical profile—what Horden and Purcell (2000: 308) call in another context 'the tyranny of the gradient'—give more reason for pause. The gradient—by which I mean the dramatic vertical decline to the valley floor from the elevated scarp of the Lower Galilee in the west and the high plateau of the Transjordan in the east—means rainfall in the valley tends to be convective (owing to the

---

16. Following Ravikovitch 1970; compare Zohary 1962: 8-9; and Dan *et al.* 1975.

17. So, for instance, Applebaum 1976: 639; and Reed 2000: 144. Singer (2007: 92, 152, 187) makes quite plain the difficult connection between typical soil characteristics and real productivity by emphasizing repeatedly the 'limitations' of particular soil composition, slope, depth, temperature, moisture, exposure and erosion. Horden and Purcell (2000: 231) are even more acute: 'Fertility, productive opportunity, and the soil itself are all of human construction . . . There is no absolute quality of land anywhere: its value and potential depend on the choices and perceptions [and here especially labour intensive management] of those who make use of it.'

upsurge of warm air) and thus particularly local, intense and brief.[18] Rainfall throughout the Galilee is highly variable from year to year, and the surround of the lake is already more susceptible to chronic drought than even the Lower Galilee, the eastern shore in particular.[19] Average annual rainfall in the valley remains above the minimum necessary for non-irrigated agriculture, more often than not, but this is not necessarily to say that rainfall in the valley is particularly effective for agricultural purposes.[20] Higher temperatures in the valley, for instance, even as regards the Lower Galilee, lead to higher evaporation levels, which mitigate the water available for agricultural use.[21] Sudden cloudbursts, similarly, do less good agriculturally than average annual figures first suggest. Especially on the 'fertile' western shoreline (but also in the Buteiha valley; cf. Singer 2007: 150), in fact, rainfall of high intensity tends to make of the deep and clayey alluvial plains a 'clinging mud' difficult to cultivate and especially susceptible to severe flooding (Karmon 1971: 170; Rubin 1978: 83; Goldreich 2003: 79). On the steep valley walls the same rainfall pattern joins with the notably strong and regular winds from especially the Mediterranean (Goldreich 2003: 139-41) to steadily erode the basaltic soil cover, already thin and because of lack of moisture without the protection of significant forest vegetation (Singer 2007: 184, 187), made worse in antiquity by the local rearing of sheep and goats, if rabbinic pressure against the practice provides accurate recall.[22]

18. So especially Orni and Efrat 1971 [1964]: 156; Karmon 1971: 170; Stanhill and Neumann 1978: 49; Rubin 1978: 83; Katsnelson 1985; and Goldreich 2003: 60, 82.

19. On variability as a general characteristic, see Karmon 1971: 24, 28; Rubin 1978: 74; and Katsnelson 1985: 19. On the disadvantage of the lake region vis-à-vis the Lower Galilee, see especially Rubin 1978: 70; and Goldreich 2003: 56-62. According to Rubin (1978: 75) the eastern shore receives on average 50 to 75 mm less rainfall per year than the western shore.

20. Goldreich (2003: 55), for instance, notes that mean annual rainfall in most of Europe (> 600 mm) falls well within the average of most Mediterranean climates (400–700 mm), modern Israel included. But the temporal concentration of rainfall in Israel (50 precipitation days compared to 151 in London), its particular characteristics (cold and intense) and the effect of higher air temperatures mean the same amount of rainfall is considerably less efficient agriculturally there than it is, for instance, in most of Europe.

21. Goldreich (2003: 120) puts the amount of evaporation in the Kinneret vicinity (measured by evaporation pans) at 240 cm/year, compared to 150 cm/year on the Mediterranean coast and 234 cm/year at Jericho. Again, however, the relationship between measurement and effect is, according to Goldreich (2003: 118), 'most complicated', depending on crop type and age, method of irrigation, soil type and variously undefined 'climatic factors'.

22. Martin Goodman (1983: 23-24, 104) finds in the rabbinic literature 'thorough disapproval' of the practice (*t. B. Qam.* 8.14; cf. *m. B. Qam.* 7.7; *t. B. Qam.* 8.11, 12). But he also notes a steady stream of complaints 'from one generation to the next' (as per

The tropical temperatures and rainfall pattern conditioned by the topography of the Lake Region have been occasionally as notable for malaria as they have been notorious for agriculture. Such was very clearly the case in the early twentieth century[23] and Reed (2008: 19) suggests that the same be applied to the first: 'we should expect much higher rates of malaria at villages like Capernaum or Magdala near the Gennosaur Plain than, say, Nazareth or Cana, which were on a slope and atop a hill . . . And surely Sepphoris . . . was better off than hot and humid Tiberias right on the lake, at least in terms of malaria.' Presumably the same would have extended to the estuaries of the Jordan at Bethsaida and the Yarmouk at Hammat Gader.[24] Evidence of morbidity and mortality rates specific to the Lake Region is necessarily limited. Reed (2008: 17-18) argues by analogy to the Egyptian Fayum, where rates are more forthcoming (Scheidel 2001: 16-19), that the hydrological situation in the valley of stagnant water and marshland be similarly correlated with substandard health in general and more specifically with the seasonal incidence of tertian and quartan fevers now associated with malaria. Such was evidently well attested in the medical corpus of the Roman Empire, diagnosed by the periodicity of intense fever, and clearly associated with wetland environments, though not yet with mosquitoes (Sallares 2002: 7-22, 55-64; Retief and Cilliers 2004). The possibility, at least, that this will have applied well to the Lake Region, and considerably less well to an environment such as Nazareth, makes particularly interesting the fevers Jesus is said to have encountered in Capernaum (Mt. 8.14-15// Mk 1. 29-31//Lk. 4. 38-39; Jn 4.46-54) as apparently nowhere else. It also directs us back to Josephus (*War* 4.455-56), now in a particularly more pessimistic mood, describing the whole Rift Valley as 'burnt up', 'excessively dry' and chronically 'pestilential'. Roman agronomists were well aware of the futility of agriculture in land susceptible to disease, no matter how fer-

---

m. B. Qam. 6.1, 2), laxity towards those who did raise sheep and goats (*t. B. Meṣ.* 2.33) and outright disregard of the regulation (*t. B. Meṣ.* 5.7; *t. Šeb.* 3.13).

23. Israel Kligler (1930: 48) calls the hydrological conditions of the Jordan valley 'undoubtedly the worst in Palestine' for the incidence of malaria and notes the classification already in 1919 of Migdal, Kinnereth and Degania as 'intensely malarious' (1930: 88, cited in Reed 2008: 19). So, more recently, Margalit and Tahori 1978.

24. Masterman (1908: 41) accounts for the remove of Bethsaida/et-Tell from the lakeshore in precisely this way: 'There is no need whatsoever to suppose that this place [i.e. Bethsaida] was necessarily, because of its name, on the shore itself. *This intensely malarious plain could never have been a suitable place for a Roman city.* Every modern analogy would lead us to suppose that the fishermen would live in the healthier site, raised above the marshes, and go to their work even as to-day [*sic*] the Tiberias fishermen do' (emphasis added).

tile its soil;[25] in fact Varro's warning in this regard—'In an unhealthy location farming is a lottery' (*Re Rustica* 1.4.3, cited in Reed 2008)—were we
to add to it the unpredictability of rainfall and the progressive soil decline
resulting from the gradient, may provide the most fitting response to an
initial impression of the valley's fertility.

The weight of literary evidence for notable agricultural production in
Galilee actually points consistently to other places—olives in Gischala
(Josephus, *War* 2.591-92//*Life* 73-76; *Sifre Deut.* 355), for instance, and
grain in the Jezreel (*Life* 24, 118-19) and Netofa valleys (*Num. R.* 18.22;
though note *y. Pe'ah* 1.20)—and other periods—flax in second-century
Tiberias (Pausanias 5.5.2; *b. M. Qat.* 18b).[26] It would be unwise to infer
from this the absence of intensive cultivation in the region; but it is also
unnecessary, even to dispute the occasional pocket of relative productivity,
such as perhaps the Gennesar valley, though I do think Josephus's vision
problematic. My argument is not with the incidence of intensive agriculture,
which I presume pervasive in the valley of the first century (as throughout
the inhabited Mediterranean), notwithstanding the very significant complications of soil, topography and climate. But I think misplaced (because
essentially abstract) the rhetoric of prosperity. Polycropping and verticality
were presumably part of the practice of agriculture in the Lake Region, as
was occasional and localized glut, but so was the unpredictability of rainfall, the risk of localized flood and drought and, as a result, the reality of
recurrent dearth.

To the challenge of production in a place of agricultural uncertainty—
high relief resulting in volatile rainfall, regular flooding, progressive soil
deterioration and perhaps also chronic disease—the diversity of the lake
environment supplies at least a partial response, which is to say that the tyranny of the gradient is met in the valley, at least in part, by the opportunities
of water. Throughout the Mediterranean, agriculturally marginal wetlands
provide diverse opportunities for gathering, grazing and even limited irrigation (Horden and Purcell 2000: 186-90) and I see no reason why this should
not apply as well to certain locales around the lake, despite the silence of

25. Hippocrates (*Airs, Waters, Places* 7, 24), Cato (*De Agricultura* 1.3), Varro (*Re Rustica* 1.12.1-3), Vitruvius (1.4.1), Columella (*Re Rustica* 1.5.6) and Pliny the Elder (*Nat. hist.* 18.7.33), cited in Sallares (2002: 55-64), all advise against situating farms on low-lying river and/or marsh land, notwithstanding the notable advantages of water.

26. If there is an exception, it may be Josephus's recall of date palm cultivation in the Gennesar valley (*War* 3.517). That Tiberias is later remembered to have imported dates from Jericho (*y. Dem.* 2.22c; cf. discussion in Safrai 1994: 139), however, suggests that even here caution is necessary.

the literati.[27] These are rather more interested in the supply of hot water endemic to the region;[28] it may even be, as Sean Freyne (2007: 158) suggests, that the valley proves attractive to urban development for precisely this reason.[29]

Rightly or wrongly, though, modern historians have been more impressed by the opportunity of the Kinneret fishery. From Strabo's notice of a fish saltery at Taricheae (*Geog.* 16.2.45), Josephus's recall of a lake heavily traversed (with an alleged fishing boat per family at Taricheae, *Life* 163; cf. *War* 2.635) and rich in fish (including one resembling the Egyptian *coracin*, *War* 3.520) and the analogies of Egypt and Asia Minor, the valley has been made a place of 'big business'—'synonymous with prosperity' (Wuellner 1967: 52, 53), 'of great importance' to at least the Jewish population of ancient Palestine (Safrai 1994: 163) but also allegedly linked by international trade to 'world markets' beyond.[30] Freyne's conclusion (2004: 52) that lake fishing in the first century was an occupation that was 'relatively lucrative' and that fishermen were 'far from the bottom rung of the social ladder' imparts to the region a rather optimistic profile of a piece with recent suggestions that fish and fish sauce played a role in the ancient consumer economy as important even as olive oil.[31]

The argument as it relates to the Lake Region is almost entirely inferential. An impressive collection of fishing implements at Bethsaida (et-Tell) evenly distributed across the excavated area and dated by archaeological context to the Hellenistic and early Roman periods suggests the importance of fishing to the local population;[32] the place-names of the valley—

---

27. Topography aside, the relative salinity of the lake water (in the range of 250 to 400 mg/litre, depending on precipitation levels; see Orni and Efrat 1971 [1964]: 451; Karmon 1971: 124; Serruya 1978a: 186-87) makes heavy irrigation in the lake basin problematic (see Reifenberg 1947 and now Singer 2007: 19), though this does not apply to the freshwater springs that feed the Gennesar and Buteiha valleys (Mero 1978: 93-94).

28. Thus especially Eunapius (*Vita Sophistarum* 459) on Hammat Gader: 'a place that has warm baths in Syria, inferior only to those at Baiae in Italy, with which no other baths can be compared'. But also Josephus (*Ant.* 18.36; *War* 2.614; *Life* 85) on Hammat Tiberias. See further Dvorjetski 1992; and Weber 1997; 1999.

29. Freyne (2007: 158) would have the reputed properties of the thermal springs at especially Hammat Tiberias, Hammat Gader and Callirhoe account for an apparent Herodian predilection *'for the whole rift region'* (emphasis added). Cf. Dvorjetski 1992; and Weber 1997; 1999.

30. Explicitly in Sawicki 2000: 27-29, 92. The language elsewhere of export (Rousseau and Arav 1995: 247), even export to Rome (Freyne 2004: 51), suggests much the same.

31. So especially Bekker-Nielsen 2002. See also Curtis 1991; and Mylona 2003; 2008, though compare Gallant 1985; and especially Purcell 1995; 2003.

32. The collection includes lead weights, iron hooks, a sail needle, two basalt sinkers, several basalt anchors and a fisherman's seal (Rousseau and Arav 1995: 19-24; Fort-

Taricheae ('Fish Salting Place', Josephus, *Life* 32; Pliny *Nat. hist.* 5.15), Migdal Nunya ('Fish Tower', *b. Pes.* 46) and Bethsaida ('House of Fisher-men')—and the various literary traditions of the New Testament suggest as much. Circumstantial observation of what appear to be ancient harbours around the lake suggests broad-based and well-organized investment at some point in the history of the region,[33] though harbours do not equal a fishery nor a fishery demand harbours, and it may be that renewed exca-vations at Taricheae will deliver a clearer material indication of a locale 'rich from fish' (Zangenberg 2001; 2003). But it is difficult without stamped amphorae, for instance, or freshwater fish bones to estimate the geographi-cal and economic extent of the lake effect in this regard.[34]

Even if we grant the material description—that the lake was the scene of intensive fishing in the first century—the usual social conclusion that the lake supported a thriving industry of entrepreneurial fishermen does not necessarily follow. Much the same has been alleged of pottery production in the Lower Galilee in an oft-cited study by David Adan-Bayewitz (1993; see also Adan-Bayewitz and Perlman 1990). Indications of intense pottery manufacture at Kfar Hananiah, in particular and its extensive distribution throughout Galilee and the Golan sponsor an irenic vision of the rural arti-san's involvement in a flourishing first-century industry (Adan-Bayewitz and Perlman 1990: 171-72). But as John Dominic Crossan has noted (1998: 223-30), increased concentration (and economic dependence) on pottery manufacture might as well denote agricultural necessity as economic spec-ulation. Adan-Bayewitz admits as much: 'When a population exceeds the carrying capacity of its available land', he concludes (1993: 235), 'there is movement into other occupations', even if these occupations prove invari-ably in the first century less satisfying (literally) than agriculture. According to Adan-Bayewitz, pottery making, in several areas of the Lower Galilee, was one such occupation; I suspect fishing, in the valley, was another.

---

ner 1999). The seal in particular, dated 'no later than 67 CE' (Rousseau and Arav 1995: 96) may substantiate the possibility of fishing collectives like the one alluded to in Lk. 5.10.

33. See especially Nun 1989b. To my knowledge none of these has been securely dated.

34. The archaeological evidence is summarized in Rousseau and Arav 1995: 96: 'Lead weights for nets have been discovered near Magdala and at Bethsaida, fish hooks at Capernaum and Bethsaida, a sail needle at Bethsaida and a net needle at Magdala, two line sinkers at Bethsaida, and several stone anchors and mooring stones in various places around the lake . . . The most significant find has been the fisherman's seal of Bethsaida, found in 1989, and dated no later than 67 C.E.' Clearly fishing was an activity of some concentration in the lake basin in the first century, but this catalogue hardly demands the usual narrative of a thriving export economy.

On the analogy of pottery making, lake fishing in the first century had more to do with a land base insufficient in quality and quantity to support the region's immediate population, which was evidently growing (Reed 2008; see above), than it did with the fish market even in Sepphoris (to say nothing of Rome) where excavations show a predilection for saltwater fish from the Mediterranean (Reed 2007: 24). The tendency throughout the Mediterranean may have been toward professionalization (Purcell 1995: 135), but this does not yet make of fishing in the first century a regional windfall, except perhaps occasionally, and even then the papyrological evidence of Roman Egypt indicates plainly that the resources of the water were as highly regulated and taxed in the empire as the resources of the land (*P.Tebt.* II, 329, 359; *P.Wisc.* I, 6; *P.Oslo* II, 47; *PSI* VIII, 901; cf. Hanson 1997).[35] Taricheae notwithstanding, the humble remains of the fishing village of Capernaum suggest that lake fishing was a poor substitute for agriculture, not often pursued as an independent subsistence strategy (as elsewhere in the Mediterranean; Horden and Purcell 2000: 194), brought about at least in part 'by the poverty of the land', to invoke Strabo's explanation of the fishery and, notably, the fish salteries in another context (*Geog.* 6.1.1, of Lucania). Let me be clear: I do not dispute the economic importance of fishing to the local population of the valley. But I find it most significant as an example of risk management—localized diversification—of the sort that made life in the surround of the lake singular and sustainable to varying degrees.

What seems more to complicate the picture of marginality typical of the Mediterranean environment and to make of the Lake Region a definite place significant beyond its ecological constraint is the mobility and the interdependence of its population by the medium of the lake. Focus on Roman roads and the 'glitter' of high commerce (Horden and Purcell 2000: 365) is typical, though not unimportant for that: 'In the time of Jesus', Rousseau and Arav (1995: 248) begin, 'the Sea of Galilee was the most important economic centre of northeastern Palestine and was connected by roads with Syria and Mesopotamia through the Via Maris linking Damascus to Ptolemais, Caesarea Maritima, and Joppa. It offered easy access to Phoenicia, Asia Minor, Samaria, Judea, and the rest of the Mediterranean world.'[36]

---

35. Reed's rejoinder (2000: 165) seems appropriate: 'For every family engaged in fishing or drying fish, there was a tax collector or official who sold the rights to fish and demanded a hefty return. The fact that Zebedee, the father of James and John, worked with hired hands (μισθωτός) in no way indicates wealth on his part or a significant entrepreneurial enterprise (Mk 1:20). Rather, it points to the common practice of seasonal, daily, or hourly hiring of peasants dispossessed from their land who sought to eke out a living in the larger villages and cities.'

36. Hyperbole aside, this might be thought sufficient to overcome any residual privilege of political boundaries. Reed (2000: 146-48) disputes the association of the *via maris* with Capernaum, with good reason, but his conclusion that Capernaum benefited

Even more telling for the imprint of the Lake Region, because more repeti-tive and routine, is the pattern of local redistribution within the basin. Ines-capable, perhaps, in an environment of limited resource and minute varia-tion in local production, local connectivity is sponsored especially by the density of settlement focused on the lake and interested, to one extent or another, in the opportunities of the water. Many of the urban centres around the lake will have been in plain view of each other—Hippos and Tiberias in particular are visible from almost any point on the opposite shore, cer-tainly to each other—and if the archaeological evidence at Taricheae is at all telling for the region, most will have had harbours, Hippos and Gadara included, to facilitate access in and out, nominally, but more significantly to announce their interest in the resource base of the lake.[37] Josephus attests (as a result?) considerable hostility between the populations of these urban centres: an assault on the eastern districts of Hippos and Gadara by the Tiberians (led by Justus) at the outset of the First Jewish Revolt (*Life* 42; *War* 2.459), a reprisal by the residents of Hippos and Gadara against those Jews already living on the eastern shore (*War* 2.478) and the flight of at least some of the remaining Jews to the western town of Taricheae (*War* 3.542). Evidently relations were strained, sometimes to excess, but it is the prior asumption of mobility in the region habitual enough to account for a significant Jewish population resident on the eastern shore by mid-first century CE and robust enough to explain spontaneous fight or flight that I find noteworthy.[38]

Josephus's account of the region in the first century suggests a people 'very effectively linked by warfare', to adopt a phrase that William Harris (2005b: 24) uses of the Mediterranean population, if nothing else. But the economic exchange and stereotyped rivalry remembered of Hippos and Tiberias, in par-ticular, contributes an even sharper image of purposeful association across the water. In the rabbinic literature, the two interact with a regularity that appears almost formulaic: the Palestinian Talmud recalls the agricultural commerce

from a regional and interregional road network points in the same direction, if consider-ably more cautiously.

37. Among those who note visibility across the water, see Rousseau and Arav 1995: 101, 127-28; and Jensen 2006: 179. An ancient harbour at Taricheae/Magdala is archaeologically attested, though as yet only tentatively dated (Rousseau and Arav 1995: 189). That Hippos and Gadara had associated harbours is suggested by Epstein (1993: 635), Rousseau and Arav (1995: 127), Zangenberg and Busch (2003: 119) and Reed (2000: 163).

38. The latter is especially evident in Josephus's account of repeated escape by lake from angry populations (*War* 2.619; *Life* 96, 153, 304) and frequent troop movement by water (*Life* 327, 406). What W. Harris says of the people of the Mediterranean 'very effectively linked by warfare' (2005b: 24) applies well to the people of the lake region

between Hippos and Tiberias as the embodiment of international trade.[39] The Midrashim (especially *Gen. R.* 31.13) consider the passage from Tiberias to Hippos so well travelled as to be marked by metaphoric 'furrows' ploughed in the water. Commercial symbiosis evidently led to rivalry—the hostility of the two centres seems to have become a type for that between Jerusalem and 'the nations' (*Lev. R.* 23.5; *Lam. R.* 1.17; *Cant. R.* 2.5)—but this should not cast their connection into doubt; quite the contrary, it confirms an interaction enduring in time if not always uniformly benign. The material tale of this interaction depends on further excavation at Hippos, in particular, but finds of Kfar Hananiah pottery (manufactured in the west and located on the west coast in particularly high proportions) point already in the same direction (Adan-Bayewitz 1993: 209, 219-20). That the lake served such exchange as a trade route rather than a trade barrier is only further suggested by a deposit of the same Kfar Hananiah ware on the lake floor, without apparent signs of use, bound for market in the east according to its excavators.[40]

There are still too few recovered shipwrecks of this sort (compared, for instance, to the Mediterranean) to elaborate much further the economic relationship sponsored by the surface of the lake. Kfar Hananiah ware has been recovered on the eastern shore further inland (at Tel Nov; Weksler-Bdolah 1998), to the north at Gamla (Adan-Bayewitz 1993) and to the south, significantly, at Gadara (Weber 2007: 460). But I would suggest that the association of Hippos and Tiberias signals the more pervasive and protracted 'background noise'[41] of mundane interaction brought about especially by the consistent requirements and possibilities of local dearth and glut.

The lake will not have been the only source of such interaction—Thomas Weber (2007) finds the 'mutual initiative' of the citizens of Tiberias and Gadara architecturally attested in the so-called 'Tiberiade' gates in each locale and the road that stretched between them—but its surface was apparently more highway than hindrance, between west and east but presumably also between communities up and down both coasts, especially if Josephus's story of his own frequent toing and froing between Tiberias, Taricheae, Capernaum and Bethsaida can be (somewhat) trusted (see note above). The shallow draft of the only ancient craft to have been extricated from the Kinneret (Wachsmann 1990a) suggests that such would likely

39. *Y.Šeb.* 8.38a. For wheat to Sepphoris and, by implication, Tiberias, see *y. B. Qam.* 9.6d (cited in Safrai 1994: 112); for dried grapes, see *y. Dem.* 2.22d; *y. Ned.* 8.41a (cited in Safrai 1994: 134).

40. Fritsch and Ben-Dor 1961; Edwards 1992: 57; Adan-Bayewitz 1993: 214.

41. The term is Horden and Purcell's (for instance, 2000: 150). They use it to privilege, in place of the usual fascination with routes, the complex web of casual, local and small-scale interactions 'more or less constant' in the history of Mediterranean exchange but always more substantial than the usual narrative implies.

have extended even to harbourless communities. The medium of water creates what Horden and Purcell (2000: 133) call an 'inside-out geography' in which the world of the lake brings opposite shores together in functional proximity while the land around becomes increasingly peripheral with its distance from the water. Which is merely to agree with Josephus (*Life* 349), who measures the trip to the eastern shore across the lake and not around it, that Tiberias belongs in the immediate vicinity of Hippos and Gadara, not despite the water but because of it.

My point in this is finally to include in the geographical articulation of the Lake Region the habitual movement of its people and their products around and especially across the lake. Because the place of the Lake Region is not simply a matter of dramatic relief or climatic peculiarity; it is as much or more a situation of human response which seems to me to include for the first century, besides farming and fishing, the regular and recurring circulation of people and product similarly premised on the interface of the lake. This qualifies somewhat the conventional definiteness of the valley—Where are its boundaries if they are not commensurate with lines of elevation (contours), temperature (isotherms) or rainfall (isohyets)?[42] It certainly complicates the cultural complexion of either shore. But I think that the interdependence of east and west across the water also points towards a place of definite historical dimensions articulated best in the variously cooperative and conflictual patterns of local environmental opportunism—fishing and ferrying, at the least—dependent on the productive opportunities of water. This is distinctive to the Lake Region. It does not speak against interaction with environs further inland (on either side of the lake), nor does it demand homogeneity within the region in cultural or economic terms. But I think it does corroborate the geological imprint of the valley. In fact, it well anticipates material resemblances within the Lake Region—of olive press design,[43] for instance, or mosaic decoration (Meyers 1976: 99)—which only come into better focus in subsequent centuries.

Jesus in a Place Called the Lake Region

If there is every reason to think that Jesus was in Capernaum, then there is every reason to take seriously the peculiarity of the Lake Region, whether or not my articulation of that place is found convincing in its detail. It may be, for instance, that the diversity of productive opportunity peculiar to the

---

42. So Braudel 1972 [1949]: 168, on the 'human unit' of the Mediterranean.
43. Thus especially Frankel 1999: 134, 169, on the so-called Tabgha screw press base (T73222; with open mortices and rounded corners) located only in the vicinity of the lake—according to Frankel because of the geological imprint (i.e., basalt rock) of the region.

valley deserves more stress or, perhaps, that the constellation of environmental conditions ought to meet with more optimism. But it should be clear
that Capernaum-by-the-sea (Καφαρναοὺμ τὴν παραθαλασσίαν), as Mt.
4.13 would have it, is not Nazareth (by what Josephus calls the Great Plain
[*War* 3.39]). The definite place of Jesus' 'headquarters' at the bottom of
the Rift Valley in a field of perception shared by Hippos and Gadara is not
the place of his reputed hometown perched between the Jezreel and Beth
Netofa valleys some 25 km in- and up-land. This is not a novel proposition;
to a considerable degree it is simply the elaboration to its logical extent of
Meyers's theory of Galilaean regionalism. But it means, as Leif Vaage suggests already in this volume, that reconstruction of 'Jesus' Galilee', if it is
to achieve its object, ought increasingly to privilege, instead of the Lower
Galilee, the geographical 'fringe' of the particular Galilaean 'border region'
otherwise known as the Lake Region.

For the reconstruction of Jesus, more particularly, taking seriously the
landscape of the Lake Region invites a corresponding shift in textual terrain
from the parables especially, of recent fascination, to the site of Mark 1–8
as the prime location for testing the recollection of Jesus. In the last two
'quests' it is the parable tradition that has become for the historical Jesus the
textual site without equal: 'There is no part of the Gospel record which has
for the reader a clearer ring of authenticity', C.H. Dodd announced (1961:
11). 'The conclusion is inevitable', Joachim Jeremias agreed (1972: 12),
'that in reading the parables we are dealing with a particularly trustwor-
thy tradition, and are brought into immediate relation with Jesus'.[44] But
the absence here of indicators of any particular place beyond very broad
notions of the Mediterranean world (Scott 1989; Oakman 1992; Rohrbaugh
1993) or the Middle East (Bailey 2008) is striking—all the more so next to
Mark's first chapters, wherein the peculiar memory of Jesus on and around
the lake intrudes forcefully and repeatedly. Scholars have often considered
the geographical resonance here part and parcel of Mark's theological landscape (Lohmeyer 1936; Lightfoot 1938; Marxsen 1956). But the specificity of the Lake Region especially in Mark 1–8, by which I mean the concentration here of proper names that seem otherwise unimportant in Mark
(e.g. Bethsaida, 6.45; 8.22; or Gennesaret, 6.53) or simply unknown (e.g.
Dalmanutha, 8.10) seems to me not compassed by this explanation. If the
geographical residue of Mark 1–8 coheres, it consists rather in a memory
of a peculiar Lake Region, on the water, to be sure, but apparently not only
for fishing or ferrying.

The pattern of located memory ensconced within the construction of
Mark 1–8 coheres rather well—Jesus of the Lake Region engages his place

44. So, variously, Funk, Scott and Butts 1988; Scott 1989; Herzog 1994; Hedrick
2004; Bailey 2008; and Snodgrass 2008.

as a local (littoral) thaumaturge. This pattern is all the more striking for its resemblance to the material that the quest has sought from the outset to discipline: more wonder-worker than wordsmith, Jesus on water has seemed dangerously unsettled and somehow unsettling. At any rate, scholarship has chosen to remember Jesus elsewhere—inland—in a discursive space more conducive to neat categorization and abstraction than cultural complexity. 'Place makes a poor abstraction', says Clifford Geertz (1996: 259); it makes a more interesting Jesus, though, and I think it also provides a significant perspective on that commemorative practice which so often includes a front seat for Galilee but as yet avoids a more definite place called the Lake Region.

DIOGENES OF CAPERNAUM: JESUS THE CYNIC IN BORDERLAND GALILEE

Leif E. Vaage

Jesus the Cynic, Now and Then

In the mid-1980s when Burton L. Mack was writing *A Myth of Innocence: Mark and Christian Origins* and I was somewhere in the middle of producing a doctoral dissertation on 'the people whom Q represents', Mack asked me to prepare a brief note for him on the topic of Jesus as a Cynic (Mack 1988: 69 n. 11). Roughly a year before this request in connection with a doctoral seminar I had taken with Mack, I had submitted to him a paper on this topic. I had become interested in the possibility of comparing the historical Jesus, namely Q, with the ancient Cynics, mainly because of the way in which Cynicism seemed to be routinely invoked by commentators on Q—most especially regarding the so-called mission instructions and, specifically, Q 10.4—only then to be immediately discarded without further ado or adequate explanation.[1]

If the comparison was so obviously beside the point, I asked myself, why did scholars keep reiterating it nonetheless as a possible option for interpretation—again, only to reject it out of hand? Gerd Theissen's initial assertion of a significant similarity between some Cynics and the earliest bearers of the Jesus tradition as a basic argument in favor of the historical possibility of Theissen's larger thesis of *Wanderradikalismus* in earliest Christianity, and then Theissen's silent retreat from this comparison, was a sterling case in point, precisely because of the lack of any clarification by Theissen why or how the Cynics subsequently had become a less likely analogy than before (see Theissen 1973; 1977; 1979: 106-41, 201-30; 1989).

Subsequently, in my book *Galilean Upstarts: Jesus' First Followers according to Q,* I used the traditions of ancient Cynicism to define the kind of persons represented by Q—this is to say, the social profile of their collec-

---

1. See, e.g., Hoffmann 1982: 318-20; Theissen 1973: 254-56; Schottroff 1975: 211-13; Schottroff and Stegemann 1978: 65; Kloppenborg 1987: 324.

tive project. I tried to make it clear that the analogy of ancient Cynicism to Q was not a claim of historical identity. Or rather, I claimed that the work of defining historical identity is actually one of 'characterization'. And if Aristotle could be believed, the work of 'characterization' would be second in importance only to that of 'emplotment' for the kind of narrative fabrication constituting, I contended, the 'scientific mythology' of modern biblical scholarship (see Vaage 1994: 1, 3-6).

As part of the theoretical justification for my use of the traditions of ancient Cynicism in *Galilean Upstarts* to re-describe the kind of persons that would be attested by Q, I invoked the theoretical work of Jonathan Z. Smith on the practice of comparison (Vaage 1994: 10; J.Z. Smith 1990: esp. 36-53). William Arnal has suggested that in doing so, I did not use Smith's work appropriately, or sufficiently, or clearly enough, to warrant the license it gives for such a 'disciplined exaggeration'.[2]

It is true that I did not invoke Smith in order to join him and his academic coreligionists in the kind of intellectual inquiry Smith himself does so well, which, to my mind, is essentially a Kantian kind of effort, first, to account for the conditions of the possibility of our claim to scholarly knowledge and, then, to articulate the rules of engagement whereby we might progressively rectify the categories otherwise defining the content of this knowledge (cf. J.Z. Smith 1992: 90-101; 1993 [1978]: 290; 2004). Such an enterprise (as I indicated in the introduction to *Galilean Upstarts*) remains, in my opinion, insufficiently attentive to the narrative nature of what historians know. This is most certainly true for modern historical-critical biblical scholarship.[3]

---

2. See Arnal 2001: 57: 'Proponents of a Cynic-like Jesus movement, Vaage in particular, seem to use Smith rather opportunistically, sliding over into a sloppy equation of the Jesus movement with Cynicism from time to time, and really failing to understand or appreciate the nuances of Smith's view of comparison. Smith makes it very clear that any comparison for non-genetic purposes implies two usually unstated qualifications or terms to the comparative pair: "x is like y" really means "x resembles y more than z with respect to . . ." or "x resembles y more than w resembles z with respect to . . ." . . . Yet the details of the repressed terms of this equation are sketchy at the best of times: Vaage, for instance, can conclude that "it would have been extremely difficult to distinguish the persons whom Q represents from *other* Cynics elsewhere in the ancient world" . . . and elsewhere refer to a "strong degree of similarity", framed absolutely . . . , but without ever telling us what theoretical factors are elucidated by the comparison, or on what specific bases it is offered.'

3. At the same time, Smith's discussion of the role of comparison in scholarly category formation struck me as germane to the work of characterization within the 'scientific mythology'—or evidence-based confabulation, or 'secular' master narrative—that otherwise is the goal of the modern Western discipline of 'history'. Because, however, Arnal disagrees, no doubt profoundly, with this view of the narrative nature of modern biblical scholarship, he finds my partial use of Smith's theory of comparison to be, in

To my own mind, the comparison of Q and ancient Cynicism in *Galilean Upstarts* was obviously a preliminary study (*Voruntersuchung*). Its main purpose was to propose the possibility of a different governing 'trope' (as Hayden White [1973] might put it) for historical reconstruction of the field of Christian origins. Under the auspices of a socio-political imaginary able to include something like ancient Cynicism, the full array of diverse utterances in Q would become, I contended, more cohesively intelligible.[4]

Without a doubt, it would have been helpful to include within the proposal of *Galilean Upstarts* a fuller demonstration of the various ways in which competing frames of reference actually fail to explain sufficiently (if at all) the specific statements in Q. Nonetheless, it remains for me strategically an open question whether it is always necessary, or even advisable, first to lay siege to whatever now may strike you as merely an imposing façade—what J.Z. Smith otherwise calls the inherently 'incredulous' (1982: 60-61). Might it not be better (at least sometimes) simply to step around the ideological roadblock presently obstructing a fuller view in order to engage more directly the hidden or lurking alternative perspective?[5] Of course, this assumes a certain capacity for lateral movement!

In any case, I now wish to probe the alleged impossibility of the Cynic analogy to Q, namely Jesus as indeed a properly 'historical' description.[6] When I do this, I am changing the nature of the argument I have previously pursued regarding ancient Cynicism and the historical Jesus, namely Q. Which is to say, for the sake of my argument here, I shall write within

---

his words, opportunistic and 'really failing to understand or appreciate the nuances of Smith's view of comparison'.

4. Implicit in this proposal was the exegetical experience of other conceivable frames of reference such as 'early Jewish apocalyptic' or 'wisdom in the ancient Near East' failing to explain adequately—with equal comprehensiveness and concreteness— the socially peculiar discourse of the document. A source of confusion for this project has been my initial use—with some modification—of Kloppenborg's thesis of a three-fold literary development for Q. See, e.g., Kloppenborg 1987; 2000: 112-65; Vaage 1992; 1994: 7-10, 107-20.

5. In this regard, what I might have done better in *Galilean Upstarts* is to articulate more clearly the nature of the political question that underlies and informs every account of Christian origins, including the historical Jesus, when speech and social behavior are characterized as 'countercultural', 'subversive', and so on.

6. Kloppenborg (2000: 420-42) has defended the Cynic analogy to Q against its facile detractors. At the same time, it is clear that Kloppenborg would not have done this if the comparison between Q and Cynicism were presented as a historical argument. The village scribes that Kloppenborg otherwise posits as the persons responsible for Q are understood by Kloppenborg to have been as real as the walls and other human artifacts exposed by archaeological excavation—even though no such evidence presently exists for the actual presence of these persons in Galilee at the time that Q was written.

the conventional scholarly conviction that by 'history' we are aiming to describe something closer to 'fact' than to 'fiction'.[7]

In a recent essay entitled 'Beyond Nationalism: Jesus "the Holy Anarchist"?' (Vaage 2007; 2010), I have tried to describe the specifically political concerns that appear to be in play whenever scholars refuse to take seriously the possibility of a Cynic analogy to the historical Jesus, namely Q. In what follows, I shall continue to explore this scholarly habit of knee-jerk refusal by asking why so many accounts of the historical Jesus (and Q) speak of ancient Galilee—specifically during the first century CE—as though there were some kind of impenetrable wall erected between the eastern and western sides of the Rift Valley in which—at Capernaum and environs—the historical Jesus typically is said to have had his—adult? professional? messianic?—home.

To speak 'historically' of Jesus as a Cynic is, basically, to imagine that at some point not recorded in any early extant account of his life, Jesus went for a little walkabout south from Capernaum around the lake (if not across it—maybe in a boat) and up the ridge that runs east to west along the south side of the Yarmouk River valley into the city of Gadara (now Umm Qés), where he then spent enough time to learn, as a number of other persons both before and after him also evidently did, a certain ancient 'Cynicism'.

The increasing insistence by different scholars on a predominantly 'Jewish' Galilee speaks against this possibility of a historically 'Cynic' Jesus— against which the insistence on a 'Jewish' Galilee often is directed, explicitly or implicitly—only if one thinks that, somehow, the eastern edge of the Rift Valley in which the Sea of Galilee resides, was, strictly speaking, out of bounds for all things 'Galilean', including the historical Jesus. This

---

7. This conviction is rooted in the assumption that the subject matter of 'history' is—ontologically—within the realm of so-called reality, to which all proper knowledge would belong, more than it is simply another type of rhetorical invention. For this reason, the discipline of history is not supposed to be confused with the less stringent epistemological demands of whatever else we might be able to imagine. At least, this appears to be the contention of most professional historians. Nonetheless, the various efforts to distinguish the epistemological substance of 'history' from other forms of fictional narrative have, in my opinion, yet to make their case successfully. The deep desire of many scholars to maintain this distinction is evident, but the reasoning that would explain how the assertion is true continues to raise more questions than it answers. Even so, I accept in this essay that to seek the historical Jesus is not merely to write another gospel about him. Under the auspices of the historical Jesus, we aim instead to discern whatever plausibly might be known 'within the bounds of (historical) reason alone' regarding the life of this particular human being. In what follows, therefore, I shall try to suggest a number of reasons—especially geographical—why calling Jesus a 'Cynic' not only is not impossible but is at least as plausible a historical claim as any number of other such descriptions.

strikes me, however, as profoundly improbable, precisely as a historical argument, on the basis of current archaeological information and especially geographical considerations.[8]

Even so, there is a clear tendency in the aforementioned scholarship to keep the historical imagination of life on the ground in Galilee at the time of Jesus focused west of a line running north to south and roughly defined by the Jordan River, the Sea of Galilee, Lake Semachontis, and the Huleh Valley. Regarding the historical Jesus, however, this is an assumption that minimally begs the question and certainly would seem to require an argument, if only because most of the literary sources that alone attest the singular life we otherwise call Jesus of Nazareth apparently had no difficulty imagining the scope of his particular existence to exceed quite matter-of-factly such a boundary.

As Though There Were a Wall Between

One might think that Jonathan Z. Smith's well-known title *Map Is Not Territory* would be a lesson long learned by New Testament scholars and other historians of the ancient Mediterranean world.[9] Smith's point, in any case, is that we should not confuse—by equating—our acts of cognitive organization with the stuff of actual existence, our mental constructions with the messier business of bodily life, the disciplined distinctions of science and knowledge with the less circumspect admixture that is, as it were, social experience by definition. Said otherwise, what we say does not describe everything we are and do, even if it may be the only way to begin a conversation about cultural identity and collective differences.

Recent scholarship on Galilee and the historical Jesus as well as on early Christian literature stemming from this region nonetheless continues to take basically the Roman administrative divisions of the area around the Kinneret as though these were concretely significant boundaries.[10] In historiographical practice, it is as though there were a wall between the eastern and

8. In part, this feature of recent scholarship is due to the extreme paucity of exploitable archaeological data and other information regarding life in the region during the Persian, Hellenistic, Hasmonean and early Roman periods. See, e.g., Weber 2007: 457. Much has to be made of very little; arguments from silence allow the mind to run in multiple directions.

9. See Smith 1993 [1978]. The title of this book was originally a dictum of Alfred Korzybski (see Smith 1993: 309).

10. In this regard, I am reminded of the weather maps that often appear on American television, which show no weather happening above the 49th parallel separating Canada and the United States. In Buffalo, New York, a blizzard is raging. Meanwhile, immediately due north of this city in southern Ontario, it is apparently unknown whether any snow is falling. Of course, the map may be meant only to track American snow.

western sides of the Rift Valley in which the Kinneret lies—even though the different archaeological data and other evidence defining the cultural zones of Galilee do not, in fact, support such a clean line of demarcation.[11]

Take, for example, the two recent books by Mark A. Chancey, *The Myth of a Gentile Galilee* (2002) and *Greco-Roman Culture and the Galilee of Jesus* (2005). In the second book, Chancey claims to work with the definition of Galilee as given by Josephus (*War* 3.35-44):

> the region between Mount Carmel and the territory of Ptolemais on the west, Samaria and the territory of Scythopolis to the south, Gaulanitis and the territory of Hippos and Gadara to the east, and the territory of Tyre, which extended as far inland as Kedesh, to the north. These borders also roughly correspond to the limits of Herod Antipas's territory (Chancey 2005: 19; cf. Aviam 2004).

Josephus himself, however, does not appear to have understood this definition of 'Galilee' to circumscribe or delimit all the places where 'Galileans' might sometimes be present, nor does it exclude people 'officially' living 'outside' Galilee from participation in the affairs of this region. In other words, Josephus did not hold as hermetically sealed an understanding of the social significance of his definition of Galilee as Chancey, with others, appears to pursue.[12] Chancey goes on to explain himself:

> This study relies primarily on Josephus's description for an obvious reason: he provides an informed first-century perspective, and my goal is to illuminate first-century Galilee. Any decision about how to define Galilee's borders has ramifications for how data is organized—what is regarded as within Galilee, and what is portrayed as outside it. Though my choice to rely on Josephus's description affects the presentation of my data, it does not affect the substance of my argument. Regardless of exactly where one draws the lines of Galilee's boundaries, the overall pattern of evidence is the same, with differences (of varying degrees of significance) between the material culture of most of Galilee and that of cities and areas on its perimeter (2005: 19-20).

If a main purpose of Chancey's work, however, is to discuss 'the Galilee of Jesus', as the second half of the title of his second book suggests, then 'the material culture of most of Galilee' would be, presumably, less relevant to this undertaking than precisely 'that of cities and areas on its perimeter' and, specifically, those within or beside the Rift Valley where the Sea of Galilee rests, since everyone seems to agree that here it is—in Capernaum and environs—where the historical Jesus actually lived and left behind whatever legacy there may be of notable sayings uttered and deeds performed. Some scholars (such as E.P. Sanders [1993a; 1993b; 2002]) may

---

11. See further Rene Baergen's essay in this volume.
12. See, e.g., Reed 2000: 26; also Moreland 2007: 157; Freyne 1980a; Cohen 1979.

dispute the significance of this fact; but no one, to my knowledge, denies that it is so. When seeking to characterize the cultural milieu of the historical Jesus, it is therefore specifically the Lake Region of the Lower Galilee or its eastern borderland that most requires attention.

Most of what has been written about Galilee and its predominantly Jewish character is thus essentially beside the point—if and when the point is to rehearse 'the Galilee of [the historical] Jesus'. The local culture of Nazareth, for example, would be important only if we were to think that everything determinative of Jesus' later life basically occurred there—a very modern nineteenth-century idea!—even though it is now virtually a truism of critical scholarship that before Jesus' baptism by John—at best—there is essentially nothing to be known 'historically' about Jesus.[13] Moreover, to imagine Jesus' baptism by John as the defining moment in Jesus' later life is implicitly to acknowledge that Jesus' start in Nazareth did not actually make him what he eventually became, namely not a normal Galilean Jew.[14]

The Lake Region

Geology alone makes it likely that Lake Genneserat defined a common environment within which the different local identities situated around the same body of water took place. The dramatic geological depression within which the Sea of Galilee sits creates a distinct (agri-)cultural zone not unlike those created by the division between the Upper and the Lower Galilee, which is, first of all, a geological fact that subsequent archaeological analysis then elaborates with architectural and other artifactual coordinates. As is well known, later rabbinical literature (*m. Šeb.* 9.2) recognized the region as a discrete area requiring its own legislation precisely because of the lake district's different growing conditions.

What do we find here if and when we make this particular place the focus of our attention as the primary cultural context of the historical Jesus? Beginning with the newly founded city of Tiberias (around 20 CE) on the southwest shore of the lake and then proceeding in a counterclockwise direction, we find, next, the 'university town' of Gadara, already in existence for a number of centuries, atop the bluffs at the southeast end of the lake, as well as the hot springs at the foot of these bluffs, just within the Yarmouk River

---

13. At least, there is no early Christian evidence regarding an earlier phase of the historical Jesus' life that would allow us to say anything at all 'historically' about this period that would not also be true for every other male of the same social group and socioeconomic status (about which, however, we know next to nothing) in the region.

14. Let me be clear: the historical Jesus definitely was a 'Jew' (whatever this concretely meant then and there). But he also definitely was not 'your average' Galilean Jew! Cf. Moreland 2007: esp. 138-39.

valley (see Wagner-Lux and Vriezen 1987; Weber 2002). Moving north-ward along the eastern shore of the lake, we come to the city of Hippos, or Susita, perched atop a butte that presently stands about 500 m above the level of the lake (see Clermont-Ganneau 1875a; 1875b; 1887; Segal 2004). Next, at the northeast corner of the lake within another wadi now known as the Nahal Dalioth, cutting through the so-called Golan Heights, between Hippos and the 'city' of Julias-Bethsaida, stood the town of Gamla, strad-dling a ridge that juts out toward the south off the ravine's north face. To the west of this settlement near the north shore of the lake, as already noted, lay the 'city' of Julias-Bethsaida (elevated in 30 CE by Herod Philip to the status of a Greek *polis*). Finally, continuing west and then south, we pass through or alongside a series of small towns, most notably, Capernaum, Chorazin, and Magdala-Taricheae, before returning once more to Tiberias. [15]

Many of these cities and settlements are visible to one another on a clear day. [16] Moreover, the majority of them maintained harbours on the lake, which now are heavily eroded or otherwise encumbered, including the cit-ies of Hippos and Gadara. [17] In the case of Gadara, its strong identification with Lake Gennesaret is attested also by some of the city's extant coins, which portray a ship. [18] Indeed, mention is occasionally made on these coins of an erstwhile 'sea-battle'. [19]

My point here is merely to underscore the a priori likelihood geopoliti-cally that the Sea of Galilee held together in some sort of symbiotic relation-ship with one another the different urban sites and other human communi-

15. This analysis of the cultural zone defined by the Kinnereth could be extended, in my judgment, also to include the cities of Pella and Scythopolis, both of which sit on the edge of the Jordan valley not far to the south of the lake. Cf. Eusebius's explanation of the term 'Decapolis': 'Δεκάπολις . . . αὕτη ἐστὶν ἡ ἐπὶ τῇ Περαίᾳ κειμένη ἀμφὶ τὴν Ἵππον καὶ Πέλλαν καὶ Γαδάραν' (Klostermann 1904: 80).

16. For such a line of sight between Gamla and Magdala-Taricheae, see Rousseau and Arav 1995: 101. From Gadara (Umm Qés) one can see the top of the ridge overlook-ing the town of Nazareth below it to the south.

17. See Nun 1989a; 1989b; 1999: 31: 'The marine suburb [of Gadara] and the city's harbor were located on the southeastern shore of the lake, at Tel Samra (now Ha-on Holiday Village)'.

18. For the coins of Gadara, see Head 1911: 787; Mionnet 1973: V, 323; VIII, 227; Saulcy 1976: 295.

19. See Meshorer 1966; his opinion however is declared 'speculative' by Schürer 1979: 134 n. 248. Lichtenberger (2000–2002) suggests that the ναυμαχία was held inside the Yarmouk River valley. See, further, Nun 1996. Cf. Clermont-Ganneau 1898b, who argues that the coins depicting a ναυμαχία may recall the X Legion Fretensis' impromptu naval triumph over the residents of Taricheae during the first Jewish war (see Josephus, *War* 3.462-70; also 3.64-69). But Clermont-Ganneau's location of the inscription under discussion (CIL III, 13589) in Gadara was later questioned as 'höchst fraglich' by Jer-emias (1932: 78).

ties sharing its shoreline during the first centuries BCE and CE (cf. Fassbeck *et al.* 2003). The existence of the so-called Tiberiade Gate, found both in Tiberias and in Gadara, certainly suggests that there was a clear connection between at least these two cities at some point in time.[20]

> [While g]ates with a single barrel-vaulted passageway and circular flank-ing towers have been excavated in various cities of northern Palestine, southern Phoenicia, and southwestern Syria, for example, Skythopolis, Caesarea Maritima, Tyre, and Hippos/Susita . . . [t]he closest parallel to the Gadarene gate is an arched monument at the southern fringe of Tibe-rias. . . The Gadarene and the Tiberias gates are related as both mark the starting points of a road linking the cities. The correspondence is also evi-dent in the architecture . . . It is probable that the gates were constructed as counterparts on the mutual initiative of the citizens of the Galilean and the Gadarene urban communities (Weber 2007: 468-69).[21]

Similarly, the western hypogaeum, or underground monumental tomb, that lies close to the Tiberiade gate in Gadara reflects architectural life around the lake. As Thomas Weber reports:

> The oldest part of the complex, dated to the 1st c. C.E., consists of an antechamber accessible by a portal in the façade. On the axis of this ante-chamber is the main hall where eighteen burial shafts in two superimposed rows are preserved in three of its walls; this is covered by a flat dome of basalt ashlars with a central light hole. The burial complex is orthogonally surrounded on three sides by a barrel-vaulted gallery, comparable to the Roman cryptoportico, with large openings to the façade. This architectural element is exceptional; the author is aware of only one parallel, located on the northwestern shore of the lake of Galilee: This is the substructure of a temple-shaped tomb at Capharnaum, published by Virgilio C. Corbo, which preserves a comparable gallery consisting of three orthogonal bar-rel-vaulted branches framing the central burial chamber (2007: 469-70).[22]

Thus, the use of Lake Gennesaret and the rivers flowing into and out of it as 'natural' administrative boundaries in antiquity, should not be taken to indicate a more profound or thoroughgoing separation between people on the ground. In this regard, Origen's description of Gadara in his *Commen-*

20. See Weber 1991: 123-26; also 2002: 330 (for BD 5); 2007: 465-69. Weber suggests a date after 66 or 100 CE for both gates versus the suggestion of the excavators of the gate in Tiberias together with other scholars that the gate in Tiberias was built between 18 and 26 CE (see, e.g., Kader 1996: 163-64, esp. n. 1077; Meynersen 2001).

21. Much more recently, Tiberias 'was the market town for the inhabitants of mod-ern Umm Qais until 1947' (Weber 2007: 454).

22. See also Corbo 1977. Corbo dates the tomb in Capernaum to the second century CE.

tary on John (6.41) is suggestive: Γάδαρα γὰρ πόλις μέν ἐστι τῆς Ἰουδαίας, περὶ ἣ τὰ διαβόητα θερμὰ τύγχάνει ...'.[23]

To be sure, there is some evidence that, as Weber writes, 'Lake Tiberias and the river Jordan marked a cultural border.' According to Weber,

> This can be best demonstrated by a large group of Syrian bronze appliqués dating to the Roman imperial period. These were attached to the long sides of wooden coffins for burial ceremonies. Such bronzes representing heads of lions . . . holding movable rings in their open mouths, have been found widely scattered in tombs in northern and western Syria, including the Phoenician coast. In southern Syria specimens hammered out of thin metal sheet prevail . . . while on the Djolan and in the Decapolitanian area more stylized circular sheets with a flat central knob seem to have been standard . . . A large number of these attachments have been found at Gadara . . . during the last decades. To the author's knowledge only two specimens of this funeral equipment, allegedly from Nablus and Jaffa . . . , have so far been found west of the river Jordan. This can only be explained by regionally different burial customs (2007: 454).

At the same time, Weber shortly observes:

> There is some evidence in the material culture of Gadara that the local Jewish diaspora maintained economical relations with the neighboring Galilee during the 1st and subsequent c. C.E. This is indicated by finds of Kfar Hananiah pottery at the site. They lead to the hypothesis that indigenous Galilean wares were continuously traded to the western Decapolitanian territories, and probably beyond. Also, the closely related Galilaean bowls have been reported among pottery finds from Gadara and Emmatha/Hammath Gader. That despite those confrontations [described by Josephus below] a peaceful mercantile exchange existed between the areas east and west of river Jordan—the geographical situation as shown strongly supports such an assumption—leads to similar considerations for other archaeological minor finds such as glassware, terracottas, and coinage (2007: 460).[24]

Josephus (*War* 2.457-60; *Life* 42) reports that at the beginning of the first Jewish revolt against Rome, the territories of both Gadara and

---

23. See Brooke 1896: 159. Also suggestive is Eusebius's description of the city: 'Γάδαρα. πόλις πέραν τοῦ Ἰορδάνου, ἀντικρὺ Σκυθοπόλεως καὶ Τιβεριάδος πρός ἀνατολαῖς ἐν τῷ ὄρει, οὗ πρὸς ταῖς ὑπωρείαις τὰ τῶν θερμῶν ὑδάτων λουτρὰ παράκειται' (Klostermann 1904: 74). This text is missing in the extant Syrian translation (see Timm 2005: 34-35).

24. In a corresponding note, Weber indicates, 'According to oral information from Karel H.J. Vriesen (communicated to the author on behalf of Jürgen Zangenberg), large quantities of sherds at Gadara have been identified as Kfar-Hananiah-type' (Weber 2007: 460 n. 41). See further Adan-Bayewitz 1993. For the closely related Galilean bowls, see Loffreda 1978 (with further bibliography); also Kuhnen 1989: 95 n. 110.

Hippos were devastated by Jewish rebels under Justus of Tiberias;[25] in response, the Gadarenes and Hippo-cenes (?) are said to have slaughtered and imprisoned *the Jews living in their towns* (*War* 2.477-80; emphasis added). This may have been due to the fact that among the armed rebels previously captured at Taricheae there were Jewish citizens of Gadara (see Josephus, *War* 3.345-49; Weber 2007: 460)—a citizenry conceivably resulting from increased Jewish settlement in this city and environs following the conquest of Gadara by the Hasmoneans around 82 BCE (see Weber 2007: 457; also 1996).

The same situation obtained in subsequent centuries. Once again, I quote Weber's summary of the evidence:

> The Talmudic narrative about the emperor Hadrian, who climbed from the hot springs [at Emmatha/Hammath Gader] up to Gadara and met a Jewish girl at the foothills of the plateau, points to the presence of diaspora [Jewish] communities in the town and on the chora. Rabbinic advice to Shabbat regulations refer [*sic*] to the forbidden ascent from the springs up to the plateau, and thus it witnesses indirectly to the frequent visits of the Jewish inhabitants of countryside villages (such as Migdal) to the town . . . A basalt relief block, acquired by Félix de Saulcy in Tiberias as coming from Gadara, displays a menorah in a wreath accompagned [*sic*] by a palm leaf (lulab) and the horn (shofar). If we take the provenance as given, this monumental block might have adorned one of the city's late antique synagogues. While the search for such a building of the Gadarene Jewish community among the ruins at Umm Qais would be in vain today, a synagogue was uncovered in Emmatha/Hammath Gader by Eliezer L. Sukenik. Of special interest is the votive inscription in front of the Torah apse because it mentions the hometowns of the persons who financed the mosaic floor, all of them settlements in Galilee: Sepphoris, Kfar 'Aqabyah, Capernaum, Emmaus, and Arbela (2007: 475-76).[26]

Thus it is entirely probable, in my opinion, that the towns of Capernaum and Chorazin also in the first half of the first century CE had commerce and conflict with the cities of Tiberias and Gadara to the south and the southeast (as well as with Hippos, Gamla, and Julias-Bethsaida to the east) as much as—if not more than—these towns did, say, with Nazareth and Cana to the southwest. Again, let me be clear: I am not suggesting that there was no contact between Capernaum and Nazareth or Cana; only that this contact, which has seemed to be so self-evident and straightforward to most scholars, is, in fact, geographically less likely than the same sort of contact with other such sites around the lake.

---

25. See Weber 2007: 457, with reference to 'recent surveys conducted by Nadine Riedl' of the villages in question.

26. Regarding the votive inscription and its reference to Capernaum, see Sukenik 1935: 47-53; Sapir and Ne'eman 1967: 12; Avi-Yonah 1976: esp. 472; Chiat 1982: 31.

Gadara, 'Attica of Syria'

For the question of ancient Cynicism and the historical Jesus (namely Q), the significance of the contiguity of Gadara and its cultural history to Capernaum and environs is obviously the crucial question.[27] The attentive reader will already have noticed that my discussion of the Lake Region anticipates this specificity. David Aune has questioned the import of previous scholarly reference to the city of Gadara and its association with a number of ancient Cynics as part of the argument for the historical Jesus (and Q) being Cynic-like. Aune writes:

> There is . . . no literary or archaeological evidence for a Cynic presence in first-century Galilee. Two famous Cynics, Mennipus and Oenomaus, together with a Hellenistic poet with Cynic sympathies, Meleager, were natives of Gadara . . . Menippus was a Phoenician who was sold as a slave to Baton in Pontus and later settled in Thebes. Some scholars have detected Semitic influence in the fragments of his writings that have survived. Meleager was born in Gadara but grew up in Tyre and retired to Cos where he probably died. However, neither figure [namely, Mennipus or Meleager] seems to have practiced the Cynic mode of life in Gadara. There is, finally, some late evidence for the awareness of Cynics on the part of rabbinic sages (1997: 188).

Aune is correct in challenging the facile use that some scholars have made of the figures of Mennipus and Meleager as though their mere mention constituted immediate proof of ancient Cynicism in Gadara and the Galilee. At the same time, Meleager is hardly to be so swiftly dissociated from his origins in Gadara as Aune implies, if only because Meleager himself repeatedly recalled and underscored them.[28]

Moreover, Aune understates the 'real presence' in Gadara of at least one Cynic, namely Oenomaus at the beginning of the second century CE.[29] Roughly a century after the historical Jesus, this 'Jewish intellectual', as he is sometimes also described,[30] wrote a widely disseminated critique of ora-

27. For Gadara and its history, see Weber 2002; also Dorandi 1987: 254-56; J.T. Fitzgerald 2004.

28. See, e.g., *Anth. Palat.* 7.417, 419; further, Luz 1988; also Weber 1996: 10: 'His [Meleagros'] renown[ed] compatriots Mennipos, Philodemos, Theodoros, Oinomaos and Apsines—as well as Meleagros himself—never refrained from keeping contact with their place of origin, despite the fact that they spent their whole lives [*sic*] abroad.'

29. For a discussion of the dating of Oenomaus, see Hammerstaedt 1988: 11-19; also 1990: 2835-36. Oenomaus is not the subject of Aune's reference to 'late evidence for the awareness of Cynics on the part of rabbinic sages' (1997: 188). For this late evidence, see *y. Git.* 7.1.48c; Lieberman 1963: 130, including n. 34; Stemberger 1979: 189.

30. See Weber 2007: 475; also Bastomsky 1974; Luz 1986–1987; Hammerstaedt 1988: 15 n. 7; 17 n. 4; 1990: 2836-39.

cles.[31] The same Oenomaus is remembered in the Talmud as having been a friend of Rabbi Meir. Indeed, in *Ruth R.* 2.13 Rabbi Meir is said to have visited Oenomaus (Abnimos) in Gadara, first, at the death of the philosopher's mother and, then, at the death of his father.[32]

Gadara was well known throughout the ancient Mediterranean world. Unknown, nonetheless, are the founding date of the city as well as the identity of its founder or founders (cf. Khouri 1997a; 1997b). The ancient city was first associated with the modern village of Umm Qés by Ulrich Jasper Seetzen in 1806 (see Seetzen 1854: 369; 1859: 188-90).[33] The acropolis or city centre sits on a flat plateau and is aligned in an east–west direction, between 7.5 and 10 km distant from the Sea of Galilee, at an altitude of roughly 350 m above sea level or approximately 550 m above the surface of the lake. The first surface survey of Umm Qés was conducted by Gottlieb Schumacher in 1886. A second survey in 1974 recorded the architectural remains of the ancient city over an area approximately 1,600 m long with a maximum width of 450 m. The second survey supersedes Schumacher's 1886 plan of the upper city. At the northern end of Gadara, steep slopes descend to the Yarmouk River valley below, where roughly 3

31. Apart from the Roman emperor Julian, who still felt compelled to respond to Oenomaus's critique roughly two centuries after its initial publication, the same writing (frag. 1.22-37 and 2.9-24 in Hammerstaedt 1988) has been shown also to inform a section of Origen's *Contra Celsum* (3.25; see Hammerstaedt 1988: 26-27; 1990: 2842, who refers to a 1910 dissertation by Fr. Jaeger, which I have not been able to see). Similarly, Clement of Alexandria (*Protr.* 11.2-3; 41.1f.; 103.2; 132.1; also 41.4) seems to reveal knowledge of Oenomaus's writing (frag. 7.18-23; 13.3-12; 6.26-29; also 5.21-23 in Hammerstaedt 1988; see Hammerstaedt 1990: 2840-41; also 1988: 22-24). Of course, it is only because Eusebius in his *Praeparatio evangelica* quoted the writing by Oenomaus as extensively as he did that we now possess the extant remains of this Cynic's work. The transfer of Origen's library in 231 CE from Alexandria to Caesarea Maritima is thought by Hammerstaedt (1990: 2842) to be the link joining together these three—Origen, Eusebius and Julian—otherwise quite different readers of the polemical essay. Hammerstaedt also writes, 'Möglicherweise ist auch Julian in den fünf Jahren nach 345, die er in seiner Jugend auf dem Fundus Macelli in der Nähe von Caesarea verbrachte, mit den Schriften des Oenomaus bekanntgeworden' (1990: 2842).

32. According to Hammerstaedt 1990: 2838, 'Sollte Abnimos mit Oenomaus identisch sein, dann wäre sein Umgang mit den Juden nicht erstaunlich, denn jene lehnten den Götzenkult, die Verehrung von Götterbildern und heidnische Orakel ab, während Oenomaus gegen den Orakelglauben und in fr. 13 gegen die Verehrung eines unförmigen Dionysusabbildes schrieb.'

33. See further Schumacher 1890: 46-80; Anonymous 1901; Warren 1901. Cf. Pliny, *Nat. hist.* 5.18.

km away the baths of the city (at Hammath Gader) could be found in later antiquity and *mutatis mutandis* still exist today.[34]

According to the ceramic finds of the surface survey conducted in 1974, there was a pre-Hellenistic occupation of the site (Wagner-Lux *et al.* 1978; 1979). When Antiochus the Great conquered the city in 218 BCE, Gadara was already a fortified *polis*.[35] Around 100 BCE, the Jewish king Alexander Jannaeus conquered Gadara after a ten-month siege. Under Jannaeus and his successors, the city officially became part of Jewish territory (Josephus, *Ant.* 13.395-97),[36] only to be 'freed' again in 63 BCE from Jewish hegemony by Pompey. In 63 BCE, Gadara became part of the so-called Decapolis and began to mint its own coins. In 30 BCE, however, Octavian gave the city 'back' to Herod the Great, which meant that once more Gadara became part of 'Jewish' territory (Josephus, *Ant.* 15.213-17; *War* 1.393-97). The Gadarenes complained about life under Herod before Agrippa at Mitylene in 22 BCE, and before Augustus himself in Syria in 20 BCE. On both occasions, however, their complaints were dismissed. Only after the death of Herod in 4 BCE did Gadara finally regain its earlier status as an 'independent' city under Rome, which it appears to have enjoyed throughout the succeeding centuries.

According to Eunapius, the late-fourth-century (346–414 CE) biographer of philosophers, in his account of Iamblichus, the leading Syrian Neoplatonist of his day, Gadara was 'a place that has warm baths in Syria, inferior only to those at Baiae in Italy, with which no other baths can be compared'—which is to say: the city had cause to be internationally 'on the map' (*Vit. Soph.* 459).[37] On the epitaph of one Gadarene named Apion, found in Saffure, southeast of Hippos, the city of Gadara is lauded as being χρηστομουσία.[38] Likewise, Meleager of Gadara recalled the city of his birth as the 'Attica of Syria'.

34. See Schürer 1979: 132-33: 'The main evidence [for the site of ancient Gadara] is provided by the warm springs, for which Gadara was famous and which are still found in those parts.' Cf. the statement by Eusebius: Αἰμάθ . . . καὶ ἄλλη δὲ κώμη πλησίον Γαδάρων ἐστὶν Ἐμμαθᾶ, ἔνθα τὰ τῶν θερμῶν ὑδάτων θερμὰ λουτρὰ (Klostermann 1904: 22).

35. See Polybius 5.71.3. For the following brief history of Gadara, see Hadas 1931: 26.

36. The Jews apparently devastated the city, since it required rebuilding when Pompey took it over. See Schürer 1979: 134.

37. Cf. Horace, *Ep.* 1.1.85: 'nullus in orbe locus Baiis praelucet amoenis'.

38. See Clermont-Ganneau 1897: 141-43 (the word 'semble être une veritable cheville'). Cf. Clermont-Ganneau 1898c: 399: 'Je me demande maintenant s'il ne faudrait pas comprendre: "aux belles mosaïques" = χρηστομουσεῖα', which then is followed by a learned but fanciful explanation of the term. See further Hengel 1989: 20; 76 n. 108;

In addition to the three Cynics already mentioned, namely Mennipus, Meleager and Oenomaus, Gadara also produced a number of other well-known philosophers and literati. These included the Epicurean philosopher Philodemus (first century BCE), a contemporary of Cicero, whose library was found at Herculaneum; the orator or rhetorician Theodorus, who lived at the end of the first century BCE and instructed the future emperor Tiberius (Suetonius, *Tib.* 57); and the rhetorician Apsines, in the third century CE.[39]

Few other provincial cities of the ancient Mediterranean world could claim to have produced such a line of intellectuals and writers as Gadara.[40] It seems improbable, therefore, that, as it were, in the city's own backyard, below its northern bluffs across the Sea of Galilee within eyeshot and walking distance, the people who lived there at the time of Jesus nonetheless would have remained culturally ignorant of such a flourishing tradition—including ancient Cynicism![41]

And, Then, He Moves!

There is something very strange about the way in which scholars have had no difficulty in imagining that the historical Jesus must have traveled at least once from Galilee to Jerusalem, at the same time that they find it apparently almost impossible to conceive that Jesus also might have walked around the Sea of Galilee and up the hill into the city of Gadara (not to mention Gamla, Hippos, Pella, and—hardly any climb at all—down the Rift Valley to Scythopolis). Equally strange is the correlative self-evidence of Jesus' traveling back and forth between Nazareth and Capernaum, since such a journey is roughly the same distance and requires more or less the same upward mobility, as a walk from Capernaum to Gadara. (In fact, the trip to Nazareth would require more of both.) Again, the scholarly imagination

Schürer 1979: 135, including n. 255. The epitaphs of other Gadarenes have been found elsewhere, including Athens. See Weber 1996; see further Maas 1942.

39. See Millar 1969: 16; also Geiger 1985; further Gatier 1993.

40. Cf. Hengel 1989: 20: 'Even if these scholars did not usually remain in the country but made their fortunes in the cultural centres of the West, we must assume that there was a firm and lasting scholarly tradition in the places [whence they came] . . . All these towns provided a solid education and also enjoyed an influence to match.' See further Josephus, *Ant.* 17.317-20; *War* 2.93-100.

41. Cf. Schürer 1979: 133: 'According to the Itinerarium Antonini (197-198), Gadara lay sixteen Roman miles from both Capitolias and Scythopolis; Roman milestones remain from both roads, as well as from [the road] leading from Gadara to Tiberias.' See further Mittmann 1970: 133-50.

has been remarkably obtuse to these basic geographical facts regarding the historical Jesus.[42]

By contrast, the canonical Gospels are strikingly able to imagine Jesus moving beyond the bounds of Josephus's definition of Galilee much more. At least in the first half of the Gospel of Mark, this is most certainly true. Of course, for some scholars this only proves that the Gospel of Mark was originally written in Rome, because the evangelist obviously did not know very much about the geography of the area in which his story of 'Jesus Christ son of God' ostensibly took place.

What happens, however, if the traditional Christian ascription of the Gospel of Mark to a colleague of the apostle Peter in Rome now fails to persuade? What happens if it makes more sense—as increasingly it has to not a few scholars—to locate the writing of the Gospel of Mark somewhere in Syria-Palestine? (see, e.g., Marxsen 1956; Marcus 1992). Then the social memory of Jesus' various movements (and his different home places) inscribed in the first half of the Gospel of Mark cannot simply be discounted as a function of ignorance or theological schemata. It may be that modern biblical scholarship on the historical Jesus still continues to follow the Gospel of Matthew when it thinks that, like his disciples, the historical Jesus went only 'to the lost sheep of the house of Israel' and not also 'into the way of the Gentiles' (see Mt. 10.5-6, 23). Logically, then, the same line of interpretation should also assert that he went to no 'city of the Samaritans'. In any case, to think that this schema has anything at all to do with the historical Jesus fails to take seriously the place of the indicated text in the redactional argument of the Gospel of Matthew as a whole, which aims to depict Jesus both as a thoroughgoing practitioner of traditional Judaism (see, e.g., Mt. 5.17-20; 23.2-3) and as a teacher of all other nations (see, e.g., Mt. 28.18-20).

None of this, of course, proves that the historical Jesus actually went to Gadara.[43] What the preceding discussion seeks to demonstrate, however, is how little the (shifting) early Roman administrative boundaries tell us about daily life around the Sea of Galilee at the time of the historical Jesus.

---

42. Is this because the history that is recounted continues to be *mutatis mutandis* a canonical tale? Or perhaps in play is just the usual historiographical habit of anachronism? In the latter case, what is being read back into the life of the historical Jesus would be the decidedly modern, closely monitored, tightly controlled boundary in place between the current State of Israel to the west of the Rift Valley and Syria and Jordan to the east.

43. Nonetheless, the text-critical problem in Mk 5.1; Mt. 8.28; Lk. 8.26 remains beguiling.

He Comes to Us as One Unknown

Regarding the historical Jesus as yet another Cynic—for example, Diogenes of Capernaum—we are clearly in the realm of the historical imagination.[44] This is not a conversation about direct or explicit evidence, if only because there is none for the historical Jesus (cf. Crossan 1991: 426). Rather, it is a conversation about what scholars are willing and able to imagine for such a person within the realm—or is it the regime?—of history; everything else is a matter of more or less probable inference.

A Cynic identity for the historical Jesus plainly exceeds the confines of what otherwise has been deemed to be both possible and appropriate for a Galilean Jew, even though the conventional location of the historical Jesus within the Rift Valley—at Capernaum and environs—puts him within eyesight and walking distance of at least one place in antiquity where more than one Cynic is known to have had his start. Historically—geographically— there is no obvious reason, therefore, why we would not consider the likelihood of some connection between that place and Jesus, too.[45]

Indeed, such an identity may turn out to be the concrete meaning of the purple prose with which Albert Schweitzer famously concluded his critical survey of the different nineteenth-century reconstructions of the historical Jesus. Ward Blanton (2007: 129-65) has proposed that this passage by Schweitzer functions as a kind of post-metaphysical *deus ex machina* for European liberal Christology. I agree. Schweitzer himself says:

> The names which were given to Jesus as a result of the late-Jewish circumstances in which he lived, such as Messiah, Son of man and Son of God, have become historical parables for us . . . We have no terms today which can express what he means for us (2000: 487).

> As a Cynic, however, in the order of Melchizedek, Menippus, Meleager and Oenomaus—one of these, I recognize, is not quite like the others—it is still strangely possible and, perhaps, even true to say, "He comes to us as one unknown, without a name, as of old, by the lakeside, he came to those men who did not know who he was (2000: 487).

44. This may also be true for the historical Diogenes of Sinope.

45. At the same time, it is important to recall, yet again, that the question of the historical Jesus as a Cynic arose, first, because of exegetical efforts to characterize more precisely certain aspects of the early Christian traditions about Jesus, specifically, the so-called hard sayings, many of which are found in Q and which otherwise have been difficult for scholars to explain adequately on the basis of the dominant theological and other categories of description. In other words, it is the specific nature of the textual terrain, in which the historical Jesus would be attested, which authorizes the geographical inquiry undertaken in this essay.

At the same time, an essay like the present one inevitably becomes, in the end, an inquiry into the specific kind of ideological work its subject matter actually has been doing, if and when the essay has succeeded in showing that what we claim to be doing—describing the historical Jesus—patently is not what we have been doing: namely describing him historically. At least the historical geography implied by recent descriptions of Jesus the 'Galilean' and 'the Galilee of Jesus' makes no sense, in my judgment, as a representation of the material environment in which someone living at the north end of the Rift Valley around the Sea of Galilee might have developed an alternate cultural identity for himself—as, it seems, the historical Jesus did once upon a time.

ENOCH POWELL AND THE GOSPEL TRADITION:
A SEARCH FOR A HOMELAND

James G. Crossley

> When we read the New Testament we all do our own expurgation
> . . . certainly every age has proceeded in this way with the Gospel.
> —Powell 1977: 59

Enoch Powell: Politician, Cultural Icon,
Classicist and New Testament Scholar

Enoch Powell (1912–1998) was one of the most notorious, controversial and learned politicians in twentieth-century British politics. Among other things, he was a Conservative Member of Parliament between 1950 and 1974, Minister of Health between 1960 and 1963, and an Ulster Unionist Member of Parliament between 1974 and 1987.

Powell is probably now best known for his controversial anti-immigration 'Rivers of Blood' speech, delivered to the Conservative Political Centre in Birmingham on 20 April 1968. Powell (1992d: 161-69), alluding to the *Aeneid*, famously said, 'As I look ahead, I am filled with foreboding. Like the Roman, I seem to see "the River Tiber foaming with much blood."' The Rivers of Blood speech was the moment when Powell would cease to be a direct influence on front bench party politics while at the same time becoming one of the most popular British politicians of the past one hundred years. To this day he remains a potent symbol—whether based on a misunderstanding or not—for English nationalists and far right groups in the United Kingdom.

Powell was also an academic. His training was in classics, a discipline in which he excelled. In 1937 he became Professor of Classics at Sydney University aged just 25, narrowly failing to beat his hero Nietzsche, who had made professor at age 24. His major published works in classics included *A Lexicon to Herodotus* (1938), *The History of Herodotus* (1939), and *Herodotus: A Translation* (1949). Powell also published studies on the Bible and

Christianity, with a combination of academic, confessional and popularist interests, most notably, *No Easy Answers* (1973) and the more developed *Wrestling with the Angel* (1977).

However, Powell's academic study of the Bible came to full fruition towards the end of his life when he published detailed studies of the Gospel tradition, something which had been an area of academic interest all his life. Powell published an article entitled 'Genesis of the Gospel' in 1991, and in 1994 *The Evolution of the Gospel* (Yale University Press), both on the origins of the Gospel tradition with particular focus on the Gospel of Matthew. *Evolution of the Gospel* further contained Powell's translation of Matthew and his own accompanying commentary. As his classical background would already suggest, Powell was no slouch when it came to New Testament studies—as a schoolboy he had already memorized the entirety of Galatians in Greek (Heffer 1998: 12)—and he certainly had one foot in the door of academic biblical scholarship. The acknowledgments in *Evolution of the Gospel* show that Powell had consulted with the highly distinguished scholars of early Christian history Henry Chadwick and William Horbury. Powell also consulted—as he did for his other work on the Gospel tradition—with Edward Ullendorff, a Semitic and Ethiopic expert and Fellow of the British Academy. In 1991, Powell gave the eighth annual *JSOT* lecture at the University of Sheffield on the 'Genesis of the Gospel', which was the basis of his 1991 article.

Enoch Powell and the Gospel Tradition

Powell's views on Matthew and the Gospel tradition were peculiar, perhaps none more peculiar than his view that Jesus was not crucified but was stoned to death by Jewish authorities. Other views were not so dramatic but were nonetheless certainly out of step with New Testament studies. For Powell, Matthew (in more or less the form we have it) was used by Luke and Mark, with Mark also using Luke. Neither Mark nor Luke had other sources, and so material particular to Mark and Luke, and not found in Matthew, was composed 'freely'. This, Powell argued (1994: xii-xvii; see also 1977: 108-21), has far-reaching consequences because Matthew, or the Matthaean tradition, is primary and is a Gospel that 'insists' on being studied alone. Furthermore, when this Matthaean tradition is studied in depth, Powell believed that it was possible to find an underlying text, a text 'severely re-edited, with theological and polemical intent', with the resulting edition then recombined with the underlying text to produce the Gospel of Matthew (1994: xi-xxii; 1991). The final form of Matthew still has certain distinctive features (e.g. contradictions, duplications, abrupt breaks) that betray a lack of smooth editing of the sort found, so Powell believed, in

Mark and Luke. These Matthaean 'blemishes' provide the clues needed to discern the compositional history of a Gospel 'produced in haste and under pressure' (Powell 1994: xviii).

One of the key ways in which Powell believed he could determine the earliest history behind Matthew's Gospel and the 'underlying book' was through duplications, which also provide insight into the earliest theological developments of the church. Powell devotes most space to the duplication of the feeding miracles, and he even suggests that there are 'vestiges at least of a duplicate execution' (1991: 9). The key to the differences can be found in the 'most portentous' of the duplications, namely the trial before the high priest and the trial before the Romans, the former being known to, and indeed ruined by, the latter. The focal point of the disputes surrounding such duplications was the identity of Jesus. For Powell, the influential underlying narrative concerned the incarnation: 'he was divine, a victim and victor not Jewish, but universal'. This in turn provoked the creation of a rival, alternative (Jewish) narrative (Powell 1991: 9).

The Gentile mission was part of the earliest reconstructed text. The Galilee of the Gentiles—'the starting point'—sat at the heart of the narrative and 'was an allegory of the great sea which united the Roman world' (Powell 1994: xxiii). Believers inherit the kingdom of everlasting life by becoming sons of God through faith in Jesus' identity, and without fulfilment of the law, because mercy and forgiveness came through Jesus' death. The lowest or earliest stratum was more or less a historical narrative preoccupied with establishing Jesus' identity as the 'son of God'. It is also a document revealing Powell's most idiosyncratic argument that Jesus was stoned to death and convicted by the 'Jewish establishment' for 'the blasphemy of allowing himself to be called "the son of God"' (Powell 1994: 207-208). Incidentally, this was a view that Powell believed reflected historical reality.

There were some hostile critical reactions to Powell's book in the British press. While critics acknowledged Powell's learning, there was also a dose of ridicule. N.T. Wright's evaluation was reported as follows:

> This is clearly a work of great erudition, which seems to have lost touch with the distinction between that which is possible and that which is plausible . . . There is something to be said for starting again from scratch, but the catty answer is that he has chosen to ignore everyone else, so he can't grumble if they return the compliment (A. Brown 1994).[1]

---

1. Online at http://www.independent.co.uk/news/uk/gospel-according-to-powell-christ-was-stoned-to-death-andrew-brown-reports-on-a-former-politician-and-greek-scholars-latest-book-which-attempts-to-reinterpret-the-foundations-of-christianity-1376685.html

More serious criticisms involved potential antisemitism,[2] especially Powell's argument that Jesus was stoned to death.[3] Hyam Maccoby was reported as saying,

> It could undoubtedly have anti-Semitic repercussions. The gospels do that already: they say that Pilate was reluctant to carry out the execution. If it is now said that the Romans did not do the executions, the Jews did, this intensifies the blame against the Jews even more (A. Brown 1994).

Maccoby is not reported as levelling claims of antisemitism at Powell personally, and it is, as we will see, worth further emphasizing that Powell's work is, at least partly, at the mercy of broader social and intellectual trends. While Powell may have had disturbing views on immigration and, contrary to many revisionists, some of his views expressed in the Rivers of Blood speech were little more than old fashioned racist language and scaremongering,[4] he was no antisemite. Indeed, Powell had once remarked that the Second World War was not against the Nazi Party but against a development among the German people because the Nazi Party shared what Powell believed were some of the strongest negative traits of the German people, such as hero worship, love of power and force for their own sake and, most significantly for present purposes, antisemitism (Heffer 1998: 60). This, Powell argued, was most unlike the English mind-set. People may want to debate whether that in itself is a fair assessment, and whether the use of English and German 'mind-sets' is helpful, but the point

2. On the spelling 'antisemitism', I follow Richard Evans (2000: 334 n. 7): 'The spelling *antisemitism* is used throughout this book in preference to the conventional *anti-Semitism*. The latter is itself an antisemitic formulation; there was, and is, no such thing as "Semitism," except in the minds of antisemites.'

3. Heffer (1998: 943) bizarrely adds, 'though the oldest teachings on this question also point to stoning', without telling us what these mysterious 'oldest teachings' might be!

4. For example, Powell recalls, "I fell into conversation with a constituent, a middle-aged, quite ordinary working man . . . he suddenly said: "If I had the money to go, I wouldn't stay in this country . . . I shan't be satisfied till I have seen them all [his children] settled overseas. In this country in fifteen or twenty years' time the black man will have the whip hand over the white man." . . . Here is a decent, ordinary fellow Englishman . . . the existing population . . . found themselves strangers in their own country. They found their wives unable to obtain hospital beds in childbirth . . . they found that employers hesitated to apply to the immigrant worker the standards of discipline and competence required of the native-born worker . . . She [an anonymous writer of a letter to Powell which he cited as an example of the "persecuted minority"] is becoming afraid to go out. Windows are broken. She finds excreta pushed through her letterbox. When she goes to the shops, she is followed by children, charming, wide-grinning piccaninnies. They cannot speak English, but one word they know. "Racialist", they chant.'

for now is that antisemitism was something that Powell saw as completely alien to himself and the English.

I say this not because I particularly want to excuse Powell's work from the charges of potential antisemitism or the like but because I think it is more fruitful to see the downgrading of Judaism as part of broader social and intellectual trend in ways that equally affect some of his critics. In other words, the importance of cultural context in analysis of scholarship is heightened because the results of scholarship can be seen to contradict personal beliefs. It certainly *is* clear that Judaism comes out a very poor second in Powell's work on the Gospel tradition and elsewhere.[5] This is no doubt in part due to the general issue of Christian supersessionism, deep-rooted European discussions of the 'Jewish question' and the 'racializing' roots of modern biblical scholarship.[6]

I would add to this my recent argument about the prominence of issues relating to 'Jewishness' in historical Jesus and New Testament studies since the early 1970s as part of a broader religious, intellectual and political turn to Israel since the 1967 Six Day War (Crossley 2008: 145-94). This broad cultural turn is rhetorically, and indeed materially, pro-Israel and pro-Jewish Israeli; but, ultimately, Israel, Jewish Israelis and Jews in general are not really loved and the positivity remains a matter of political expediency, as in the case of US and British administrations since the 1970s, and a matter of religious expediency, as in the case of movements such as Christian Zionism: Jews and Israel are deemed wonderful now but they will burn with the rest of hardened humanity if they do not convert before the return of Jesus. N.T. Wright (1996) himself is a very good example of this cultural tension. Repeatedly he tells us what Jewish identity was like at the time of Jesus, repeatedly he tells us how positive this identity was, repeatedly he tells us how 'very Jewish' Jesus was . . . and repeatedly he tells how Jesus subverts everything Wright constructs as central to Jewish identity! Wright is an excellent representative of a broad trend in contemporary historical Jesus scholarship: for all the emphasis on Jesus the Jew, Jesus regularly comes out over against Judaism in one way or another (Crossley 2008: 179-80).

---

5. Compare Powell's comments on Jewish and Christian eschatology: 'This, like so much else that is Christian, represents a reinterpretation of the Jewish revelation so profound as to be a contradiction of it. The Jew looked forward—still does look forward—with the practical, earthbound, matter-of-factness characteristic of the Jew, to the actual establishment of his own theocracy in the world . . . The Christian is at once more humble and more realistic, and his hope is of a different sort' (1977: 61).

6. See, e.g., Keeley 2002; Arnal 2005; Penner 2008: 429-55; Vander Stichele and Penner 2009: 145-52.

Enoch Powell and Homelands

While acknowledging these broader cultural and scholarly trends concerning a continual downgrading of Judaism in different guises, I think there are further reasons underlying Powell's peculiar reconstruction of the Gospel tradition. While these further reasons help explain Powell, an analysis of Powell in turn can help us understand some of the trends further affecting New Testament scholarship.

Most immediately, something significant that helps us understand Powell's reconstruction of Christian origins is very much at the heart of the theme of this book, namely homeland. Powell's construction of a cultural and political homeland in the twentieth century is, I would argue, at the heart of his construction of homeland and his reconstruction of the Gospel tradition purportedly reflecting issues and events two thousand years earlier. I will turn first to Powell's construction of homeland in the twentieth century.

Powell's first great construction of what he called, as a young man, his 'spiritual homeland' involved all things German (Heffer 1998: 24; Pedraza 1986: 83-84). Powell started to develop his love of German language and culture as a teenager. He was intoxicated by what he saw as Germanic scientific rigour, deemed not so typical of English scholarship, coupled with a certain romance for the poetic qualities of the language (Heffer 1998: 10). Ultimately, this love affair, alongside his ever growing atheism, which in turn was one product of his early New Testament study, would lead to Nietzsche (he had read all of Nietzsche's works by his early twenties), who would lead to a hard atheism (Heffer 1998: 22-23). However, during the inter-war years, Powell was also certain there would be another war, with Germany as the great enemy, though Powell did not think that the rise of Hitler in 1933 was a decisive moment (Heffer 1998: 22; Pedraza 1986: 83-84). Still, Powell was worried about the future of Germany in particular because of his love for German culture. The major turning point for Powell's creation of a *new* homeland, and the shattering of the *old*, was in 1934 and the 'Night of the Long Knives'. Powell was devastated:

> . . . it had all been an illusion, all fantasy, all a self-created myth. Music, philosophy, poetry, science and the language itself—everything was demolished, broken to bits on the cliffs of a monstrous reality. The spiritual homeland had not been a spiritual homeland after all, since nothing can be a homeland, let alone a spiritual homeland, where there is no justice, where justice does not reign . . . overnight my spiritual homeland had disappeared and I was left only with my geographical homeland (cited in Heffer 1998: 24; cf. Pedraza 1986: 83-84).

While he never lost his interest in German culture, it was the mythology of Powell's geographical homeland that would utterly dominate his thought and deeds for the rest of his life. At first this meant fighting in World War II and the upholding of the British Empire, including an ambition to be viceroy of India. He was worried that, with talk of disintegration, the British Empire would ultimately fall and so he was determined to save the empire. So, in 1944, and significantly in India, he decided to become a Member of Parliament (Pedraza 1986: 89).

However, with independence for India and Sudan among other things, Powell soon realized that the empire was no longer the force it had been, and he believed that the Commonwealth was little more than a 'gigantic farce' (Pedraza 1986: 95, 106-107; Heffer 1998: 350, 132, 335-40). Powell opposed the 1956 intervention in Suez partly on the grounds that Britain should face reality and stop behaving as a power in the Middle East when it manifestly was not, a view not typical of the nostalgia of much of the Conservative Party thinking of the time. Despite entering Parliament with the intention of saving the empire, by the end of the 1940s he was shifting towards a deep nationalism *without* empire, or even anti-empire (Heffer 1998: 119-21, 335, 431-32).

Despite Powell's post-war pessimism concerning the British Commonwealth and immigration, he was always optimistic about the English nation and developed ideas of Englishness based on values, culture, a state of mind, economics and institutions understood as a result of a peculiarly English evolution, such as Parliament and the church.[7] At times this could be sentimental idealism, but concrete details illustrated this for Powell. For instance, Powell believed that the 1982 Falklands War showed that Britain could fight a war on its own terms as a nation—just as the nation could compete economically—with its own resources (Pedraza 1986: 147). Powell also *really* disliked the United States and, alongside his criticisms of America itself, this dislike was tied with his concept of British nationhood. Moreover, unlike the dominant Conservative Party thinking of the 1980s, Britain could be, and should be, distinct from the United States, which, he argued, did not really care about Britain. It followed that, for Powell, a healthy distance had to be kept from other potentially dominant institutions such as NATO and the UN (Pedraza 1986: 147-50; Heffer 1998: 57, 579-80). Powell's views on nation in relation to the European Economic Community (EEC) were so powerful that in 1974 he advised people to vote Labour over against his 'natural' home, the Conservative Party, and over against his dislike for anything that might smack of socialism. This was because Labour promised to renegotiate terms of entry into the EEC followed by a referendum (Pedraza 1986: 118; Heffer 1998: 579-80).

---

7. For useful overviews, see Pedraza 1986; Heffer 1998: 334-40.

For Powell, the nation was worth living, fighting and dying for, and was the ultimate political reality (Pedraza 1986: 125, 167; Heffer 1998: 5, 153, 334-40, 580, 822, 843). Powell was dedicated to the concept of nation, his 'guiding principle', as Howard Pedraza put it (1986: 92), embodied in Parliament and applied to just about anything political, from Powell's vigorous opposition to the European Common Market to immigration, from Ulster to the head of the Church of England.[8] Anglicanism was interwoven with his idealized concept of the nation. 'Perhaps the Celtic Church, distinctive though it was, cannot be thus classified [as a national church]', Powell speculated, 'but there was certainly a Gallican Church and an Anglican Church before the Reformation was dreamt of'. Powell stressed that in the twelfth century the king, like any modern prime minister, was insistent on the right to nominate bishops, and in the Middle Ages, the *Ecclesia anglicana* 'was an accepted political as well as ecclesiastical reality . . . the Church, the universal, catholic church, could also be a national church'. When England shook off the last remnants of external dependence it was the monarch—first Henry VIII—who asserted spiritual authority through Parliament, a decisive movement in English history (Powell 1992c: 73).[9]

The church in and of England evolved through compromise and debate, and with particularly English product to show, but with authority grounded in the Crown, and in a not dissimilar way to Powell's other major symbol of English nationhood, Parliament. Powell's thoughts on the 1981 legislating of the entrenchment of the Book of Common Prayer are significant. He believed that too much stress has been placed on the 'literary and linguistic excellences of the Prayer book' because the real gain is that Parliament is the guardian of the Prayer Book, which 'embodies forms of worship and expressions of faith that are broad, generous and deep enough to embrace the wide spectrum which a national church must comprehend . . . a Church of all the English' (1992c: 73-74).

Enoch Powell and the Origins of 'the Church'

> Christianity does not, repeat not, look forward to a gradual betterment of human behaviour and society or to the progressive spread of peace and justice upon earth. Still less does Christianity purport to offer a scheme or general outline for bringing that about. Quite the reverse . . . (Powell 1977: 61).

8. See also Pedraza 1986: 103; Heffer 1998: 116, 119, 338-39.

9. It is significant that the opening essay in Powell's book of sermons, exegesis and religious reflection (1977) begins with an essay on 'Patriotism'. See also his essay 'God Save the Queen' (1977: 74-82).

> One night . . . I passed St Peter's Church and the bells were ringing for
> Evensong . . . I opened a prayer book and I thought to myself . . . 'This is
> wonderful' . . . (Powell 1992b: 30-31).

Returning to Powell and the Gospel tradition, we see clearly the rhetorical links with his views on church and nation despite claims such as the
following, where Powell reflected on distance between the church then and
now:

> I do think that I have been travelling. The principal change that I believe
> I notice is that words of the Gospel which previously I took as given
> starting-points for comparison or contrast with conventional morality or
> conventional Christianity now present themselves to me in a more and
> more mysterious guise, as if they themselves were rather the end-products
> of processes or chain of events of which I can yet form only a dim con-
> ception. The absolutes which they address to me are no less imperious
> than before . . . but the Christ who confronts me with these absolutes has
> become more and more like a traveller from an unknown country, whom,
> if I dared, I would fain question whence and how he came hither (1977:
> ix-x).[10]

Powell was also explicit on the point that worship does not stand or fall
by textual history but 'derives its authority and its persuasiveness from the
immemorial practice and experience of the Church itself' (1994: viii). However, his analysis of the Gospel tradition, while hardly forsaking the former,
certainly shows clear intellectual influence from the latter. Powell, perhaps
contradicting his earlier statements, claimed that 'the most surprising experience has been to be led to perceive from how early a period in the evolution of the gospel the forms and ideas of worship were recognizably the
same as they have continued down the ages' (1994: viii). This could equally
have been said of Powell's concept of the origins of the Church of England.
It also comes through in the details of his analysis of the Gospel tradition.
Perhaps the Christ of this tradition was not so strange, after all.

As mentioned, duplications in Matthew were central for Powell's reconstruction, in particular his reconstruction of the tradition history of the feeding miracles.[11] These miracles also betray the evolution of church history
grounded in compromise and cohesion. The feeding miracles were certainly
not to be understood as historical events. Rather, the terminology in the
Feeding of the Five (or, in the alternative, Four) Thousand 'unmistakably'
alludes to 'the liturgical act of the Church known as the holy communion
or mass. That statement is one which I make as self-evident to anybody not

---

10. Compare Powell 1977: 121: '. . . I have offered only a small specimen of the
riches that the textual treasure-house known as Matthew has hardly begun to yield to an
unbiased critical analysis.'

11. See Powell 1977: 95-98 for his earlier interest in the feeding miracles.

determined to avoid its implications . . . Those who originally read or heard the narrative could not fail to understand what it was about' (Powell 1991: 6). The large surplus created by Jesus, including the consecrated bread, can now be taken up after the multitude had their fill and remains 'supernaturally' equal to the food consumed by the multitude (1991: 6-7). For Powell, the feeding miracle was composed in an 'already existing Church with an already recognizable liturgical practice' (1991: 6). However, the feeding miracle was also once part of a dispute over the significance of the consecrated elements. This underlies the reason for the duplication of the miracle. The duplication of the miracle is evidence of reconciliation, in this instance of a dispute over eucharistic details, between two opposing schools ('dare I say churches?') (1991: 8-9).

But tracing the history of the earliest church was important for Powell, just as it was for Powell's understanding of Anglicanism, because these origins in the depths of time add weight to the concept of a movement evolving to reflect the culture and interests of its people. The 'church' (the anachronistic ἐκκλησία) of the influential narrative underlying the Gospel of Matthew was none other than the Church of Peter with some suspiciously orthodox theology. The alternative version lost out but was, naturally, absorbed into the Gospel of Matthew (Powell 1991: 11). The Church of Peter was the church of the incarnation and the church of the Mass. The Church of Peter was also the church of the Gentiles, the church for all the world. Works of the law and personal merit are no longer required in this church. Faith in the propitiation and the identity of Jesus brought an end to that. And, of course, this church already possessed a book. The Church of Peter had been in sharp conflict with a Jewish 'church' that insisted on the role of the law and *created out of* the Gentile gospel an alternative myth of origins where Jesus was a prophet hero and martyr for Israel. So, a 'concordat' or compromise with the Gentile church was reached, and the mutual agreement was sealed with a new single Gospel of the different books.

Powell's reading of the Gospel tradition thus pushes the idea of a church of consensus, a gospel of societal cohesion. Moreover, it would have been necessary, Powell argued, for there to be a book or narrative for missionaries of the sort who would have converted Gentiles such as the addressees of Paul's letters. 'It would be well', Powell added, 'if it were a book accepted by every section of Christianity—in Jerusalem as well as in Rome. That would be a book such as might have evolved by AD 100 into the document which we possess under the title of "the gospel according to Matthew"' (1994: xxviii). Unsurprisingly, perhaps, and in stark opposition to much of New Testament scholarship, Paul and Matthew are part of the same strand of Christianity which would become orthodoxy. The Pauline Epistles could assume familiarity with the Matthaean traditions: 'the theology of the principal Pauline epistles is quite at home in the environment where Matthew

originated' (Powell 1994: xxvii-xxviii). What we clearly have here then
is the gradual evolution of orthodox Christian theology crystallized in the
Gospel of Matthew in a coming-to-terms with the realities of the secular
world. *Precisely* why this came about is not, Powell admitted, easy to determine but it is 'impossible to avoid the fact' that the Gentile church had
been validated by the Roman victory in Jerusalem: 'the *imperium Romanum*
could be seen as, however involuntarily and unconsciously, the executant of
the divine purpose' (Powell 1991: 15).

There is further evidence to boost the argument that Powell's history of
the Gospel tradition is less about disinterested textual analysis and more
about the social function of religion, namely Powell's religious convictions
and their relationship to his views of the state.[12] Powell converted from
atheism to Anglicanism in 1949 and was known to answer 'Anglican' when
asked about being a Christian (Heffer 1998: 131). Powell would become
identified with the High Tory, Anglo-Catholic wing of the church, which
placed greater emphasis on the role of tradition in worship and held to some
distinction from the evangelical and literalist believers (Heffer 1998: 135-
36; Powell 1977: 87-94; 1991). But Powell consistently emphasized the
social function of religion and worship and was not strong on issues of
personal faith and belief. Powell, at the end of his life, stressed that religion
was important in the history of human survival, and with this stress in mind
perhaps we should not be surprised at some of Powell's personal views
about faith.[13]

Powell's recollection of his conversion from atheism to Anglicanism in
1949 is significant here because it is tied up with his views of a distinctly
English church. For a start, it was the Evensong bells of St Peter's church
in Wolverhampton that called him (Powell 1992b: 30-31). The corporate
nature of the significance of his conversion and its tying in with political
ideas is typical Powell:

> However, ashamed or not, I came again and again, until presently I real-
> ised that I was caught fast . . . by an inner logic or necessity . . . once got
> within the walls, physical and liturgical, of the Church of England, I was
> proud enough to see that it was a goodly inheritance from which, like a
> prodigal son, I had so long deliberately exiled myself . . . like someone
> who returns after a long absence to an ancestral home, I looked at the half-
> familiar scenes with new eyes . . . I had stepped inside the Church Uni-
> versal . . . compelled to acknowledge a truth that is corporate . . . I noticed
> that the loyalties I had lived with in war and peace had been corporate too
> (cited in Pedraza 1986: 91).

12. A helpful summary is found in Heffer 1998: 134-38.
13. In this light, Powell's earlier remarks (1977: 65-70) on immortality in different
historical and cultural contexts, including Christian contexts, make particularly interesting reading.

The image of a conversion immersed in Powell's nationalism perhaps ought to alert us to issues of belief. Powell's most detailed biographer to date, Simon Heffer (1998: 134-36), records that 'one of his [Powell's] closest friends, himself deeply religious', suggested that Powell never ceased to be an atheist and that the role of the church as a social and national institution kept him within the fold. Furthermore, another close friend and Powell archivist, Richard Ritchie, said that the aging Powell at least did not believe in an afterlife, while another friend, the Member of Parliament and churchman Frank Field, claimed that Powell had no concern for the mission of the church.[14] As a Member of Parliament, Powell's concerns for the church consistently related to issues of the church–state relationship (Heffer 1998: 136). It is always worth recalling that the young Powell idolized Nietzsche and that the latter's influence would never fully leave him. Furthermore, in 1962 Powell was still recalling the influence of J.G. Frazer's *The Golden Bough* on his own thought and his boyhood atheism (Heffer 1998: 11).

It is difficult, then, to underestimate just how important the social function of the church was for Powell. In a related way, Powell was not a supporter of the relevance of the Bible and Christianity for contemporary political issues. For Powell, things such as 'faith in action' were, at best, meaningless or, at worst, dangerous.[15] Not only was this concern due to what Powell saw as a misreading of the Bible but was due also to what Powell believed were naïve understandings of politics and the role of the nation. In 1977, he even accused the Archbishop of Canterbury, Donald Coggan, of 'bad elementary economics . . . economic errors . . . damaging to this nation and its people', when Coggan spoke about issues of neglecting the needs of other nations (Powell 1977: 20). For Powell, the modern clergy had no authority to provide guidance for an earthly kingdom, only preparation for the kingdom to come. As Powell said of Coggan and his role as Archbishop of Canterbury,

> I owe respect to Dr Coggan, as Archbishop of Canterbury, a respect which I gladly yield. I also owe him more than respect when he speaks with the voice of his Master, to tell me that the blessed are the poor, the hungry, the thirsty and the oppressed, and that a rich man—and presumably a nation of rich men—cannot by any contrivance enter into his Kingdom. But it is not with that voice that his Grace was speaking in the words I have just quoted. He was speaking the language of materialism and bad elementary

14. Compare Pedraza 1986: 103. See Powell (1977: 52-58, 65-70) for his intellectualized reflections.

15. See, for example, Powell's chapters 'Christianity and the Curse of Cain', 'Action for World Development', 'My Country, Right or Wrong', and 'Christianity and Social Activity' (1977: 12-13, 14-19, 20-24, 30-51). See also Powell 1977: 63-64: 'Christianity . . . does not help me decide to vote for or against a United Kingdom in the European Community, or for or against the capital penalty for murder, or for a flat-rate or graduated system of state pensions or, for that matter, for or against state pensions at all.'

economics, and when he so speaks, it is the right and duty of a politician
. . . to refute and to rebuke (Powell 1977: 20).

Likewise, Powell condemned what he saw as the hijacking of Christianity by welfarism and equality of opportunity, and he strongly opposed the use of the Bible in understanding foreign policy. But Powell went further still. He could not accept the reading of the story of the Rich Man and Lazarus at face value where the rich man was punished for being rich and the poor Lazarus saved for being poor. Such readings will inevitably put people off reading the Bible (Heffer 1998: 137)! Unsurprisingly, then, in his work on Matthew, the Gospel tradition did not condemn the rich in verses such as the famous eye-of-the-needle saying, but rather this saying becomes an attack on personal merit and reliance on works, which in turn of course is, for Powell, something more typical of Judaism and/or the Jewish church (Powell 1991: 12; cf. 1977: 30-34, 39-40).

Enoch Powell and Empire

There is one curious feature about using Powell's nationalism to understand his reconstruction of the Gospel tradition: the Roman Empire, as we have seen, comes out positively, seemingly in sharp distinction from his views of the British Empire (Powell 1991: 15). In fact, constantly hovering in the background of Powell's reconstruction is the importance of Rome and the empire. Some of the language even puts Jesus in Romanesque garb: 'like the centurion ordering soldiers, Jesus designates missionaries to do his bidding, and dispatches them to work in the mission field' (1994: xxiv). Even the geography of Matthew's narrative, or at least in the underlying book, is more reflective of the Roman Empire than Palestine, and, in one sense, Powell effectively conquers Galilee for Rome. In addition to being an 'allegory of the great sea which united the Roman world', the 'sea' is a code word 'which often, if not always, represents the Mediterranean and signifies the gentile mission field' (Powell 1994: xxii, xxvi). From this perspective, it is perhaps not so surprising that Powell confidently ('there would be little hesitation about the answer') places the location of the underlying book in the heart of the empire—Rome. This, Powell argues, is due to the Roman bias and Gentile mission. From this Petrine origin in Rome, the other Gospels evolve, 'presumably in other quarters of the Mediterranean world', though here Powell gives no indication as to how he would account for pro-Roman bias and concern for Gentiles in other Gospels (1994: xxvii). This point is, I think, doubly significant because, in New Testament scholarship, by far the dominant view of the place of writing for Matthew's Gospel and Matthaean traditions is somewhere in the eastern Mediterranean, such as Antioch. Powell's idiosyncrasies again suggest that something other than mere scholarly curiosity is dictating the results.

Indeed, the idiosyncratic Roman bias in Powell's reconstruction makes it extremely difficult to avoid the conclusion that something else must be dictating the results. The authors of the underlying book were 'sensitive' or even 'apprehensive' about the relationship between Rome and the mission to the Gentiles, and here we return to that peculiar argument that the historical Jesus and the Jesus of the earliest reconstructed text was not crucified but stoned to death: Rome had nothing to do with it; Jesus was emphatically not a threat to Roman power. This pattern continues. The substitution of crucifixion for stoning was 'made conditional' upon Pontius Pilate being exonerated from blame (Powell 1994: xxiii, 207-208). The crucifixion is not the only problem for those who wish Rome to be exonerated. The kingdom of heaven, as Powell realized, is 'not self-evidently compatible with the *imperium Romanum*'. However, Powell stressed that the kingdom is 'painstakingly distanced' from the Jewish uprising (Mt. 24.27) and is 'allowed to remain in an unexplored limbo between individual immortality and a new world order', a view not dissimilar, it should be noted, to Powell's view of the role of the Anglican clergy noted above. Ultimately, with Pilate not really believing Jesus to be guilty (Mt. 27.23), 'Caesar's judgement-seat was in no imminent danger of being replaced by God's'. The blame for Jesus' crucifixion, as it was for the stoning and as it is for the destruction of the temple, is laid upon 'the Jews themselves' (Powell 1994: xxii).

Surely Powell was protesting too much! Why such a spectacularly pro-empire reading from a man who had become profoundly anti-imperialistic and profoundly anti-American empire? For a start, it ought to be observed that Powell's anti-imperialism was born out of a stark reality: Britain really was *not* the imperial force it had once been. Moreover, while Powell may have disliked American culture and its form of imperialism, he had a profound admiration for the Roman Empire (Heffer 1998: 28). There is presumably also some influence of Powell's view that the church does not dictate secular power but vice versa. This is, in fact, a view that Powell derives not only from church history but from his reading of the New Testament and with, of course, direct reference to Rome:

> 'Fear God, honour the king' in the First Epistle General of St Peter (2.17), or St Paul's injunction (Rom. 13.1-4) to 'be subject unto the higher powers' because 'the power' 'is the minister of God', who 'beareth not the sword in vain', will get us nowhere. Those are admonitions that were addressed to a tiny religious community who 'confessed that they were strangers and pilgrims on the earth' (Heb. 11.13), advising them that it was not their duty therefore to revolt against the Roman world-empire. Good behaviour and passive obedience were to be their proper attitudes towards it (Powell 1977: 79).

But perhaps most importantly, and despite his practical honesty, Powell still held a nostalgic view of the British Empire. After all, what if Britain had *not* given up India . . . ? In 1991, around the time that his published work on the Gospels was coming to fruition, Powell spoke to the Institute of Contemporary British History's Summer School at the London School of Economics, making the following revealing romanticizing remarks:

> When I resigned my chair in Australia in 1939 in order to come home to enlist, had I been asked 'What is the State whose uniform you wish to wear and in whose service you expect to perish?' I would have said 'The British Empire' . . . I also know that, on my deathbed, I shall still be believing with one part of my brain that somewhere on every ocean of the world there is a great, grey ship with three funnels and sixteen-inch guns which can blow out of the water any other navy which is likely to face it. I know it is not so. Indeed, I realised at a relatively early age that it is not so. But that factor—that emotional factor . . . will not die until I, the carrier of it, am dead (cited in Hennessy 1992: xiv-xv; see also Heffer 1998: 172-73).

Underlying Powell's Roman Gospel is not, then, simply an idealized picture of what the British or English *nation* was but also what the *Empire* was, and how it had a formative role in English and British identity. In one sense, Jesus, Peter, and Matthew, alongside Powell himself, were all *like*, and I stress *like*, the Roman. So, one imagined homeland, Galilee, is replaced by another imagined homeland, the empire, in support of Powell's contemporary imagined homeland, England, and refracted through the memory of Powell's homeland at its peak: British Empire. And all this was fought out on the text of the Gospel of Matthew.

Making an Example of Enoch Powell

Various contributions to this book show how concepts of nationalism and nation-state have affected biblical studies more generally and Gospel studies more specifically. Similarly, as the rise of postcolonial studies has shown, the role of empire runs deep in intellectual thought and biblical studies more generally and Gospel studies more specifically.[16] It is not difficult to show how many academic studies clearly reflect a coming to terms with shifting imperial powers. The Nazi Jesuses are a glaring example of imperialism and nationalism combined.[17] In post-war Germany, Günther Bornkamm (1960: 102, 223) devoted some space to what may seem an unusual debate for a book on the historical Jesus—namely an attack on Bolshevism—illustrating obvious Cold War concerns. From the UK, a type of engagement with

---

16. See, e.g., Sugirtharajah 2002; Moore 2006.
17. For discussion with further bibliography, see, e.g., Head 2004: 55-89; Heschel, 2008.

empire different from Powell's (and one, no doubt, that Powell would have deeply disliked) was Scott Brandon's nationalistic, anti-Roman revolutionary Jesus, where Brandon's publications tie in with some of the feelings of de-colonialization in the 1960s (Brandon 1967; 1968). Even more recently concerns with empire are present. It is perhaps no surprise that the anti-imperialistic Jesus (and Paul) really came to the forefront of New Testament scholarship from American scholars such as Richard Horsley, among many others. Most significantly, while American cultural and physical imperialism was taking off, a streak of self-denial has been common, from politics through to the superficial anti-imperialism of films about the ancient world coming from that bastion of cultural imperialism, Hollywood.[18] In a different way, and with the culturally prominent rise of the not-always-loved American Empire, it is perhaps no surprise that prominent British scholars such as N.T. Wright have willingly taken up an anti-imperial Jesus (and Paul).

Again in North America (largely), the extensive work of Bruce Malina and the Context Group have repeatedly given us constructions and tabulations of supposed individualist US culture over against the ancient and contemporary Mediterranean and Arab world. The intention may be to show the alien nature of the New Testament documents, but regularly such descriptions replicate the clash-of-civilizations rhetoric so prominent in US intellectual and popular culture. Malina and certain others have made some outrageous generalizations about the contemporary 'Arab world', such as endorsing claims, in a book on Jesus and the Gospels, that contemporary Arabs are likely to interpret life's difficulties as 'personal humiliations', to join extremist political movements, to revolt against legal governments, and so on (Malina 1996: 63).[19] The location of this rhetoric in contemporary American imperialism hardly needs spelling out here.

The static 'Mediterranean world' of certain imaginations is an increasingly popular backdrop in scholarship on the historical Jesus and Christian origins, though some scholars are much more careful and avoid some of the highly dubious stereotyping of contemporary Mediterraneans and Arabs. John Dominic Crossan is a good example of this, and his work is tied in with goals of liberation. Yet, for all the anti-imperial rhetoric of scholars such as Crossan, including anti-British Empire rhetoric, it is noticeable that Crossan's Jesus stands over against the alien Mediterranean world as a noticeably liberal figure (Crossan 1991; 1998). Many have criticized Crossan's Jesus for being too liberal, and, though this is often for the polemical reason to prove historically a more Christianized conservative Jesus rather

18. Compare Davies 2004: 142-55.
19. For further discussion of Malina and the Context Group in the context of contemporary US politics and culture, see Crossley 2008: 101-42.

than establish the political locations of scholarship, the general criticism can
be taken up: I do not think it is going too far to see Crossan's liberal Jesus
as a representation of liberal America constructed over against the 'other'
civilization represented by the grand 'Mediterranean'.[20] Crossan's Jesus is
as much a product of the new American Empire as it is a critique of it.

Concluding Remarks

Powell is undoubtedly worth studying as an insight into English and
British political culture. Yet there is also some advantage to studying figures
such as Powell for help in our understanding of the issues dictating questions in New Testament studies because his political and academic lives
make him a lightning conductor for crucial political trends. In his book
on eighteenth-century French cultural history, *The Great Cat Massacre*,
Robert Darnton advocates a more anthropological approach to history and
the importance of a perception of distance from the culture under investigation. For Darnton, the best starting point in attempting to penetrate an
alien culture is 'where it seems to be most opaque'. By 'getting' the joke,
proverb, riddle, ceremony or whatever it is possible to start grasping a 'foreign system of meaning' (Darnton 1984: 77-78). While I am an advocate of
investigating those parts of contemporary culture that seem so normative, it
is worth turning Darnton's suggestion on our own general cultural contexts
in looking at parts of our culture that seem alien to the investigator and how
they help us understand our own systems of meaning. Powell is an excellent
example of this.

20. See also Keeley 2002: 182-210 for the intellectual influences on Crossan's
work from nationalistic and racializing discourses through Heidegger and Bultmann and
modern American biblical scholarship.

HOMELESSNESS AS A WAY HOME:
A METHODOLOGICAL REFLECTION AND PROPOSAL*

Todd Penner and Davina C. Lopez

Method as Home

As scholars, theoreticians, and analysts of early Christian phenomena, method is our home. It is the habitat or, rather, *habitus*[1] within which we

We wish to thank Director John B. Weaver and the staff of the Burke Theological Library at Columbia University in New York for providing the space for us to collaborate on this project as Scholars-in-Residence during the Summer of 2010. The Burke staff have opened up their 'home' to us, and we are most grateful for their many kindnesses, professional and personal. We are grateful to Austin College and Eckerd College for providing continued institutional support toward our collaborative efforts. The original paper on which this essay is based was presented in March 2009 at the 'Holy Land as Homeland? Models for Constructing the Historic Landscapes of Jesus' seminar as part of the 'Jesus in Cultural Complexity' project. Halvor Moxnes was a most gracious and welcoming host. Thanks also to James Crossley, Ward Blanton, Signhild J. Stave Samuelsen, and Marianne Bjelland Kartzow for their contributions to making that trip possible. The core idea regarding the new or 'younger' German scholarship (particularly Martin Hengel's students) as representing a site for critical investigation and serious concern was first raised by Susannah Heschel in a conversation several years ago (she was indeed quite prescient in this regard). As a result of the boundless hospitality of Marc Ellis, we were able to develop some of the ideas articulated here through a presentation entitled 'Encountering the Apostle Paul's Jewish Future through His Christian Past', our contribution to the 'Encountering the Jewish Future' seminar held at the Center for Jewish Studies at Baylor University in September 2010. Lastly, we presented a portion of this essay as part of a Friends of the Burke Library Lecture entitled 'Birthing Modern Narratives with Ancient Worlds: The Histories and Heresies of Introductory Textbooks on the Bible' at Union Theological Seminary in February 2011. We thank Mim Warden for her generous hosting of that event. On the occasion, David M. Carr posed some challenging questions for our epistemological and ethical project, and we are appreciative of his frank and open engagement. Finally, Keith Whitelam, the editor of this volume, deserves to be singled out for special recognition for his inordinate and, indeed, superhuman capacity for patience and persistence. This essay exists largely because of his insistence and perseverance.

1. For an elaboration of *habitus* as mediator, see Bourdieu 1977. For an attempt to theorize *habitus* as additionally mediating between religious practices and ideologies,

organize data, analyze filiations in our subjects and/or objects of study, highlight (or perhaps downplay) attendant complexities, configure the paradigms that will construe (our) meaning, and, to be sure, also establish value (ethical, social, cultural, and, perhaps most importantly, economic). Method, as home, as symptom (or symptomatic) of tradition, enables us both to pursue origins (Where did we come from? How did we get to be this way?) and, in so doing, as Michel Foucault suggests, to 'isolate the new against a background of permanence' (Foucault 1972: 21). In this respect, the *telos* of method is always already about our ability to circumscribe and thereby comprehend our world, to make it familiar, to make it 'homey', stabilizing, in the process, emergent newness, and no doubt also warding off potential intrusions into the spaces and places that we call 'home'. Method is the means, finally, by which we are able to reconfigure what we might experience as instability and fluidity within a framework that (re)locates change within a predictably consistent habitat. Method, as home, as *habitus*, can be a comfortable and comforting mediating space between social relations and individual behaviors, in this case between professional hermeneutical and interpretative practices situated within the social relations and hierarchies of professional disciplinary orientations (e.g. 'New Testament Studies', 'Christian Origins', 'Late Antiquity'). Method is thus not only home; it also makes home visible to us, provides a map to find our way (back?) home and gives us a familiar place to hang our proverbial hats.

One would assume it ill-advised to imagine any serious scholarly endeavor venturing forth into the terrain of the study of early Christian literature, discourse, history, social and cultural contextualization and so forth without explicit attention being given to the method(s) by which the material will be engaged—to the *habitus* that will mediate such interaction. Scholars believe it is critical that doctoral students learn about method as an essential component of their guilding process, as a disciplining effect (and affect) of their pedagogical regimen toward making the guild a home. Of course, in this context, we are well aware that there is not a single method per se, so we are wont to speak about methods and theories in the plural, even experimenting with (or at least talking about) hybridic methodological models. We can delineate clearly the use of correlative 'traditional' methodologies, for example, historical, source, form, redaction, genre and literary criticisms. At other times divergent analytic paradigms—for example, 'queer criticism', 'postcolonial reading', 'literary deconstruction'—are deployed, which are evidently departures from, and sometimes at odds with, the aims related to what we might configure as more traditional historical methodological modalities (at least this is how such innovations are positioned

see Mahmood 2005. It could be said that Mahmood's strategies vis-à-vis Bourdieu's work invite the kinds of methodological questioning we aim to do in this essay.

against the 'background of permanence' that the 'older' methods represent). We might think of the latter as new urban subdivisions, which do sometimes appear as a threat to the 'old downtown' homes but which, nevertheless, offer something fundamental about the 'old' now in a 'new' frame. It might be the case that discourses about newer methodologies employ the rhetoric of departure and innovation, or of fragmentation over against the wholeness and purity of more traditional methods. We submit, however, that the perennial question, which is at once geographical and genealogical, still needs to be posed: Where do you live, and who are your people/ancestors/parents? The answers, even from proponents of newer hermeneutical configurations such as queer and postcolonial criticisms, reveal spaces and histories of some aspects of home while simultaneously obscuring others.

Method is our home. And yet, along with Theodor Adorno, who perhaps stated it most clearly in his famous aphorism on private property—'it is part of morality not to be at home in one's home' (Adorno 1978: 39), we raise a serious caution against being and becoming too comfortable with and comforted by such homeliness, by that *habitus* we desire to cultivate, keep, and pass on to others in the quest for continued relevance, perhaps even aspiring to immortality by hanging our portraits in the hallways of the mediating places we inhabit. Adorno identifies a seemingly contradictory ethics about home: 'home is where the heart is', and yet it is desirable, even necessary, to be out of place at home in order for a higher—or highest—form of morality to be reached. Of course, many of us leave our homes—some of us run away from home. Whether we can ever really leave home is another question. By running away, we embark on a search for, and sometimes think we are able to establish, what we might frame as new homes—sometimes much grander structures than the ones we left behind (or into which we were born). Sometimes, the structure is more modest, and at other times it is situated in a neighborhood that makes us a little uneasy. Ultimately, though, structure is the unifying constant in all such construction.

Like all homes, method has a formal structure and logic that need to be identified and understood, even (perhaps especially) when such structure seems natural or the way it should be since it always has been. The boundaries of home are circumscribed by the limits of language, constrained by the extent of conceptuality and, of course, also opened up at times by the possibilities inherent in creative and (re)imaginative thought, which can push the limits of language itself. Still, without structure there is no home—whether we think of home as a house, as a different kind of metaphorical space, as a local community, as our country, as friendship, as family, as the body of a lover . . . and so on. Sometimes we are not always clear what home we are in or whether we are even welcome there. Whatever we believe to be home, such a place has to be built and structured and ordered, and even in those moments of extreme chaos the palpable outlines of structure remain. In the story of the tower of Babel in Genesis, language becomes something of a curse on humanity, making human communication difficult or even impossible. The gods are saved through language—which becomes an interesting metaphor for how language functions—it 'saves the appearances' (to steal a line from Owen Barfield's famous book) or, at the very least, it 'keeps up the appearances' very much in line with Hyacinth Bucket's desires. Of course, the gods are 'saved' precisely because of the distinction and division that language brings—the otherness that language can and does create. In some ways, then, language is the curse of method, as much as it is also the very (re)source that makes our ability to conceptualize methodologically possible—and perhaps, most importantly, language makes it possible for us to fully and finally distinguish between an 'I' and 'thou' . . . a 'self' and 'other', to 'let there be light', to make order out of chaos—that is to say, to take raw material and to make it a home (whether of mud, straw, brick, cement). Yet, at the same time, as in that moment of mass language diffusion (and confusion) at Babel, language of necessity distinguishes, divides, limits, constrains—it disrupts, corrupts, baffles. Still, language also creates the power for translation, intuition, empathy, transformation, and the creation of imaginative spaces in which we can encounter ourselves through relating to otherness (Buber 1958) and therein also come to understand better not the nature of the infinite but the material structures of our own homes.

And it is here, at this juncture, that we must forefront the most important aspects of home in relation to who we are as humans. That is, if 'home is where the heart is', then it stands to reason that it is the home that shapes our selves, that provides the structure in which our daily actions and thoughts are shaped and reconfigured in relationship to our environment.[2] So 'home' is much more than a 'place'—it is, finally, a site from which and in which we construct self-identity and social relations. One only need think here of the numerous studies of late that have tried to show a relationship between the re-situating of homes and houses in our urban environment and the types of societal reconfigurations that have taken place as a result (see especially Farrelly 2008; Harvey 2009; Putnam 2000). As larger structural shifts take place in terms of the situation of homes and their relationship to one another, our very conceptions of self and other—and especially the relationship of the self to the other—are changed gradually but nonetheless radically (so David Harvey asks us to reimagine space in order to change our social relationships [2000]). As Judith Butler argues,

---

2. Georg Lukács offers a helpful formulation of our point, here related to the ways in which ideas and actions in history change over time: '. . . the essence of history lies precisely in the changes undergone by those *structural forms* which are the focal points of man's interaction with environment at any given moment and which determine the objective nature of both his inner and his outer life' (Lukács 1971: 153).

the question of ethics emerges precisely at the limits of our schemes of
intelligibility, the site where we ask ourselves what it might mean to continue in a dialogue where no common ground can be assumed, where one
is, as it were, at the limits of what one knows yet still under the demand
to offer and receive acknowledgement: to someone else who is there to be
addressed and whose address is there to be received (2005: 21-22).

There are old homes and new homes, red homes and blue homes, homes
in old towns and those in new suburbs, homes that are shacks and those that
are mansions—but in all cases, in this metaphorical framework, the relationship of the self-produced in such homes stands in relationship to those
selves produced in other places and spaces, and, in the case of us historians,
in other times and places. The desires that are produced in these structures,
then, have multifaceted dimensions in as much as they can move in multiple
directions, some that produce, from a particular ethical standpoint, better
social relations or worse social relations. The self so produced is a desir-
ing self, and for this reason it is imperative to examine closely the kinds
of desires (in this case for larger social relations) that are produced in and
through our methodological homes and structures, and the selves and social
relations to the other that are produced therein.

How Is your Home Built? Method and Structure

We may not be able to escape the 'prison house of language', to borrow a
phrase from Fredric Jameson, but we can and should spend time reflecting on
and trying to locate and decipher its blueprints, particularly keeping in view
our professional disciplinary orientations and how those are configured at
this world-historical moment of considerable social and cultural complexity. Indeed, it also seems to us that any serious consideration and engagement of such 'cultural complexity' in our time needs to take into account the
nature of methodology itself, perhaps even demanding that methodologies
provide an account of themselves. Given the seemingly little reflection on
method among scholars of early Christianity, one could assume that there
exists a general consensus, or at the very least an overarching assumption,
that methods themselves are neutral in origin and use.[3] We consider this to

---

3. One certainly receives this impression in reading Larry Hurtado's programmatic
statement in his summary of the main issues in biblical criticism at the turn of the millennium (Hurtado 1999), wherein there is no serious reflection on method itself, only
the religious impulses behind the New Testament writings, conclusions that, of course,
are produced by Hurtado's own religious positioning. Jacques Berlinerblau (2002) has
helpfully identified some of the inherent problems with this form of scholarship, noting
in particular the failure of biblical scholars to be fully shaped by the secularism of the
modern university system (and also the failure of the university itself in this respect).
Hence, religious commitments abound in the practice of biblical historical work with

be one of the more dangerous assumptions circulating (even if somewhat unwittingly) among modern critics. Taking methodology at face value, as a harmless structure of meaning and meaning making, occludes the forging of the self that it enacts and reifies. Thus, the danger, as we see it, lies in the failure among scholars to perceive and to analyze critically the connections among the use of particular modes of thinking, the methodologies that produce those and the ways in which we inhabit our world(s).

Discourses about methodological matters often posit that 'others' such as feminist and gender theorists, postcolonial critics and similar ideological-critical scholars tend to pay more attention to the embedded value systems of method, as well as the social, cultural and economic values encased in the forms that give expression to our thoughts, and which, in turn, our thoughts then reconfigure and reshape. Nevertheless, it can be questioned whether or not this is a fair representation of non-conventional methodologies or, as we are now fond of saying, those methodologies that are produced as a result of the 'linguistic turn'. More often than not such 'newer' methodologies are structured on the same logic as so-called traditional approaches. The interventions posed by proponents of feminist hermeneutics provide an excellent example. Feminist criticism, which is largely a theological and ecclesial project (here betraying a continued indebtedness to its primary roots), focuses on engaging 'male-stream' scholarship for its failure to cultivate a desire for the recovery of female voices from the past—in the service, of course, of providing redress in the present and, in some cases, a better future for all people. In other words, the issue is not one of fundamental reorientation of method but a deployment of the very same method in question toward a different end. Queer and postcolonial theorists are essentially involved in the same enterprise. Seeking to recover the 'voices' of the 'voiceless' in the ancient past (which is itself 'voiceless') or to expose assumptions by modern scholars is certainly not something to dismiss—in its own right it is a valuable and important undertaking. Our concern is rather that such methods envision themselves as having broken with past methodologies. By so doing, critics in this vein of analysis occlude their own self-production by and through the very methods they are criticizing. In fact, the 'home' is the same—it is a matter of how one chooses to decorate that home that is fundamentally at stake in such conversations. Do we use historical investigation to recover the 'great men' of the past? Or do we utilize the same scholarly tools and procedures to detect ancient male bias toward and denigration of women, or to discover and then to give voice to females and others from the past who have been 'hidden' from our view by ancient male writers? It might

relatively little thought given to the impact such convictions have on the products of scholarly inquiry.

seem trite to say, Do you prefer lighter or darker colored walls? And yet it is difficult to see how much else is, in fact, going on in such conversations.

Fundamental to our argument at this juncture is that the self produced in either feminist or more traditional forms of historical criticism, as well as the relationship with other selves, is in fact not as different as we would like to believe.[4] The structure that shapes the method that produces the self is the same, because the material world in which the structure exists is the same. One might well argue that the antagonism with which some of the interaction between competing scholarly methods is carried out reveals something fundamental about the types of relationships between the self and the other that the methodologies of our field produce—but this need not imply that the selves in and of themselves are fundamentally different. Adorno's thoughtful commentary on these dynamics illustrates the larger themes addressed here and throughout the rest of this essay:

> The sword dance is rigged. No matter whether it is the Categorical Impera-
> tive which triumphs or the Rights of the Individual—whether the can-
> didate succeeds in freeing himself from faith in a personal God or in
> reconquering it, whether he confronts the abyss of Being or the harrowing
> experience of the Senses, he falls on his feet. For the power which steers
> the conflicts, the ethos of responsibility and integrity, is always authoritar-
> ian, a mask of the State. If they choose acknowledged blessings, all's well
> in any case. If they come to rebellious conclusions, they go one better as
> the fine, independent men who are in demand. In either case they approve
> like good sons the authority which might call them to account, and in
> whose name the whole trial has really been fought out: the gaze under
> which they have been seemingly scrapping like two rowdy school boys is
> from the outset a frown (Adorno 1978: 134).

Whatever our methodological inclinations, whichever fights we pick in the schoolyard, the question is this: How might we turn our attention from dodging the next thrown punch toward the overarching gaze that creates the context for the scrapping itself?

---

4. For a recent illustration of our point, see Scholz 2010. Ironically, her criticism of German white male scholarship is found in that most-German of scholarly forms: the *Festschrift*. In short, even these front-runners of hermeneutical suspicion tend to identify the problems with 'other' traditional methods while failing to see how their own meth-odological approaches frequently reinscribe and mimic the very 'failings' of that under critique. A different end to which one deploys a particular method does not in anyway engage the formal structure and logic of the methodological home. In this way, it is not clear that feminist criticism of male-stream scholarship can actually be more 'ethical' than the latter's focus on establishing a reliable, stable and consistent historical ground-ing for modern individual and social existence. Both approaches, in effect, are reflective of ethical systems and value choices.

No matter the problems engendered in our little corner of the playground, one should not think that these methodological matters are somehow limited to the field of biblical scholarship. All methodologies in all academic disciplines produce categorization and classification and, as a result, produce a self and other in separation and in relation. Similarly illustrative is the larger umbrella field of religious studies, under which biblical scholarship stands on occasion and has lately been invoked as that which might serve as a remedy or balancing mechanism to the insularity of biblical studies methods (e.g., Arnal 2010). Tomoko Masuzawa's recent provocative book, *The Invention of World Religions* (2005), falls prey to the very same complex of issues we associate with the study of, for example, Christian origins. Masuzawa adeptly points out the ways in which the founding figures of the discipline of the scientific study of religion were conceptually limited in their framing and articulation of religion. In her critical assessment of earlier scholarship, she argues that the concept of 'world religions' was essentially a construct forged within Western language constraints and connected to emergent Orientalist perceptions grounded in colonial expansion and the rise of a secular state. The concept of 'religion' in its origin, then, is very much a Western construction, one that is decidedly shaped by the Judeo–Christian impulses embedded in the discourses and paradigms of early scholars of religious phenomena (see especially T. Fitzgerald 2007; similarly Cavanaugh 2009). Indeed, one of the critical underlying commitments of these early scholars of religion was to shore up a form (even if increasingly secularized) of Protestantism. In the largely taxonomic approach to the study of world religions, the emphasis on locating 'founders', 'scriptures', and 'rituals' as artifacts of 'religions' that can, in the end, be compared to Protestant Christianity, proved to be profoundly useful in terms of articulating regimes of liberal Protestantism as well as emergent secular versions of the nation-state that arose from within the very same (for similar observations with respect to biblical scholarship, see Marchand 2009; Penner 2008).

Masuzawa has clearly hit the proverbial nail on the head—and into the house—with respect to the ways in which Western categories of interpretation have shaped the ways we both define 'religion' and then identify the very same. Masuzawa fails to explicitly recognize, however, that all academic study of religion is fundamentally encased within this framework, and that even so called postcolonial approaches can do little to shed the shackles (if we choose to think of them that way) of Western, colonizing systems of classification and categorization. The 'subaltern' that is frequently propped up by scholars situated in or influenced by Western institutions (be it Gayatri Chakravorty Spivak or Fernando Segovia; Homi Bhabha or R.S. Sugirtharajah; Chinua Achebe or Musa Dube) becomes a medium for configuring an 'other' that is both a vanishing point and, at the same time, an object that helps one decipher Western codes and concepts. We would be willing to go so far as to say that if one is engaging in something approximating 'religious studies', regardless of what specific methods are employed therein, one is ultimately working from within a colonial conceptuality. Even the designation 'postcolonial' is predicated on an understanding of and entanglement with colonialism and colonial frameworks, no matter the identity, historical positioning and social location of the interpreter (cf. Lopez 2011).[5] To be sure, the interplay of interpreter and chosen methodological framework matters, but an important question to posit over and over again is, What exactly is at stake in such alignments and intersections? What is at stake in the production of a 'queer reading' or a 'postcolonial interpretation' alongside of or in opposition to 'colonial' or 'non-queer' modes of engagement? What difference does the difference make, to whom, and to what end? While it is the case that the position of the interpreter matters in their choice of method (thus, 'colonial subjects' might be drawn to 'postcolonial interpretation'), we would also like to suggest that methodology is not, and cannot be, constructed in a historical and social vacuum. Home, as structure, is never built on neutral ground. The people who live there can, and do, have agency in how the home looks, how it shelters, how it is financed, but we are nonetheless still shaped and produced by those very same aspects (that is, home makes us as much as we make home).

The position we are delineating here, that methodological stances and the interpreters who use them are both shaped and re-shaped by each other, stands in stark contrast to the proposition that methods are neutral, that it is only the practitioners of methods who are the 'problem'. This is, in effect, one of the main affirmations of a host of scholars who consider themselves to be 'post-linguistic-turn-interpreters': it is the particularity of the self that shapes the ways in which methods are deployed and by which data are interpreted. We have no quarrels with and no doubt about the position that the ideologies of those who use methods shape the way in which that method is

---

5. R.S. Sugirtharajah (2008) provides an excellent demonstration of some of the larger complications we are identifying here. In his semi-autobiographical account of his interaction with traditional German historical-critical scholarship on the Bible, he makes it clear that his issue from a colonial standpoint is not that the Bible came to Sri Lanka, but that the simple, more personal appropriation of the biblical text by the colonized subjects was challenged and ultimately ruined by the theological educational commitments of biblical criticism and the methods deployed therein. The Bible in his context was already a colonial product, but there is a latent postcolonial nostalgia for a time when its interpretation was less convoluted and complicated and, essentially, less critical as far as a personal theological orientation is concerned. This same nostalgic impulse plays out in Sugirtharajah's more recent work, where he insists that the Bible needs to be wrested from the hands of biblical critics and put (back) into the hands of non-trained interpreters who are 'still at the margins' and who will 'get back to basics'.

employed, the manner in which the data are organized and the results determined by such interactions. Nevertheless, we think it imprudent to accent the biases and values of readers and interpreters while ignoring the methodologies used by such biased readers and interpreters, which is tantamount to suggesting that these lenses are themselves value-neutral. Within the framing of 'cultural complexity', we want to insist on the complex intersection (and mutually interactive) interrelationship between the ideologies of methods and the ideologies of the selves of interpreters produced therein (and the vast network of social and cultural contextualities that play into that relationship). One might consider our emphasis here to be one of 'truth telling'; a process wherein the self is called upon to account for itself. Perhaps the act of giving an account of oneself is ultimately the task of any reflection on method as home, particularly as the self has no choice but to do so from within the confines of the house itself.

Let us clarify. We are not suggesting that biases or value-laden interpretative strategies are avoidable or necessarily problematic in themselves. Nor are we calling for a rehearsal of the politics of identity among biblical scholars and other disciplinarians (that very liberal type of confessional project that never leads to an actual analysis and engagement of the formal and logical structures that bolster that confession and perhaps, masking, in the process, the underlying identities that that personal acknowledgment overlays[6]). Rather, we are suggesting that the construction of the self and the relationality of that self to other selves be fronted first and foremost in our thinking and our work (and our thinking about our work). As Butler has aptly stated, 'when I tell the truth about myself, it is not only my 'self' that I consult, but the way in which that self is produced and producible, the position from which the demand to tell the truth proceeds, the effects that telling the truth will have as a consequence' (Butler 2003a: 79). In other words, the self can be fully valued and assessed only in terms of its worldly effect, in terms of its incarnation and the consequences thereof. In this sense, Butler, in line with both Adorno and Foucault, would suggest that the self cannot be known or evaluated in and of itself, but only in relationship, and only in assessment and recognition of the effects of such relationship. In terms of our reflective methodological focus in this essay, then, the methodological self is itself impossible to evaluate apart from some form of assessment of the consequences that are created by its deployment in the world. Put another way, if one were to situate this epistemological project within an ethical framework (as we aim to do), then the self of particular methodologies is called to give an account of itself in order to demonstrate the manner

---

6. This insight regarding 'liberal confession' was clarified for us in conversation with Jeremy Kirk, a Ph.D. candidate at Union Theological Seminary.

in which, in a world such as ours, this self serves to foster a fundamentally different and better world than the one we inhabit.

Home and 'Homeland': Nationalist Impulses in the Study of Early Christianity

One may ask, then, How is all of this reflection on methodology as 'home' related to studying the landscapes of early Christianity, or, for that matter, construing the various intersectionalities that the memories of Jesus might engender in our scholarly and popular imaginations? One of the themes of this volume has to do with the intersections of nationalism and the construction of our own modern identities in and through the figuration of ancient world 'realities' (see Penner 2008; Lopez 2008). If early Christianity is to 'mean' anything to us, it seems, we ought to pin down its genesis to one home(land) or another. Alas, the search for an ancient home(land) is always already about where we might like to hang our hats now. To that end, much greater attention to methodology itself will yield critically important results for thinking about how our selves are produced in and through conceptualizing the ancient world as we do and, in the process, how our own selves in turn are productive of relations with other selves. If we take seriously a genealogy of methodologies—admitting that methods do not arrive on the scene *ex nihilo*—it therefore becomes imperative to give serious attention to the origin, development, and continued deployment of particular methodologies and their embedded and attendant ideological formulations and conceptions.

In examining the structure of our discourses and the form of the methods we employ for the study of early Christianity, we may well be surprised, for instance, to find just how close we stand to earlier forms of scholarly inquiry that we have since judged to be incomplete or, worse, insidious. When the matter is simply one of interpretation, then modern scholars would eschew very quickly any connections they might have to, say, Third Reich scholarship on the Bible. But if methodology itself is acknowledged as a *habitus* that shapes and molds not only the questions we ask and the ways in which we use these questions to align and interpret the data but also, finally, the very self of the interpreter inhabiting that interpretative space, then we are able to open some windows on a very different set of questions. We tend to reflect on method all the less when we resonate with a particular set of ideas, when we feel that the methods are being used by the 'right' people toward the 'appropriate' ends. Drawing on a Foucauldian model of power, one could suggest that methods (here in the active tense) convey as much authority as they do precisely because they are made to appear to be completely divested of any power in and of themselves—in dominant scholarly discourses, they attain such authoritative power only through their *use* by an interpreter (who is also 'powerless' until s/he learns the 'language' of method and other 'house rules' of the discipline). We submit that this position is palpably illusory, substantively problematic and potentially very dangerous with respect to the political and social consequences in the material world that can emanate from such positions.

For example, today we will generally find the work of a scholar such as Walter Grundmann to be highly problematic. His reconstructions of a Galilee devoid of any kind of Jewish influence, in order to produce a Jesus that was for all intents and purposes non-Jewish, finds little support among contemporary New Testament scholars (see Heschel 1994; 2008). It is no overstatement to suggest that we contemporary interpreters consider ourselves much more informed, better educated and possessing more superior and enlightened values, and even in some respects further evolved and more civilized. Indeed, while there are attempts at present, particularly by German scholars, to recover something of the usefulness (even if cautiously) of Grundmann's scholarly legacy (Deines *et al.* 2007), overall most scholars would shy away from that reclamation. Naturally, a consensus position on 'now' is shaped by consciousness about the horror and humanity of the events of 'then', particularly the systematic mass extermination of Jews in Europe, an act that cannot be fully disconnected or disembodied from the intellectual work of Third Reich scholars of all fields. Thus, scholars of Christian origins these days are much more attentive to the Jewish dimensions of 'Jesus places' such as Galilee, 'Jesus activities' such as communal meals, and 'Jesus words' such as parables. This considerate attentiveness to and ecumenical interest in the thoroughgoing Jewishness of Jesus and the New Testament more broadly could be understood as a result of, and therefore genealogically linked to, much of the implicitly and explicitly anti-Jewish interpretations of earlier Northern European, mostly German, scholarship of the late eighteenth and early nineteenth centuries. Still, what is interesting in both of these cases is the similarity of the position that the character of 'Jewishness' is perceived to be readily identifiable and distinguishable—that a 'Jewish' essence of one kind or another, in singularity or plurality, is identifiable, recoverable, definable in relation to other essences, and that identification ultimately makes all the difference for efforts toward a 'fuller' theological reconstruction of Christian origins. The difference is simply that in the former case the de-Judaized Galilee was the work of a well-trained scholar who happened to live and work during the Third Reich, and the latter is likely not to be a product of the same exact historical moment.

We further note that, while someone like Grundmann—or at least his political activity and also much of his work toward framing Jesus and early Christianity as devoid of Jewish impulses—is manifestly repudiated by modern scholars of all persuasions, very few might take a similarly uncompromising stance toward someone like Martin Hengel. It is hard to deny that some of the basic patterns of earlier German biblical scholarship still affect our modern scholarly paradigms (see the recent engagement of this issue in Lapin and Martin 2003). Indeed, in many respects, Hengel's voluminous scholarly output on ancient Judaism in relationship to early Christianity (from his classic *Judaism and Hellenism* to manifest other publications) effectively accomplishes something akin to the agenda of Grundmann's work. In some ways, we might even say that Hengel's corpus betrays, even more fully than Grundmann's, a fairly consistent effort toward a subordination of Jewish identity, belief and practice with respect to the rise of early Christian belief and practice (see Penner 2005).

While Hengel has gone to great scholarly lengths to show how even a fully 'hellenized' (read: 'less barbaric') ancient Judaism (in contradistinction to a more legally lessopen form of Judaism) ultimately surrenders to an even more civilized early Christianity, he has gone to equally great lengths to articulate, and perhaps even overdetermine, a critical distance from the political, social, and theological sympathies characteristic of scholars of Grundmann's ilk (see his later-in-life confessional essay, 'A Gentile in the Wilderness'; Hengel 2010). Nevertheless, Grundmann and Hengel employ similar methodologies in terms of how they go about doing their historical work and how they perform 'at home' as historical-critical biblical scholars. Modern biblical scholars, moreover, tend not to see the problematic nature of Hengel's work—in fact, it is most often lauded for its breathtaking voluminousness and diversity, its deep immersion in a full range of primary sources and its incisive critical acumen (see Hurtado 2008, as well as the essay by his foremost pupil and 'anointed disciple', even 'apostle', Jörg Frey [2010]). We simply have been trained not to see the problem (and not in small part because our training and our scholarship are complicit to greater and lesser degrees in these seemingly unseemly projects). In turn, we will readily perceive the problematic nature of Grundmann's work not because of some inherent flaw in his method itself, but in the judgment of history on his Third Reich context, which then implicates the scholarship of that era (and the interpretations derived from the use of said method). However, in so far as the methodologies themselves have not changed with time, and in so far as the selves produced in relationship to otherness are embedded thoroughly within the methodological home of historical-criticism itself, then it is hard to imagine that the *habitus* has fundamentally changed in any way. It would be naïve to assume, we think, that since we are no longer gassing Jewish bodies that somehow our inherited interpretative methods are any more ethical than when we were doing so. The two may in fact be relatively unrelated—the self in relation to the other may still exist as it once did; it is only that now that relationship manifests itself in different ways (given the differing political, social, and economic realities of our own time).

One might apply this standpoint to what would appear to be a form of scholarship dramatically different from that of the German tradition. For instance, scholars of the New Testament and early Christianity generally applaud the work of Mark Nanos, not in small part because he is a self-identified Jewish interpreter of Paul who, following the largely Protestant 'New Perspective' interpretative trajectory, reads the apostle as a first-century Jew thoroughly enmeshed in the conceptual, legal and social contexts of the Judaism of his day. Not by his own doing or by any necessary desire on his part, Nanos's work enjoys a singular resonance and reception as "Jewish" among those invested in Pauline studies and other scholars of Christian origins, and particularly among those who might tend to be a little more theologically conservative (see Elmer 2009; for a critical engagement of Nanos's categories, see Elliott 2008). The social-scientific models adapted by Nanos are grounded in the work of Philip Esler, who tends to use such approaches within a decidedly theological framework. The strategic deployment of such 'scientific' models offers a discourse that posits something of a solid historical grounding for this reading of Paul's Jewishness. In some sense, this trend in Pauline studies is considered by contemporary scholars to provide a necessary counterbalance and response to the anti-Jewish readings of Paul or Jesus of earlier periods. And, undeniably, it is exactly that. If we are talking here only about the ideology of scholars—their particular social, cultural, political, perhaps even religious leanings—as determinative for delineating the contours, structures and logics of our methodologies in the study of early Christianity, then we can clearly state that Mark Nanos has a radically different ideological bent from that of Hengel or Grundmann. But, in fact, that is not what we have been arguing. If what we are suggesting here is cogent, then the work of Nanos (or, at the very least, its reception) may well be (inadvertently of course) even more problematic than that of Hengel, because the former's use of the 'conventional' methods of the field as a Jewish interpreter provides the illusion of the 'value neutrality' of the methods so employed.

Indeed, a figure like Nanos creates significant desire on the part of Christian theo-historical interpreters of early Christianity. There is a desire for Jewishness, a desire for Protestant Paul scholars to be friends with Jews (a desire Hengel himself expresses [2010]) and a desire for a more authentic Jewish Paul who is given the Jewish stamp of approval by a practicing Jewish scholar employing predominantly Protestant methods (employing, no less, these methods better than Protestant scholars themselves). Not unlike the observations made above with respect to Masuzawa's work, the relationship between the self and the other created through conventional methods in the field of early Christian studies *produces* an acceptable Judaism— affirmed by Jewish scholars themselves—in which the other helps bolster the identity and essential commitments of a generally Protestant worldview. Judaism, in that respect, is the 'world religion'. It is not simply that this is an Orientalist reading of Judaism, but that, ultimately, this reading establishes a proximate other, which in turn now affirms the one doing the reading, shoring up the sometimes caving walls of the methodological homes of most scholars of early Christianity. The methods cannot be anti-Jewish if, in effect, the methods are used and accepted by Jewish scholars themselves— or so it is believed. And this use and acceptance then create a substantive desire for the whole home—and the backyard! Our methodological correlations, in this respect, are, in the end, about the creation of our self-identity and the establishment of that necessary relationship with an other that we do not welcome as the 'stranger', but, in effect, most frequently assimilate to our very selves. The desire, then, is about sustaining and nurturing our own homes, irrespective of the costs to others.

We do not think one can emphasize strongly enough the radical effects such conceptions of methodology—as neutral, natural, objective—have had on the construction of Jews and Judaism in cultural, religious, and political thinking, especially in the post-Reformation period. In the logic and structure of our current methodological *habitus*, the body of the Jew becomes something like the body of text: it can be manipulated, regulated, ordered and objectified. Indeed, its origin can be delineated; its transmission, including deviations and deformations, can be traced out; and its essential nature can be recovered and redeployed. And in those moments, the landscape of early Christianity—that not-so-foreign territory—comes to life precisely against this highly textualized Jewish body. Judaism hence emerges as that thing which Christianity is not—and could never be. But the method that distinguishes and divides, that separates out and contains, that stabilizes and regulates—that method would continue even after the Western world stands in post-Shoah horror. And the question of ethics and politics, it seems to us, rests in the evaluation of the method as much as if not more than the assessment of its usage or of its instrumentality. We say this because the instrumentality of the method always bears an imprint of the original impulse—of that desire for purity and wholeness through the creation of alterity and distinction. Thus, since 'home is where the heart is', the methods we deploy for historical study say much about where our hearts lie.

To illustrate our point further, we turn now to the fairly striking appearance of Jörg Frey on the contemporary scholarly scene in New Testament and early Christian studies, whose apparent (desire for) home(land) aptly betrays some important contours of the broad strokes we have been painting above. Frey, perhaps more than any other scholar working in the discipline at this moment, has participated in the orchestration of historical and theological—or rather, theo-historical—intellectual machinery that is unrivaled and unparalleled in the field (although we note that the final determination of such claims can be assessed only years out, in retrospect). Frey is one of the last students that Martin Hengel produced, and, more than any of his genealogical 'brothers', has dedicated himself to the preservation and perpetuation of the 'father's' intellectual and theological legacies. Indeed, it is evident that Hengel himself passed on his scholarly mantle and blessing to Frey, who has shown himself to be the good and faithful 'son' and heir. And why shouldn't he be? Our concern here is not with the personhood or personality of Frey or any other scholar. We cannot criticize or fault Frey for his unwavering fidelity to a Hengelian tradition of scholarship *per se*, or, put another way, we cannot blame the son for moving into the father's home. Rather, we are more interested in what the perpetuation of that tradition, now in an adapted and reconfigured form, might look like for the field as a whole in light of the methodological reflections we offer below.

Since we are invested in the epistemological effects of scholarly discourses and the ethical implications embedded therein, it stands to reason that our concerns should start at home, so to speak, with the allegiances made through scholarly interaction. And so, as Hengel forged relationships and intercontinental alliances by inviting scholars of all ranks and nationalities into his legendary den in his home, Frey has followed suit. For Frey, however, the forging of relationships is on a much grander scale, which includes running numerous conferences at his home institution where senior and junior scholars alike are invited to share their work around various themes related to early Christian literature. (As of the writing of this essay, we are still waiting for our invitations!) Alongside the home-grown conference circuit on the European continent, reinforcement of the allegiances made there through regular participation in larger international guild activity, and a variety of publications that have come out of these gatherings, Frey is also the editor of the Wissenschaftliche Untersuchungen zum Neuen Testament series, published by Mohr Siebeck, the 'flagship' series with which every New Testament scholar is familiar. With access once mediated by Hengel, Frey's leadership has taken this series to a new ideological level by providing a rather large platform for, and the legitimizing *wissenschaftliche* stamp on, scholarship that is fairly theologically conservative and traditionally dogmatic in its conclusions, some of which displays a seeming historical amnesia about the field and is questionable in terms of its exegetical merit by guild standards. Frey also belongs to other editorial boards, and definitely, with a small group of collaborators who appear to share a similar theo-historical vision as well as comparable aspirations, has embarked on a level of theo-historical publication and scholarly industriousness that is reshaping the topography of the study of early Christianity in both Europe and the United States.[7] Ambition and hospitality are, again, nothing to criti-

---

7. We would also note that the often uniquely contoured scholarly pockets outside of German and North American contexts, such as the English and Scandinavian traditions, are similarly succumbing to the 'sweet wine' offered by Frey.

cize; in fact, we would say that Frey models an intentional international hospitality rarely seen in scholarship across disciplines. However, we are also wary of the long-term effects of such endeavors as those orchestrated by Frey and his colleagues. One is reminded here of Adorno's cautious words about the 'culture industry':

> The concepts of order which it [the culture industry] hammers into human beings are always those of the status quo. They remain unquestioned, unanalyzed and undialectically presupposed, even if they no longer have any substance for those who accept them. In contrast to the Kantian, the categorical imperative of the culture industry no longer has anything in common with freedom. It proclaims: you shall conform, without instruction as to what; conform to that which exists anyway, and to that which everyone thinks anyway as a reflex of its power and omnipresence (Adorno 1991: 104).

Indeed, as Adorno later states, 'The total effect of the culture industry is one of anti-enlightenment, in which, as Horkheimer and I have noted, enlightenment, that is the progressive technical domination of nature, becomes mass deception and is turned into a means for fettering consciousness' (Adorno 1991: 106). The theo-historical program that Frey supports, encourages and manages may appear to many scholars as a 'natural' development in the field that has no particular agenda. Admittedly, there does seem to be a certain randomness to this larger so-called scientific historical program apart from simply trying to 'tell the story of Christianity' or 'get to the bottom' of the great mysteries that underlie the origin and development of early Christian theological impulses and literary production. Still, we propose here, that more is going on than meets the eye.

The disciplinary contributions and merits of Frey's own published scholarly corpus, which rivals the most prolific exegetes of the last century and spans a range of subfields from Johannine eschatology to Pauline literature to Qumran studies, is not of primary concern here and, in some ways, this output is much less important than the scholarly ties that Frey would, by all appearances, be seeking to forge. Nevertheless, brief attention to two exemplary entries might help illuminate some of our argument regarding his larger influence as a 'man of the (Hengelian) house', or, rather, as a chief proponent of a Hengelian legacy now reconfigured in a different historical moment and sociopolitical scene than in Hengel's periods of greatest productivity. Frey's recent essay (2007) concerning the apostle Paul's Jewish identity, for instance, provides an important glimpse into his larger project, its *Heimat* methodological orientation and home-ward boundedness, and ethical implications in the world beyond scholarship. On the surface, this essay is simply a brief reflection about how scholarship might locate and understand Paul's Jewishness, given all the different Jewish options available in the ancient world. Methodologically, this argument would appear to be in complete agreement with the contributions of, say, the New Perspective in Pauline studies, which is situated in the recent history of New Testament scholarship as a range of responses to how Christianity's 'second founder' might be interpreted and appropriated in relation to Judaism given the pernicious historical uses of New Testament texts to justify violence and other means of anti-Jewish sentiment and oppression, particularly during and after the Holocaust.

While the New Perspective might have its own shortcomings, the consensus in this scholarly trajectory is around a more responsible interpretative framework for Paul through aligning his activity within, and not against, ancient Judaism(s). Along these lines, Frey seems to have no problem with thinking about Paul as a Jewish person; it is the 'type' of Jew he proposes Paul to be that is at issue, and in his essay he goes to great lengths to distinguish Paul *qua* Jew from other, more legalistic types. One can readily perceive why Frey, along with many other scholars who do not, in the end, fully acknowledge or value the insights of the New Perspective, would make this move in terms of seeking to keep Paul Jewish but also to make him unlike a particular conception of Judaism that, in the German Protestant tradition of interpretation, Paul himself criticizes from a purportedly 'Christian' understanding that is often configured through a 'converted' self-representation and a new theological program such as 'justification by faith'. To that end, in this essay Frey identifies Paul as a 'cosmopolitan Jew', that is to say, someone who is indeed Jewish, but also one who 'fits in' within a larger non-Jewish, 'hellenized' Greco-Roman society. In other words, this Paul is an ethnic foreigner in a dominant colonial society who manages to adapt and to assimilate to that larger culture, unlike the other Jews in his midst, perhaps even some 'Jewish Christians', who refuse to 'get along' and are, at the end of the day, 'stubborn'. Leaving such stubbornness behind, Paul, and the 'Gentile Christians' who are naturally the object of his so-called mission, evolve as a community with seamless ties to their larger milieu. As the 'fittest' in this environment, they ultimately are the ones who survive.

Such a proposal about Paul's identity and immediate environment engenders a significant resonance with Hengelian views on the relationship of early Christianity to Judaism, although, to be sure, Frey's Jewish apostle is not appropriated in precisely the same way. Perhaps not unlike Grundmann's assessment of Jesus being situated in a non-Jewish Galilee, Frey claims that Paul's relationship to Judaism is to be mediated through his ethnic assimilation to the decidedly non-Jewish city and social life of the Roman Empire, and in so doing he affirms a semiotic, if not genealogical, link between the two scholarly epochs. We are aware that, regarding specific historical and theological details, Frey and Grundmann are saying something different from each other, in distinct historical contexts, and with divergent social and political outcomes. Even as this is the case, the hermeneutical effort to create and sustain a distance of early Christianity from a particular 'type of Judaism' is evident in both scholarly configurations. Indeed, Grundmann's Jesus and Frey's Paul might be said to be Jewish non-Jews, or more civilized/evolved Jews than their corrupt contemporaries—albeit the former might be more pastorally inclined and the latter more urbanely so. Nevertheless, the (re)positioning of Jesus and/or Paul as 'better', and *therefore in hierarchical relationship to or in a position to supersede*, the lesser Jews of their day represents an important proximity between these two arguments that is significant for methodological reflection, and it is that larger signification that matters for the purposes of this essay.

Even more recently, Frey has undergone somewhat of an evolution himself and, in addition to merely assuming editorial leadership of a long-standing flagship book series, has been involved in co-founding a new academic journal project that carries potentially significant methodological consequences for the study of the New Testament and early Christianity. Frey 'of Zurich', together with an international team including Clare Rothschild 'of Chicago', Jens Schröter 'of Berlin', and Francis Watson 'of Durham', has inaugurated *Early Christianity* (published by Mohr Siebeck) with a jointly and boldly written 'Editorial Manifesto' (Frey *et al.* 2010), which is both interesting and rare in the field. The stated aims of the manifesto, which we must admit sparked our own interest in Frey as a 'player' in the contemporary New Testament and early Christian studies arena, are wide-ranging and multivalent. One of the most transparent agenda items is the editors' desire to stem a 'drift' that has happened between English-language and German-language scholarship in the name of *Wissenschaft*. At the same time, there is also something of a declaration of 'war' on that scholarship having connections to methodological shifts represented by the deployment of, for example, postmodernist and poststructuralist literary analysis. *Early Christianity*'s manifesto makes it apparent that this inaugural editorial board, through and with this journal's proceedings, intends to usher in a new period of scholarly activity that is in essence a 'return' to something from an earlier time. Whether to a more robust form of scholarship or a more pure form of analyzing the New Testament as evidence of the origins and uniqueness of Christianity, the manifesto insinuates that something important has been lost in the methodological morass of contemporary studies of the New Testament and early Christianity—and what is lost should be recovered and reinvigorated.

While we might be inclined to agree with such a sentiment, we would add that the manifesto reads as somewhat nostalgic not for methodological clarity or accountability but perhaps for a time when scholars were 'men', or, at the very least, simply 'real' interpreters with explicit theological and historical commitments. We are especially curious about the manifesto's dialectical movement between radical inclusion and an equally radical disavowal, between 'friendship' and 'war'. Such an articulation resonates with someone like Hadrian, the savvy Roman emperor from the second century CE, who, according to secondhand literary sources and visual representation, both offered up discourses (and acts) of friendship and collaboration with subject peoples and also, in that same moment, used such alliances to aid in his fateful war on the restive province of Judea. We use Hadrian here purely as a metaphor, if only to underscore that acts of 'friendship' can be intimately related to declarations of 'war'.[8]

Furthermore, we observe that, for the group of scholars involved in founding and editing *Early Christianity*, there is an acknowledgment that the study of the New Testament and early Christianity has made methodological maneuvers that now position a more traditional Hengelian interpretative strategy as but one among many frameworks available to contemporary scholarship. Such maneuvers include attention to the discovery of new texts and other artifacts, reflection on the tasks of hermeneutics and the incorporation of theoretical discourses into critical exegetical work. The collaborators of the manifesto have, additionally, conflated the usually safeguarded 'New Testament' with a whole array of literature typically separated out and isolated as 'noncanonical'. In an undoubtedly brilliant move of appropriation and assimilation, and in the name of 'rethinking New Testament studies', Frey and the other editors of *Early Christianity* have claimed all early Christian literature as part of a legitimately 'friendly' theological enterprise of theo-historical hermeneutics. In other words, there is *no one context* for the literature of early Christianity, no one congregation out of which it arises, but the complex of writing, reading and *Sitz im Leben* is admittedly multivalent and multicontextual, even phenomenologically oriented. In some respects, then, every 'evolved' New Testament exegete or scholar of early Christianity can fit within the paradigm set up in the manifesto—we can all be extended the hand of 'friendship' on these terms. Further, there is no real threat to the core theological identity of early Christianity from, say, Gnostic texts or the apocryphal Gospels and Acts. All these 'barbarians' are welcome at the table—and, no doubt, 'Paul, the cosmopolitan Jew' is the one at the head.

---

8. We quite emphatically intend 'war' to be read in a nonliteral, metaphorical sense, signifying a scholarly enterprise of seeking to root out a troubling force that has, supposedly, contaminated scholarly agendas and brought about a certain impurity or contagion in the field. While we have criticized poststructuralist methodological commitments above by essentially suggesting that they have not gone far enough, and certainly have not gone as far as they think they have in terms of offering a challenge to conventional scholarship, we ourselves, as is evident from this essay, are probably located somewhere near or perhaps in the 'province of Judea' according to what we might call a 'Frey-ian topography of scholarship'.

Of course, as Frey's larger methodological mission indicates, and as the manifesto notes, at *this table* there is a 'welcome' theological core to the scholarly content. We might not be evaluating and judging that theological content at all times, and yet the primary criterion for the framing of early Christianity, if one is to enjoy this meal, must be theologically oriented (aptly stated in the latest issue of *Early Christianity* by Deines [2011]). It could be said that such a shift removes the final hurdle in the Hengelian trajectory: Tübingen *Tendenz* criticism. Herein there is *no final conflict* and *theology needs no justification;* the mere presence of Francis Watson on the journal's editorial board makes this agenda palpable, as he has been so insistent in his own writings on the crucial role of theological interpretation as a core principle of New Testament studies. And it is here where we are reminded again of Adorno, who aptly states about such individuals:

> They only unroll the whole spiritual paraphernalia because they were not allowed to vent their frenzy and fury anywhere else, and they are ready to reconvert the struggle against the enemy within into a deed, believing as they do that the latter was there 'in the beginning' in any case. Their prototype is Luther, the inventor of inwardness, throwing his ink-pot at the devil, who does not exist, and already meaning it for the peasants and the Jews (Adorno 1978: 134-35).

Of course, the 'peasants' and 'Jews' are no longer those of Luther's day (or the ancient world for that matter), but we cannot exclude the likelihood that such figures as 'peasants' and 'Jews' continue to exist in the socio-political scholarly imagination, and it is the existence of such that should give us serious pause. While there is a common table to which everyone—contemporary scholars willing to practice 'legitimate' and 'pure' historical methods, and ancient writers/texts/communities offering differing theological interpretations with respect to Christian concepts and themes—is invited, there is still an implied hierarchical seating arrangement that must be obeyed: there are rules to dining in this home. And, to be sure, there are purity laws, ones that would undoubtedly still cause 'Peter' to leave 'that table', and perhaps justifiably so.[9]

---

9. Although space does not permit a more elaborate treatment of this very important theme, it bears noting that another element excluded from 'the table' is a decidedly nontheological approach to the religion and literature of the ancient world. The legacy of scholars like William Wrede and others who sought to create a distinction between 'religion' and 'theology', and between 'theology' and 'history', is here collapsed in this emergent framework offered up by Frey and his comrades (on the former's legacy, see Penner 2005: 7-10). This is a critically important hermeneutical trajectory that is herein being suppressed or, more precisely, reconfigured, since part of Wrede's program is in fact taken up by the manifesto, particularly in its eradication of the boundaries between New Testament literature and other early Christian texts. It is the Wredian legacy, however, that would prevent or at least intervene in this Frey-ian program, which runs the

There is much more to say about Frey's influence, his ideas, and his assured legacy. There is also much to explore about his reconfiguration of Hengel's earlier agenda in a much more persuasive logical form, which, in this current social and political climate, can be highly seductive and persuasive to scholars of many different nationalities and countries. Our most substantive concern at present, in this meta-reflection on methodological issues in the study of the New Testament and early Christianity, is Frey's ability, with seeming ease, to assimilate all types of differing forms and formulations of scholarship into a common vision and project. Indeed, as we note in our conclusion to this essay, we consider the underlying assumptions behind this project, behind the *habitus* that structures and encloses it, to be both potentially dangerous and, we propose, also somewhat insidious. At the very least, we submit, the project is methodologically regressive.

However bold a claim our readers might take the above to be, and for whatever reasons they might do so, it is our position that, as humanistically grounded, publicly inclined scholars of conscience, we acknowledge the imperative to constantly raise sets of ethical questions that aim to get all of us to think about what kinds of selves and others are produced by inhabiting our homes in the ways that we do. We therefore deem it unethical to avoid raising a series of critical ethical challenges about the work that Frey and others are doing in a seeming quest to raise a 'standard' for the field to follow. Scholars of conscience cannot and ought not to stand idly by, even as many scholars at present are doing just that or, at the very least, wanting to know 'what is all the fuss about? So long as we get to present at conferences and get our ideas published, what's the problem?' In our imagination, and in the home in which we choose to make our scholarly lives, scholarship is about cultivating human flourishing, about giving an account of ourselves, who we want to be, what kinds of others we want to construct, and what kinds of relations we choose to have with other humans and the world. Let us be clear: Frey and his collaborators are not 'evil' or 'wicked' or involved in some kind of cosmic war between the 'darkness' of their methods and the 'lightness' of others. Like all of us, though, they do construct and deploy frameworks that, perhaps unwittingly on their end, perpetuate highly problematic conceptions of the self, other selves, and relationships between the two. Further, perhaps most unethically, the *Early Christianity* editors' manifesto betrays a methodological position that precludes having to offer an account of themselves, failing to represent their set of premises and pre-

---

risk of fully returning (perhaps 'handing over' or 'back', even if unwittingly) early Christian studies to the field of dogmatics. This possibility alone should create great dis-ease among scholars of early Christianity who are inclined to eschew theological methodological commitments, and hopefully will foment resistance to these current and fast-becoming-dominant trends in scholarship.

scriptions as in any way responsible to communities of accountability in the present. We are, as invested members of the same guild, challenging them, and all of us, to acknowledge such responsibility.

Concluding Meditations: Leaving Home to Go Home?

In what follows we return to Jörg Frey's broader program for the formation of scholarly alliances toward a rehabilitation of traditional scholarship, and, in so doing, we offer a few concluding points for reflection and some questions for further thought. *First*, and foremost, it is our view that to be attentive to method means to give an account of one's self. The recent desire for a *Wissenschaft* of New Testament and early Christian studies that is linked to a more traditional theological German historical program and not devoid, moreover, of nationalist impulses (see below), is, essentially, a desire to (re)turn to a methodological position that 'needs no defense'. This desire evidences a nostalgia for homes and neighborhoods of an earlier time, perhaps when the structure of life was simpler, more concrete, more stable, when there was a clear-cut political and social identity, or at least the rhetoric thereof. Moreover, to make the case (or simply to take the stance) that something needs no defense is a methodological choice in its own right, a choice shaped by social and historical circumstances. That choice is not self-evident. It is, rather, an arbitrary choice, a faith commitment, if you will, to a set of propositions that are, ultimately, a product of the material world we occupy.

Second, such a decision about the positioning of a *wissenschaftliche* program says more about the material circumstances of the person(s) making such claims than the 'ancient world' as such. In this sense, the designation of subdisciplines as 'New Testament' or 'Christian origins' are really just red herrings, or, as Adorno would have it, anachronisms, deployed in the service of articulating a present (Butler 2005: 8-9). Studying the New Testament and early Christianity, then, is, methodologically speaking, never simply about giving an account of the ancient world. Nor is it about giving an innocent account of our interpretations of the ancient world. All discussion of the ancient world is about negotiating the relationships in our world through debating relationships in and to that world. Studying the New Testament and early Christianity, then, must also give an account of how modern scholars use the ancient world to construct a home in the present.

Third, the recent identification of 'others' (e.g. postcolonial exegetes, feminists, 'reception history' scholars) as representing a 'decline' in scholarship and the realignment of *wissenschaftliche* New Testament and early Christian Studies with theological interests represents an earnest effort to reposition current scholarship within a framework that resonates with scholarship of nearly one hundred years ago, a form of scholarship that, despite its flaws, is believed to be more pure and more concrete in its assessment of the ancient world. As the 'Editorial Manifesto' for *Early Christianity* or the identification of Paul as a 'cosmopolitan Jew' suggests, a resurgence of theological investment is to use the language of 'science' and 'authority' to create power hierarchies, with those making such claims positioned at the top. Scholars of conscience cannot ignore such hierarchy-making agendas.

Fourth, since all method is occasioned by the historical and social contexts in which methodological questions arise, there is no method outside of a scholar's own social and historical context, including contexts imbued with nationalist tendencies. The shift we propose is to move from confessional notions of personal or social identity (e.g. woman, colonial subject) to a response to the conditions of the present that make certain configurations of personal or social identity possible, that is to say, a response to the world now. Thus, in terms of a set of questions, we might ask what kinds of circumstances produce a methodological interest in the assertion and stabilization of 'home' in any number of ways. The desire for a 'home' from the past, renovated for the present, might well be an interesting shift in scholarship. But our task is to pose the challenge: Why in this moment? Why in this way? Thinking dialectically for a moment, but without any assertions of 'improvement' or 'evolution', it is intriguing to see how the Third Reich positing of a non-Jewish Jesus and a non-Jewish Paul was confronted with its oppositional premise of a Jewish Jesus and a Jewish Paul. A synthesis, however, emerges in the work of Hengel and is now more fully entrenched in the scholarship of Frey. Such a synthetic position thus seeks to mediate between what was essential about the earlier epoch of scholarship (e.g., the superiority of Protestant Christianity over a perceived legalistic set of values, be they Jewish or Catholic) and that which is critical about the later epoch (e.g., a negative judgment on the political claims and outcomes of the Third Reich). In other words, one could argue that Frey, building on Hengel's legacy, wants the 'best' of both worlds, or wants to build a comfortable home from two sets of blueprints.

But there is more. One cannot exclude the effect that the current social and political situation in Northern Europe might have, even if unwittingly, on the formulation of such paradigms. In Germany, for instance, both the chancellor and other high-profile leaders have recently and publicly discussed the 'failure of multiculturalism' in conversations about possible socioeconomic futures in troubled times. A continued Muslim and Turkish presence, in particular, has posed what is perceived to be a significant challenge to Northern European principles of liberal democracy. The apparent 'stubbornness', which in this context is understood to be the willful *lack of integration* on the part of these immigrant populaces, who were expected to assimilate into the larger social and political fabric, is seen as a serious threat to a coherent political-national identity. In this light, Frey's 'stubborn

Jews' opposed to Paul's 'cosmopolitan' form of Judaism bears a striking resemblance. We are not intuiting Frey's state of mind or his position on any of these political realities. We are noting, rather, that the increasing scholarly interest in Frey's programs is arising within this very context, and that context has to be taken into account in terms of assessing the construction, even if implicit and unconscious, of the formal logic and structure of the methods employed in this research.[10]

Tensions about nationalism and identity in Europe are not new; they have been going on for decades (see, e.g., Peck 1992; Morley and Robins 1990; Butler 2003a), if not for centuries. And, to be sure, such conflicts are not limited to Europe. In the United States, for instance, the rise of the 'Tea Party' and of harsh anti-illegal immigrant laws (such as in the state of Arizona), alongside a highly vitriolic divide between a 'right' and 'left' in social and political discourses, evidences a similar structural desire for a purer and simpler time, when there was a more cohesive national and social identity among those who were called 'Americans' and less 'disenfranchisement' from a perceived time of more equality and unity among the 'people'. It should, thus, come as no surprise that we see at this time, in both Europe and the United States, a desire for purer forms of New Testament scholarship and studies of early Christianity, for an older, more reliable logic of historical inquiry, for a more honest theological *Heimat*, for a cultivation of nostalgia for a period of more cohesive and unified social identities. The relationship between methodologies for the study of the New Testament and early Christianity and these larger social and political contexts is, without a doubt, profoundly complex. There is not a simple correspondence, and there is no one to blame here. We would not want to be read as suggesting that there is. Nevertheless, a relationship between method and context in this case likely does exist, and it falls on scholars of conscience to begin to raise a set of questions that would explore the interrelationship between the methods that we use for the study of the past and the social and political realities in which we live. Without doing so, we might, willingly or unwittingly, feed into a complex of global national, political and sociocultural configurations that could, potentially, prove to be quite unsettling to many of us when we think about them on our own, alone at home, in our armchairs.

---

10. It falls to another venue to discuss further our own take on the nature of that 'formal logic and structure' in the methodologies of much of this scholarship on the New Testament and early Christianity. We would suggest that one fruitful area of investigation, though, would be to look more closely at the connection between philology and its embedded logics of identity and opposition. Text-critical methods similarly embody logics of social identity and historical development. And these logics, to be sure, also have a politics.

Fifth, and finally, we raise the matter to which Adorno, at the opening of this essay, drew our attention: there is a correlation between a desire for higher morality and ethics and a willingness to be uncomfortable in one's own home, perhaps, even being willing to become homeless (cf. Morley and Robins 1990). At the very least, we might recognize that the desire for home itself is shaped by our present and is not somehow a moral obligation or personal privilege that exists without a context. Granted, our pushing for a homelessness in methodology also has to be understood as an ethical stance that is fully forged in the present. There is, ultimately, in the framework we have articulated in this essay, no outside of the present. One might raise the question whether, then, there is any outside of 'home'. Our response to that is a measured yes, fully realizing that the conditions of our epistemological commitments make it very difficult to enact such. Admittedly, it is easier to be discomforted at home than it is to conceptualize a world without a home. Yet it is possible, we submit, to reimagine a world and a series of methods in which homelessness, and not homeboundedness, functions as a mediating force in the production of the self, the other and the relationship between the two. In this framework, one is always already a stranger to the self, and the other thus stands similarly as a stranger. The relationship of stranger to stranger, in the absence of home, homeland and *Heimat*, creates interesting possibilities for imagining not just better relationships between individuals but a more just world.[11] Of course, it also poses challenges to many if not most forms of liberal democratic visions of the future. And, to be sure, such constructions of the self and other in a context of homelessness constitute a major threat to methodologies in the study of the New Testament and early Christianity that are insistent on saving home, homeland, and *Heimat* at all costs.

---

11. We want to single out Marc Ellis (2010) as a particularly profound thinker in this regard. Like Edward Said, Ellis has accented 'exile' as a hermeneutical and ethical framework through which to view one's relationship to the world and, out of that, one's constructions of justice. In his more radicalized version of 'homelessness' as 'exile', Ellis is clear to articulate the complicity and compromise that exist in this state as well. There is no pure or simple existence 'outside' of home—it is always complicated, it is always a matter of ever vigilant negotiation of the 'troubled waters'.

BIBLIOGRAPHY

Abbott, L.
 1871 'The Recovery of Jerusalem', *Harper's New Monthly* (July), p. 206.
 1896 'Christianity and Democracy', *Outlook* 53: 97-100.
Adan-Bayewitz, D.
 1993 *Common Pottery in Roman Galilee: A Study of Local Trade* (Jerusalem: Bar-Ilan University Press).
Adan-Bayewitz, D., and I. Perlman
 1990 'The Local Trade of Sepphoris in the Roman Period', *Israel Exploration Journal* 40: 153-72.
Adorno, T.
 1978 *Minima Moralia: Reflections from Damaged Life* (trans. E.F.N. Jephcott; London: Verso).
 1991 *The Culture Industry: Selected Essays on Mass Culture* (ed. J.M. Bernstein; London: Routledge).
Aharoni, Y.
 1979 *The Land of the Bible: A Historical Geography* (trans. and ed. A.F. Rainey; Philadelphia: Westminster Press, revised and enlarged edn).
Ahlström, G.W.
 1986 *Who Were the Israelites?* (Winona Lake, IN: Eisenbrauns).
Albright, W.F.
 1921 'Mohammedan and Christian Sanctuaries', *Bulletin of the American School of Oriental Research* 4: 4-5.
 1922 'Archaeological Discovery in the Holy Land', *Bibliotheca Sacra* 79: 401–17.
 1923 'Rediscovering Ancient Palestine', *Sunday School Times* 65: 7-8.
 1924 'Notes from the School in Jerusalem', *Bulletin of the American Schools of Oriental Research* 15: 12-13.
 1932 *The Archaeology of Palestine and the Bible* (New York: Fleming H. Revell).
 1933 'How to Study the Archaeology of Palestine', *Bulletin of the American Schools of Oriental Research* 52 (December): 12-15.
 1947 'Chester Charlton McCown: An Appreciation', in *An Indexed Bibliography of the Writings of Chester Charlton McCown* (Berkeley, CA: Pacific School of Religion).
 1957 *From the Stone Age to Christianity* (Garden City, NY: Doubleday, rev. edn).
 1967 *Archaeology and the Religion of Israel* (Garden City, NY: Doubleday, rev. edn).
Alcalay, A.
 1993 *After Jews and Arabs: Remaking Levantine Culture* (Minneapolis: University of Minnesota Press).

Anderson, A.
   1997   *The Treatise of the Three Impostors and the Problem of Enlightenment* (Lanham, MD: Rowman and Littlefield).
Anonymous
   1901   'Gadara', in *Encyclopaedia Biblica: A Critical Dictionary of the Literary, Political, and Religious History, the Archaeology, Geography, and Natural History of the Bible* (ed. T.K. Cheyne and J. Sutherland Black; London: A. & C. Black), II, 1587-88.
Applebaum, S.
   1976   'Economic Life in Palestine', in *The Jewish People in the First Century: Historical Geography, Political History, Social, Cultural and Religious Life and Institutions* (ed. S. Safrai and M. Stern; Compendia rerum iudicarum ad Novum Testamentum; Philadelphia: Fortress Press), I, 631–700.
Arav, R.
   1988   'Et-Tell and el-Araj', *Israel Exploration Journal* 38: 187-88.
   1997   'Bethsaida', in *Oxford Encyclopedia of Archaeology in the Near East* (ed. E.M. Meyers; New York: Oxford University Press), pp. 302–305.
   2006   'Bethsaida', in *Jesus and Archaeology* (ed. J.H. Charlesworth; Grand Rapids: Eerdmans), pp. 145–66.
Arnal, W.
   2001   *Jesus and the Village Scribes: Galilean Conflicts and the Setting of Q* (Minneapolis: Fortress Press).
   2005   *The Symbolic Jesus: Historical Scholarship, Judaism and the Construction of Contemporary Identity* (London: Equinox).
   2010   'What Branches Grow Out of this Stony Rubbish? Christian Origins and the Study of Religion', *Studies in Religion* 39: 549-72.
Atlas of Israel: Cartography, Physical and Human Geography
   1985   (Tel Aviv: Survey of Israel, 3rd edn).
Aune, D.
   1997   'Jesus and Cynics in First Century Palestine: Some Critical Considerations', in *Hillel and Jesus: Comparative Studies of Two Major Religious Leaders* (ed. J.H. Charlesworth and L.L. Johns; Minneapolis: Fortress Press), pp. 176-92.
Aviam, M.
   2004   'Borders between Jews and Gentiles in the Galilee', in *Jews, Pagans and Christians in the Galilee: 25 Years of Archaeological Excavations and Surveys. Hellenistic to Byzantine Periods* (Land of Galilee, 1; Rochester: University of Rochester Press), pp. 9-21.
   2007   'Distribution Maps of Archaeological Data from the Galilee: An Attempt to Establish Zones Indicative of Ethnicity and Religious Affiliation', in *Religion, Ethnicity, and Identity in Ancient Galilee: A Region in Transition* (ed. J. Zangenberg, H.W. Attridge and D.B. Martin; Wissenschaftliche Untersuchungen zum Neuen Testament, 210; Tübingen: Mohr Siebeck), pp. 115-32.
Avi-Yonah, M.
   1976   'Hammat Gader', in *Encyclopedia of Archaeological Excavations in the Holy Land* (ed. M. Avi-Yonah and E. Stern; Jerusalem: Israel Exploration Society/ Massada Press, 1976), II, 469-73.
   1977   *The Holy Land from the Persian to the Arab Conquests (536 B.C. to A.D. 640): A Historical Geography* (Grand Rapids: Baker Book House, rev. edn).

Bagehot, W.
1905   *Physics and Politics: Or Thoughts on the Application of the Principles of 'Natural Selection' and 'Inheritance' to Political Society* (London: Kegan Paul).

Bailey, K.E.
2008   *Jesus through Middle Eastern Eyes: Cultural Studies in the Gospels* (Downers Grove, IL: InterVarsity Press).

Baird, W.
1922   *History of New Testament Research: From Deism to Tübingen*, II (Minneapolis: Fortress Press).

Baly, D.
1974   *The Geography of the Bible* (Guildford: Lutterworth, rev. edn).

Barton, G.
1904   *A Year's Wanderings in Bible Lands* (Philadelphia: Ferris & Leach).
1916   *Archaeology and the Bible* (Philadelphia: American Sunday-School Union).

Bastomsky, S.J.
1974   'Abnimos and Oenomaus: A Question of Identity', *Apeiron* 8: 57-61.

Bauer, W.
1967   'Jesus der Galiläer', in *Aufsätze und Kleine Schriften* (ed. W. Bauer; Tübingen: J.C.B. Mohr), pp. 91-108.

Baynton-Williams, A., and M. Baynton-Williams
2006   *New Worlds: Maps from the Age of Discovery* (London: Quercus).

Becker, C.L.
1932   *The Heavenly City of the Eighteenth Century Philosophers* (New Haven: Yale University Press).

Bekker-Nielsen, T.
2002   'Fish in the Ancient Economy', in *Ancient History Matters: Studies Presented to Jens Erik Skysgaard on his Seventieth Birthday* (ed. K. Aslani and V. Gabrielsen; Rome: L'Erma di Bretschneider), pp. 29–37.

Ben-Arieh, Y.
1989   'Nineteenth-century Historical Geographies of the Holy Land' *Journal of Historical Geography* 15: 69–79.

Berlinerblau, J.
2002   'Poor Bird, Not Knowing Which Way to Fly': Biblical Scholarship's Marginality, Secular Humanism, and the Laudable Occident', *Biblical Interpretation* 10: 267-304.

Berti, S.
1998   'Unmasking the Truth: The Theme of Imposture in Early Modern European Culture, 1660–1730', in *Everything Connects: In Conference with Richard H. Popkin* (ed. J.E. Force and D.S. Katz; Leiden: E.J. Brill).

Besant, W.
1889   *Twenty-One Years' Work in the Holy-Land: (A Record and a Summary) June 22, 1865–June 22, 1886* (London: Palestine Exploration Fund).

Betz, H.D.
1991   'Wellhausen's Dictum "Jesus was not a Christian, but a Jew" in Light of Present Scholarship', *Studia theologica* 45: 83–110.

Blackburn, S.
1994   'Deism', in *The Oxford Dictionary of Philosophy* (Oxford: Oxford University Press), p. 97.

Blanton, W.
    2007   *Displacing Christian Origins: Philosophy, Secularity, and the New Testament* (Chicago: University of Chicago Press).
Bloch, J.
    1952   'Max L. Margolis' Contribution to the History and Philosophy of Judaism', in *Max Leopold Margolis: Scholar and Teacher* (ed. R. Gordis; Philadelphia: Alumni Association of Dropsie College), pp. 53-57.
Blount, C.
    1695   *The Oracles of Reason* (London).
Bolingbroke, Henry St John(Lord Viscount)
    1752   *Letters on the Study and Use of History* (2 vols.; London: printed for A. Millar).
Bornkamm, G.
    1960   *Jesus von Nazareth* (Stuttgart: Kohlhammer).
    1960   *Jesus of Nazareth* (trans. Irene and Fraser McLuskey with James M. Robinson; London: Hodder & Stoughton).
Bossuet, J.B.
    1785   *An Universal History from the Beginning of the World, to the Empire of Charlemagne* (Dublin: printed and sold by R. Marchbank).
Bourdieu, P.
    1977   *Outline of a Theory of Practice* (trans. R. Nice; New York: Cambridge University Press).
Brandon, S.G.F.
    1967   *Jesus and the Zealots: A Study of the Political Factor in Primitive Christianity* (Manchester: Manchester University Press)
    1968   *The Trial of Jesus of Nazareth* (London: B.T. Batsford).
Braudel, F.
    1972   *The Mediterranean and the Mediterranean World in the Age of Philip II,* I (New York: Harper & Row, 2nd rev. edn).
    2002   *The Mediterranean in the Ancient World* (London: Penguin).
Brewster, C.B.
    1910   'The Democratic Ideal and the Christian Church', *North American Review* 191: 302-10.
Brooke, A.E. (ed.)
    1896   *The Commentary of Origen on S. John's Gospel* (Cambridge: Cambridge University Press).
Brown, A.
    1994   'Gospel according to Powell: Christ was Stoned to Death', *Independent* (August 16, 1994).
Brown, C.
    2008   *Jesus in European Protestant Thought: 1778–1860* (Pasadena, CA: Full Seminary Press).
Buber, M.
    1958   *I and Thou* (trans. R.G. Smith; New York: Charles Scribner's Sons).
Burckhardt, J.L.
    1822   *Travels in Syria and the Holy Land* (London: John Murray).
Bushell, T.L.
    1967   *The Sage of Salisbury: Thomas Chubb 1679–1747* (New York: Philosophical Library).

Butler, J.
2003a *Giving an Account of Oneself: A Critique of Ethical Violence* (Assen: Van Gorcum).
2003b 'Reflections on Germany', in *Queer Theory and the Jewish Question* (ed. D. Boyarin, D. Itzkovitz, and A. Pellegrini; New York: Columbia University Press), pp. 395-402.
2005 *Giving an Account of Oneself* (New York: Fordham University Press).
Butlin, R.
1988 'George Adam Smith and the Historical Geography of the Holy Land', *Journal of Historical Geography* 14: 381–404.
Cappelletti, S.
2007 'Non-Jewish Authors on Galilee', in *Religion, Ethnicity, and Identity in Ancient Galilee: A Region in Transition* (ed J. Zangenberg, H.W. Attridge and D.B. Martin; Wissenschaftliche Untersuchungen zum Neuen Testament, 210; Tübingen: Mohr Siebeck), pp. 69–81.
Cassirer, E.
1955 *The Philosophy of the Enlightenment* (trans. Fritz C.A. Koelln and James P. Pettegrove; Boston: Beacon Press).
Cavanaugh, W.T.
2009 *The Myth of Religious Violence: Secular Ideology and the Roots of Modern Conflict* (Oxford: Oxford University Press).
Chamberlain, H.S.
1899 *Die Grundlagen des Neunzehnten Jahrhunderts,* I (Munich: F. Bruckmann).
Champion, J.
1996 'Legislators, Impostors, and the Political Origin of Religion: English Theories of "Imposture" from Stubbe to Toland', in *Heterodoxy, Spinozism and Free Thought in Early Eighteenth-Century Europe* (ed. S. Berti, F. Charles-Daubert and R.H. Popkin; Dordrecht: Kluwer Academic Publishers), pp. 333-56.
Chancey, M.A.
2002 *The Myth of a Gentile Galilee* (Society for New Testament Studies Monograph Series, 118; Cambridge: Cambridge University Press).
2005 *Greco-Roman Culture and the Galilee of Jesus* (Society for New Testament Studies Monograph Series, 134; Cambridge: Cambridge University Press).
Chiat, M.J.S.
1982 *Handbook of Synagogue Architecture* (Brown Judaic Studies, 29; Chico, CA: Scholars Press).
Christie, C.
1998 *Race and Nation: A Reader* (London: I.B. Tauris).
Chubb, T.
1738 *The True Gospel of Jesus Christ Asserted: Wherein Is Shewn What Is and Is Not That Gospel—To Which Is Added a Short Dissertation on Providence* (London: Tho. Cox).
1748 *'Of Divine Revelation in General and of the Divine Original of the Jewish, Mohometan, and Christian Revelations in Particular'*, in *The Posthumous Works of Mr Thomas Chubb: Containing 1. Remarks . . . II. Observations . . . III. The Author's Farewell./.With an Appendix, Including a Postscript . . . To the Whole if prefixed, Some Account of the Author: Written by Himself in Two Volumes* (London: Printed for R. Baldwin, jun.; sold by E. Easton, Sarum), pp. 3-138.

Clarke, D.
    1982   *Descartes' Philosophy of Science* (Manchester: Manchester University Press).
Clermont-Ganneau, C.
    1875a   'Où était Hippos de la Décapole?', *Révue archéologique* 29: 362-69.
    1875b   'The Site of Hippos', *Palestine Exploration Fund* 7: 214-18.
    1887   'Hippos of the Decapolis', *Palestine Exploration Fund* 19: 36-38.
    1897   'Nouvelles inscriptions grecques & romaines de Syrie', in *Études d'archéologie orientale* (Paris: Bouillon), II, 141-50.
    1898a   *Recueil d'archéologie orientale*, II (Paris: Leroux).
    1898b   'Gadara et la Xe legion Fretensis', in Clermont-Ganneau 1898a: 299-302.
    1898c   'Gadara χρηστομουσῖα [*sic*]', in Clermont-Ganneau 1898a: 399.
Cohen, S.J.D.
    1979   *Josephus in Galilee and Rome: His Vita and Development as a Historian* (Columbia Studies in the Classical Tradition, 8; Leiden: E.J. Brill).
Collins, A.
    1713   *A Discourse of Free-Thinking* (London).
    1724   *A Discourse of the Ground and Reasons of the Christian Religion. In two parts . . . To which is prefix'd an apology for free debate and liberty of writing* (London).
Conder, C.R.
    1878   *Tent Work in Palestine: A Record of Discovery and Adventure* (2 vols.; London: Richard Bentley & Son).
Corbo, V.C.
    1977   'Il Mausoleo di Cafarnao', *Studii biblici franciscani liber annuus* 27: 145-55.
Coudert, A.P., *et al.* (eds.)
    1998   *Leibniz, Mysticism and Religion* (Dordrecht: Kluwer Academic Publishers).
Craffert, P.F.
    2008   *The Life of a Galilean Shaman: Jesus of Nazareth in Anthropological-Historical Perspective* (Matrix—the Bible in Mediterranean Context, 3; Eugene, OR: Cascade Books).
Crossan, J.D.
    1991   *The Historical Jesus: The Life of a Mediterranean Jewish Peasant* (San Francisco: HarperSanFrancisco).
    1998   *The Birth of Christianity: Discovering What Happened in the Years Immediately after the Execution of Jesus* (San Francisco: HarperSanFrancisco).
    1999   *The Birth of Christianity: Discovering What Happened in the Years Immediately after the Execution of Jesus* (London: T. & T. Clark International).
Crossan, J.D., and J.L. Reed
    2001   *Excavating Jesus: Beneath the Stones, Behind the Texts* (New York: HarperSanFrancisco).
Crossley, J.G.
    2008   *Jesus in an Age of Terror: Scholarly Projects for a New American Century* (London: Equinox).
Curtis, R.I.
    1991   *Garum and Salsamenta: Production and Commerce in Materia Medica* (Studies in Ancient Medicine, 3; Leiden: E.J. Brill).
Dahl, N.A.
    1953   'Problemet den historiske Jesus', in N.A. Dahl, *Rett laere og kjetterske meninger* (Oslo: Land og Kirke), pp. 152-202.

1991. 'The Problem of the Historical Jesus', in N.A. Dahl, *Jesus the Christ: The Historical Origins of Christological Doctrine* (ed. D.H. Juel; Minneapolis: Fortress Press), pp. 81-111.

Dan, J., Z. Raz, H. Yaalon and H. Koyumidjisky
1975   *Soil Map of Israel* (Tel Aviv: Survey of Israel).

Darnton, R.
1984   'Workers Revolt: The Great Cat Massacre of the Rue Saint-Séverin', in *The Great Cat Massacre and Other Episodes in French Cultural History* (London: Allen Lane), pp. 75-104.

Davies, P.R.
2004   *Whose Bible Is It Anyway?* (London: T. &T. Clark International, 2nd edn).

Davis, J.
1996   *The Landscape of Belief: Encountering the Holy Land in Nineteenth-Century American Art and Culture* (Princeton, NJ: Princeton University Press).

Davis, M.
1995   *America and the Holy Land* (With Eyes Towards Zion, 4; Westport, CT: Praeger).

Dawes, G.W. (ed.)
2000   *The Historical Jesus Quest: Landmarks in the Search for the Jesus of History* (Louisville, KY: Westminster/John Knox Press).

Dawson, J.F.
1966   *Friedrich Schleiermacher: The Evolution of a Nationalist* (Austin, TX: University of Texas Press).

Deines, R.
2011   'Jesus and the Jewish Traditions of His Time', *Early Christianity* 1: 344-71.

Deines, R., V. Leppin and K.-W. Niebuhr (eds.)
2007   *Walter Grundmann: Ein Neutestamentler in Dritten Reich* (Arbeiten zur Kirchen-und Theologiegeschichte, 21; Leipzig: Evangelische Verlagsanstalt).

Descartes, R.
1985a *The Philosophical Writings of Descartes* (ed. and trans. J. Cottingham, R. Stoothoff and D. Murdoch; Cambridge: Cambridge University Press)
1985b 'Discourse on the Method', in Descartes 1985a: I, 109-76.
1985c 'Meditations on First Philosophy', in Descartes 1985a: II, 1-62.

Dickens, C.
1995   *Hard Times* (London: Penguin Books).

Dodd, C.H.
1961   *The Parables of the Kingdom* (London: James Nisbet, rev. edn).

Dorandi, T.
1987   'La patria di Filodemo', *Philologus* 131: 254-56.

Duncan, J., and D. Ley (eds).
1993   *Place, Culture, Representation* (London: Routledge).

Dvorjetski, E.
1992   'Medical Hot Springs in Eretz Israel and in the Decapolis during the Hellenistic, Roman and Byzantine Periods', *ARAM Periodical* 4: 425-49.

Edwards, D.R.
1992   'The Socio-Economic and Cultural Ethos of the Lower Galilee in the First Century: Implications for the Nascent Jesus Movement', in *The Galilee in Late Antiquity* (ed. L.I. Levine; New York: Jewish Theological Seminary of America), pp. 53–73.

Ehrman, B.
    2008   *The New Testament: A Historical Introduction to the Early Christian Writings* (Oxford: Oxford University Press, 4th edn).
Elliott, N.
    2008   *The Arrogance of Nations: Reading Romans in the Shadow of Empire* (Paul in Critical Contexts; Minneapolis: Fortress Press).
Ellis, M.
    2010   'Exile With/Out God: A Jewish Commentary in Memory of Edward Said', in *Edward Said: A Legacy of Emancipation and Representation* (ed. A. Iskandar and H. Rustom; Berkeley: University of California Press), pp. 354-65.
Elmer, I.
    2009   *Paul, Jerusalem, and the Judaisers: The Galatian Crisis in its Broadest Historical Context* (Wissenschaftliche Untersuchungen zum Neuen Testament, 2.258; Tübingen: Mohr Siebeck).
Epstein, C.
    1993   'Hippos', in *The New Encyclopedia of Excavations in the Holy Land* (ed. E. Stern; Jerusalem: Carta), II, 634-36.
Evans, R.J.
    2000   *In Defence of History* (London: Granta, 2nd edn).
Farrelly, E.
    2008   *Blubberland: The Dangers of Happiness* (Cambridge, MA: MIT Press).
Fassbeck, G., S. Fortner, A. Rottloff and J. Zangenberg (eds.)
    2003   *Leben am See Gennesaret: Kulturgeschichtliche Entdeckungen in einer biblischen Region* (Sonderband Antike Welt; Mainz: von Zabern).
Faust, A.
    2006   *Israel's Ethnogenesis: Settlement, Interaction, Expansion and Resistance* (London: Equinox).
Fiensy, D.A.
    2007   *Jesus the Galilean: Soundings in a First Century Life* (Piscataway, NJ: Gorgias Press).
Finkelstein, L., et al.
    1941   *Science, Philosophy, and Religion: A Symposium* (New York: Conference on Science, Philosophy and Religion in their Relation to the Democratic Way of Life).
Finley, J.H.
    1919   *A Pilgrim in Palestine: Being an Account of Journeys on Foot by the First American Pilgrim after General Allenby's Recovery of the Holy Land* (New York: Charles Scribner's Sons).
Finnie, D.
    1967   *Pioneers East: The Early American Experience in the Middle East* (Cambridge, MA: Harvard University Press).
Fitzgerald, J.T.
    2004   'Gadara: Philodemus' Native City', in *Philodemus and the New Testament World* (ed. J.T. Fitzgerald, D. Obbink and G.S. Holland; Supplements to *Novum Testamentum,* 111; Leiden: E.J. Brill), pp. 343-97.
Fitzgerald, T.
    2007   *Discourse on Civility and Barbarity: A Critical History of Religion and Related Categories* (Oxford: Oxford University Press).
Flusser, D.
    1968   *Jesus in Selbstzeugnissen und Bilddokumenten* (Reinbek bei Hamburg: Rowohlt).

Flusser, D., in collaboration with R.S. Notley.
1998   *Jesus* (Jerusalem: Magnes Press, 2nd augmented edn).
Fogarty, G.P., S.J.
1989   *American Catholic Biblical Scholarship: A History from the Early Republic to Vatican II* (New York: Harper & Row).
Fortner, S.
1999   'The Fishing Implements and Maritime Activities of Bethsaida-Julias (et-Tell)', in *Bethsaida: A City by the North Shore of the Sea of Galilee*, II, *Bethsaida Excavations Project Reports & Contextual Studies* (ed. R. Arav and R.A. Freund; Kirksville, MO: Truman State University Press), pp. 269-80.
Foucault, M.
1972   *The Archaeology of Knowledge and the Discourse on Language* (trans. A.M. Sheridan Smith; New York: Pantheon).
Frankel, R.
1999   *Wine and Oil Production in Antiquity in Israel and Other Mediterranean Countries* (JSOT/ASOR Monograph Series, 10; Sheffield: Sheffield Academic Press).
Freedman, D.N.
1975   *The Published Works of William Foxwell Albright: A Comprehensive Bibliography* (Cambridge, MA: American Schools of Oriental Research).
Frei, H.W.
1974   *The Eclipse of Biblical Narrative: A Study in Eighteenth and Nineteenth Century Hermeneutics* (New Haven: Yale University Press).
Frey, J.
2007   'Paul's Jewish Identity', in *Jewish Identity in the Greco-Roman World* (ed. J. Frey, D.R. Schwartz and S. Gripentrog; Ancient Judaism and Early Christianity, 71; Leiden: Brill), pp. 285-322.
2010   'Martin Hengel als theologischer Lehrer: Persönliche Erinnerungen an einen väterlichen Wegbegleiter', in Martin Hengel, *Theologische, historische und biographische Skizzen* (ed. C.-J. Thornton; Kleine Schriften, 7; Wissenschaftliche Untersuchungen zum Neuen Testament, 253; Tübingen: Mohr Siebeck), pp. xi-xxix.
Frey, J., C.K. Rothschild, J. Schröter and F. Watson (eds.)
2010   'An Editorial Manifesto', *Early Christianity* 1: 1-4.
Freyne, S.
1980a   *Galilee from Alexander the Great to Hadrian 323 B.C.E. to 135 C.E.: A Study of Second Temple Judaism* (University of Notre Dame Center for the Study of Judaism and Christianity in Antiquity, 5; Notre Dame, IN: University of Notre Dame Press).
1980b   'The Galileans in the Light of Josephus' Vita', *New Testament Studies* 26: 397-413.
1997   'Town and Country Once More: The Case of Roman Galilee', in *Archaeology and the Galilee* (ed. D.R. Edwards and C.T. McCollough; South Florida Studies in the History of Judaism, 143; Atlanta: Scholars Press), pp. 49-56.
2004   *Jesus a Jewish Galilean: A New Reading of the Jesus-Story* (London: T. & T. Clark International).
2007   'Galilee as Laboratory: Experiments for New Testament Historians and Theologians', *New Testament Studies* 53: 147–64.

Friedman, J.
1978   *Michael Servetus: A Case Study in Total Heresy* (Travaux de humanisme et renaissance, 163; Geneva: Droz).

Fritsch, C.T., and I. Ben-Dor
1961   'The Link Expedition to Israel, 1960', *Biblical Archaeologist* 24: 50-59.

Fulton, J.
1891   *The Beautiful Land, Palestine: Historical, Geographical and Pictorial, Described as It Was and as It Now Is, Along the Lines of Our Saviour's Journeys* (New York: T. Whittaker).

Funk, R.W., R.W. Hoover and The Jesus Seminar
1997   *The Five Gospels: What Did Jesus Really Say? The Search for the Authentic Words of Jesus* (San Francisco: HarperCollins).

Funk, R.W., B.B. Scott and J.R. Butts (eds.)
1988   *The Parables of Jesus: Red Letter Edition. A Report of the Jesus Seminar* (Sonoma, CA: Polebridge Press).

Gallant, T.W.
1985   *A Fisherman's Tale: An Analysis of the Potential Productivity of Fishing in the Ancient Mediterranean* (Miscellanea Graeca, 7; Brussels: Gent).

Gatier, P.L.
1993   'À propos de la culture grecque à Gérasa', in *Arabia Antiqua: Hellenistic Centres around Arabia* (ed. A. Invernizzi and J.F. Salles; Rome: Istituto italiano per il Medio ed Estremo Oriente), pp. 15-35.

Gavish, D.
1994   'French Cartography of the Holy Land in the Nineteenth Century', *Palestine Exploration Quarterly* 26: 24–31.

Gay, P.
1967–70   *The Enlightenment: An Interpretation* (2 vols.; London: Weidenfeld & Nicolson).

Geertz, C.
1996   'Afterword', in *Senses of Place* (ed. S. Feld and K.H. Basso; School of American Research Advanced Seminar Studies; Santa Fe, NM: School of American Research Press), pp. 259–62.

Geiger, J.
1985   'Athens in Syria: Greek Intellectuals of Gadara' (in Hebrew), *Cathedra* 35: 3-16.

Gibbon, E.
1994 [1787–89]   *The History of the Decline and Fall of the Roman Empire* (ed. D. Womersley; 3 vols.; London: Allen Lane).

Gillin, J.L.
1919   'The Origin of Democracy', *American Journal of Sociology* 24: 704-14.

Goldman, S.
1997   'The Holy Land Appropriated: The Careers of Selah Merrill, Nineteenth Century Christian Hebraist, Palestine Explorer, and U.S. Consul in Jerusalem', *American Jewish History* 85: 151-72.

Goldreich, Y.
2003   *The Climate of Israel: Observation, Research and Application* (New York: Kluwer Academic/Plenum Publishers).

Goodman, M.
1983   *State and Society in Roman Galilee, A.D. 132–212* (Oxford Centre for Postgraduate Hebrew Studies; Totowa, NJ: Rowman & Allanheld).

Goodspeed, E.J.
1900   'From Haifa to Nazareth', *Biblical World* 16: 407-13.
Gordis, R. (ed.)
1952   *Max Leopold Margolis: Scholar and Teacher* (Philadelphia: Alumni Association of Dropsie College).
Goren, A.
1996   'Spiritual Zionists and Jewish Sovereignty', *The Americanization of the Jews* (ed. R. Seltzer and N. Cohen; New York: New York University Press), pp. 165-92.
Gottwald, N.
1976   'Nomadism', *Interpreter's Dictionary of the Bible Supplementary Volume* (Nashville: Abingdon), 629-31.
Greene, H.B.
1880   *Wild Flowers from Palestine* (Lowell, MA.: Dumas).
Greenspoon, L.
1987   *Max Leopold Margolis: A Scholar's Scholar* (Biblical Scholarship in North America, 15; Atlanta: Scholars Press).
Grotius, H.
1689   *The Truth of Christian Religion: In Six Books. Written in Latin by Hugo Grotius. And Now Translated into English, with the Addition of a Seventh Book* (trans. S. Patrick; London: printed for Luke Meredith).
Grundmann, W.
1941   *Jesus der Galiläer und das Judentum* (Leipzig: G. Wigand).
Hadas, M.
1931   'Gadarenes in Pagan Literature', *The Classical Weekly* 25.4: 25-30.
Hale, M.
1677   *The Primitive Organisation of Mankind Considered and Examined according to the Light of Nature* (London: printed for W. Shrowsbury).
Halpern, B.
1979   'The Americanization of Zionism, 1880–1930', *American Jewish History* 69 (September): 15-33.
Hamel, G.
1990   *Poverty and Charity in Roman Palestine, First Three Centuries* C.E. (Berkeley: University of California Press).
Hammerstaedt, J.
1988   *Die Orakelkritik des Kynikers Oenomaus* (Frankfurt am Main: Athenaeum).
1990   'Der Kyniker Oenomaus von Gadara', in *Aufstieg und Niedergang der römischen Welt: Geschichte und Kultur Roms im Spiegel der neueren Forschung* II 36, 4 (ed. H. Temporini; Berlin: W. de Gruyter), pp. 2834-65.
Hanson, K.C.
1997   'The Galilean Fishing Economy and the Jesus Tradition', *Biblical Theology Bulletin* 27: 99–111.
Harland, E.H.
1965   *Christian Seed in Western Soil: Pacific School of Religion Through a Century* (Berkeley, CA.: Pacific School of Religion).
Harley, J.B.
1992   'Deconstructing the Map', in *Writing Worlds: Discourse, Text and Metaphor in the Representation of Landscape* (ed. T.J. Barnes and J.S. Duncan; London: Routledge), pp. 231-47.

Harris, W.V. (ed.)
 2005a *Rethinking the Mediterranean* (Oxford: Oxford University Press).
 2005b 'The Mediterranean and Ancient History', in Harris 2005a: 1-42.
Harrison, P.
 1990 *'Religion' and the Religions in the Early Enlightenment* (Cambridge: Cambridge University Press).
Harsnet, S.
 1603 *Declaration of Egregious Popish Impostures, to With-draw the Harts of her Maiesties Subjects from their Allegiance, and from the Truth of Christian Religion Professed in England, under the Pretence of Casting out Devils* (London: printed by James Robets).
Harvey, D.
 2000 *Spaces of Hope* (California Studies in Critical Human Geography; Berkeley: University of California Press).
 2009 *Social Justice and the City* (Geographies of Justice and Social Transformation; Athens, GA: University of Georgia Press, rev. edn).
Head, B.V.
 1911 *Historia Numorum: A Manual of Greek Numismatics* (Oxford: Clarendon, 2nd edn).
Head, P.
 2004 'The Nazi Quest for an Ayrian Jesus', *Journal for the Study of the Historical Jesus* 2: 55-89.
Hedrick, C.W.
 2004 *Many Things in Parables: Jesus and his Modern Critics* (Louisville, KY: Westminster / John Knox Press).
Heffer, S.
 1998 *Like the Roman: The Life of Enoch Powell* (London: Weidenfeld & Nicolson).
Hengel, M.
 2010 'A Gentile in the Wilderness: My Encounter with Jews and Judaism', in M. Hengel, *Theologische, historische und biographische Skizzen* (ed. C.-J. Thornton; Kleine Schriften, 7; Wissenschaftliche Untersuchungen zum Neuen Testament 253; Tübingen: Mohr Siebeck), pp. 532-45.
Hengel, M., with C. Markschies
 1989 *The 'Hellenization' of Judaea in the First Century after Christ* (London: SCM Press).
Hennessy, P.
 1992 *Never Again: Britain 1945–51* (London: Jonathan Cape).
Herrick, J.A.
 1997 *The Radical Rhetoric of the English Deists: The Discourse of Skepticism, 1680–1750* (Columbia: University of South Carolina Press).
Herzfeld, M.
 2005 'Practical Mediterraneanism: Excuses for Everything, from Epistemology to Eating', in Harris 2005a: 45-63.
Herzog, W.R.
 1994 *Parables as Subversive Speech: Jesus as Pedagogue of the Oppressed* (Louisville, KY: Westminster / John Knox Press).
Heschel, S.
 1994 'Nazifying Christian Theology: Walter Grundmann and the Institute for the Study and Eradication of Jewish Influence on German Church Life', *Church History* 63: 587-605.

2008 *The Aryan Jesus: Christian Theologians and the Bible in Nazi Germany* (Princeton, NJ: Princeton University Press).

Hillquit, M., and J. Ryan
1913 'Socialism: Promise or Menace?' *Everybody's Magazine* 29.4 (October): 482-89.

Hobsbawm, E.J.
1991 *Nations and Nationalism since 1780: Programme, Myth, Reality* (Cambridge: Cambridge University Press).

Hoffmann, P.
1982 *Studien zur Theologie der Logienquelle* (Münster: Aschendorff, 3rd edn).

Hollywood, A.
2004 'Reading as Self-Annihilation', in *Polemic: Critical or Uncritical* (ed. J. Gallop; New York: Routledge), pp. 39-102.

Horden, P., and N. Purcell
2000 *The Corrupting Sea: A Study of Mediterranean History* (Oxford: Basil Blackwell).
2005 'Four Years of Corruption: A Response to Critics', in Harris 2005a: 348-75.

Horsley, R.A.
1997 *Jesus and the Spiral of Violence: Popular Jewish Resistance in Roman Palestine* (San Francisco: Harper & Row).
2003 *Jesus and Empire: The Kingdom of God and the New World Disorder* (Minneapolis: Fortress Press).

Hurtado, L.W.
1999 'New Testament Studies at the Turn of the Millennium: Questions for the Discipline', *Scottish Journal of Theology* 52: 158-78.
2008 'Martin Hengel's Impact on English-Speaking Scholarship', *The Expository Times* 120: 70-76.

Israel, J.I.
2001 *Radical Enlightenment: Philosophy and the Making of Modernity: 1650–1750* (Oxford: Oxford University Press).

Jacob, M.C.
1981 *The Radical Enlightenment: Pantheists, Freemasons and Republicans* (London: George Allen & Unwin).

Jensen, M.H.
2006 *Herod Antipas in Galilee: The Literary and Archaeological Sources on the Reign of Herod Antipas and its Socio-Economic Impact on Galilee* (Wissenschaftliche Untersuchungen zum Neuen Testament, 215; Tübingen: Mohr Siebeck).

Jeremias, J.
1932 'Eine neugefundene Inschrift in Gadara', *Zeitschrift des deutschen Palästina-Vereins* 55: 76-80.
1972 *The Parables of Jesus* (London: SCM Press, rev. edn).

John, E.S.
1963 'Protestant Clergymen and American Destiny: Prelude to Imperialism, 1865–1900', *Harvard Theological Review* 56: 297-311.

Joosten, J.
2002 'The Gospel of Barnabas and the Diatessaron', *Harvard Theological Review* 9: 73-96.

2010   'The Date and Provenance of the *Gospel of Barnabas'*, *Journal of Theological Studies* 61: 200-15.

Kader, I.
1996   *Propylon und Bogentor: Untersuchungen zum Tetrapylon von Latakia und anderen frühkaiserzeitlichen Bogenmonumenten im Nahen Osten* (Mainz: von Zabern).

Kark, R. (ed.)
1990   *The Land that Became Israel: Studies in Historical Geography* (New Haven: Yale University Press).

Karmon, Y.
1971   *Israel: A Regional Geography* (London: Wiley-Interscience).

Katsnelson, J.
1985   'Annual Rainfall, 1932/33–1975/76', in *Atlas of Israel: Cartography, Physical and Human Geography* (Tel Aviv: Survey of Israel, 3rd edn).
2007   'Rain', in *Encyclopedia Judaica* (ed. M. Berenbaum and F. Skolnik; Detroit: Macmillan, 2nd edn), pp. 70-73.

Kee, H.C.
1992   'Early Christianity in Galilee', in *The Galilee in Late Antiquity* (ed. L.I. Levine; New York: Jewish Theological Seminary of America), pp. 3-22.

Keeley, S.
2002   *Racializing Jesus: Race, Ideology and the Formation of Modern Biblical Scholarship* (London: Routledge).

Kelly, D.R.
1998   *Faces of History: Historical Enquiry from Herodotus to Herder* (New Haven: Yale University Press).

Kent, C.F.
1919–20   'The Birth of Democracy', *Yale Review* 9: 131-42.

Khouri, R.G.
1997a   'German Excavations Continue to Clarify the Long Historical Development of Gadara (Umm Qais)', *Jordan Antiquity Annual* 1/18 (6 July).
1997b   'German Team Identifies, Excavates First Known Roman Era Temple at Gadara (Umm Qais)', *Jordan Antiquity Annual* 1/35 (2 November).

King, P.J.
1983   *American Archaeology in the Mideast: A History of the American Schools of Oriental Research* (Philadelphia: American Schools of Oriental Research).

Kippenberg, H.G.
2002   *Discovering Religion in the Modern Age* (trans. B. Harshaw; Princeton, NJ: Princeton University Press).

Klausner, J.
1989   *Jesus of Nazareth: His Life, Times and Teaching* (New York: Bloch).

Kligler, I.J.
1930   *The Epidemiology and Control of Malaria in Palestine* (Chicago: University of Chicago).

Kloppenborg V., J.S.
1987   *The Formation of Q: Trajectories in Ancient Wisdom Collections* (Philadelphia: Fortress Press).
2000   *Excavating Q: The History and Setting of the Sayings Gospel* (Edinburgh: T. & T. Clark).

Klostermann, E. (ed.)
1904 *Das Onomastikon der biblischen Ortsnamen* (Eusebius Werke, 3.1; Leipzig: Hinrichs).

Knauf, E.A.
1992 'Bedouin and Bedouin States', in *The Anchor Bible Dictionary* (ed. David Noel Freedman; 6 vols.; New York: Doubleday), I, 634-38.

Knight, S.G.
1888 *Ned Harwood's Visit to Jerusalem* (Boston: Lathrop).

Kraeling, E.G.
1963 'Gadara', in *Dictionary of the Bible* (ed. J. Hastings; rev. edn by F.C. Grant and H.H. Rowley; New York: Charles Scribner's Sons), p. 310.

Kuhn, H.W., and R. Arav
1991 'The Bethsaida Excavations: Historical and Archaeological Approaches', in *The Future of Early Christianity: Essays in Honor of Helmut Koester* (ed. B.A. Pearson; Minneapolis: Fortress Press), pp. 77–106.

Kuhnen, H.-P.
1989 *Studien zur Chronologie und Siedlungsarchäologie des Karmel (Israel) zwischen Hellenismus und Spätantike* I (Wiesbaden: Reichert).

Kuklick, B.
1996 *Puritans in Babylon: The Ancient Near East and American Intellectual Life, 1880–1930* (Princeton, NJ: Princeton University Press).

Kümmel, W.G.
1973 *The New Testament: The History of the Investigation of its Problems* (London: SCM Press).

Lachmann, K. and F. Muncker,
1897 *Gotthold Ephraim Lessings sämtliche schriften, XXII (Berlin/Stuttgart/Leipzig: J.G. Goschen.*

Lagarde, P. de.
1878 *Deutsche Schriften* (Göttingen: Dieterische Verlagsbuchhandlung).

Lapin, H., and D.B. Martin (eds.)
2003 *Jews, Antiquity, and the Nineteenth-Century Imagination* (Bethesda, MD: University Press of Maryland).

Lechler, G.V.
1841 *Geschichte des englischen Deismus* (Stuttgart: J.G. Cotta'scher Verlag).

Leibner, U.
2006 'Settlement and Demography in Late Roman and Byzantine Eastern Galilee', in *Settlements and Demography in the Near East in Late Antiquity: Proceedings of the Colloquium, Matera, 27–29 October 2005* (ed. A.S. Lewin and P. Pellegrini; Rome: Istituti editoriali e poligrafici internazionali), pp. 105-30.

Levi, C.
1982 *Christ Stopped at Eboli* (Harmondsworth: Penguin).

Lichtenberger, A.
2000–2002 'Reading a Hitherto Lost Line and the Location of the Naumachia at Gadara', *Israel Numismatic Journal* 14: 191-93.

Lieberman, S.
1963 'How Much Greek in Jewish Palestine?', in *Biblical and Other Studies* (ed. A. Altmann; Cambridge, MA: Harvard University Press), pp. 123-41.

Lightfoot, R.H.
1938 *Locality and Doctrine in the Gospels* (London: Hodder & Stoughton).

Loffreda, S.
   1978   Review of *Ancient Synagogue Excavations at Khirbet Shema, Upper Gali-
          lee, Israel, 1970–1972* (Durham, NC: ASOR/Duke University Press, 1976),
          by Eric M. Meyers, A. Thomas Kraabel and James F. Strange, in *Studii biblici
          franciscani liber annuus* 28: 274-80.
Lohmeyer, E.
   1936   *Galiläa und Jerusalem* (Göttingen: Vandenhoeck & Ruprecht).
Long, B.O.
   2003   *Imagining the Holy Land: Maps, Models and Fantasy Travels* (Bloomington:
          Indiana University Press).
Lopez, D.C.
   2008   *Apostle to the Conquered: Reimagining Paul's Mission* (Paul in Critical Con-
          texts; Minneapolis: Fortress Press).
   2011   'Visualizing Significant Otherness: Reimagining Paul(ine Studies) through
          Hybrid Lenses', forthcoming in *The Colonized Apostle: Paul through Post-
          colonial Eyes* (ed. C. Stanley; Paul in Critical Contexts; Minneapolis: Fortress
          Press).
Lukács, G.
   1971   *History and Unconsciousness: Studies in Marxist Dialectics* (trans. R. Living-
          stone; Cambridge, MA: MIT Press).
Lundsteen, A.C.
   1939   *Hermann Samuel Reimarus und die Anfänge der Leben-Jesu Forschung*
          (Copenhagen: Olsen).
Luz, M.
   1986–87 'Abnimos, Nimos and Oenomaus: A Note', *Jewish Quarterly Review* 77.3:
          191-95.
   1988   'Salam Meleager', *Studi italiani di filologia classica* 6: 222-31.
Lynch, W.F.
   1849   *Narrative of the United States' Expedition to the River Jordan and the Dead
          Sea* (Philadelphia: Lea & Blanchard).
Lyon, D.
   1911   'Archaeological Explorations of Palestine', *Journal of Biblical Literature* 30:
          1-17.
Maas, P.
   1942   'The Philinna Papyrus', *Journal of Hellenic Studies* 62: 33-38.
Mack, B.L.
   1988   *A Myth of Innocence: Mark and Christian Origins* (Philadelphia: Fortress
          Press).
Mahmood, S.
   2005   *Politics of Piety: The Islamic Revival and the Feminist Subject* (Princeton, NJ:
          Princeton University Press).
Malina, B.J.
   1996   *The Social World of Jesus and the Gospels* (London: Routledge).
Marchand, S.L.
   2009   *German Orientalism in the Age of Empire: Religion, Race, and Scholarship*
          (Washington, DC: German Historical Institute).
Marcus, J.
   1992   'The Jewish War and the Sitz im Leben of Mark', *Journal of Biblical Litera-
          ture* 111: 446-56.

Margalit, J., and A.S. Tahori
1978   'Insects: Mosquitoes', in Serruya 1978a: 377-79.

Margolis, M.L.
1902   *'The Central Thought of the Book of Job': Papers Presented at the Fifth Annual Session of the Summer Assembly of the Jewish Chautauqua Society* (Philadelphia: Jewish Publication Society).
1907a   'The Message of Moses', *Maccabaean* 12 (February): 41-46.
1907b   'Professor Max Margolis a Zionist: An Open Letter Defining his Position and Offering his Active Co-operation', *Maccabaean* 12 (March): 97-99.
1908   *Micah: The Holy Scriptures with Commentary* (Philadelphia: Jewish Publication Society).
1910–11 'The Scope and Methodology of Biblical Philology', *Jewish Quarterly Review* NS 1: 32-33.
1915   'The Jewish Defense of the Bible', *B'Nai B'rith News* (June): 10.
1917   'The Leadership of Herzl', *Maccabaean* 22 (August): 23.
1924–25 'A Year in the Holy Land', Parts 1-5, *B'nai B'rith Magazine* 39.1 (October 1924): 8-10 (part 1), 44-45 (part 2); 39.2 (November 1924): 74, 86 (part 3); 39.3 (December 1924): 106-107 (part 4); 39.4 (February 1925): 167, 182-83 (part 5).
1925   'Oriental Research in Palestine', *Jewish Institute of Religion Bulletin* 3 (November): 1-17.

Margolis, M.L., and A. Marx
1927   *A History of the Jewish People* (Philadelphia: Jewish Publication Society).

Marxsen, W.
1956   *Der Evangelist Markus: Studien zur Redaktionsgeschichte des Evangeliums* (Forschungen zur Religion und Literatur des Alten und Neuen Testaments, 67; Göttingen: Vandenhoeck & Ruprecht).

Masterman, E.W.G.
1908   'The Fisheries of Galilee', *Palestine Exploration Fund* 40: 40-51.

Masuzawa, T.
2005   *The Invention of World Religions: Or, How European Universalism Was Preserved in the Language of Pluralism* (Chicago: University of Chicago Press).

Mathews, S.
1903   'A Reading Journey through Palestine: Going Up to Jerusalem', *The Chautauquan* 43.6 (August): 493-560.

McCown, C.C.
1912   'New Year's among the Mohammedans of Calcutta', *Epworth Herald* 23: 5-23.
1919   'The Temptation of Jesus Eschatologically and Socially Interpreted', *Biblical World* 53.4: 402-407.
1921   *The Promise of his Coming* (New York: Macmillan).
1927   'Climate and Religion in Palestine', *Journal of Religion* 7: 5-6, 520-39.
1929   *The Genesis of the Social Gospel: The Meaning and Ideals of Jesus in the Light of their Antecedents* (New York: Alfred A. Knopf).
1933   'The Social Gospel', in *The Church Looks Ahead: American Protestant Christianity, an Analysis and Forecast* (ed. C.E. Schofield; New York: Macmillan).
1940a   *Search for the Real Jesus* (New York: Charles Scribner's Sons).

1940b 'The Kingdom of God and the Life of Today', in *Theology and Modern Life: Essays in Honor of Harris Franklin Rall* (ed. P.A. Schilpp; Chicago: Clark, Willet,).

1940c 'The Major Emphasis in Preaching—Social', *Christian Advocate* 106: 54.

1943 *The Ladder of Progress in Palestine: A Story of Archeological Adventure* (New York: Harper & Brothers).

1947 'The Geographical Conditioning of Religious Experience in Palestine', in *The Story of the Bible Today and Tomorrow* (ed. H.R. Willoughby; Chicago: University of Chicago Press), pp. 231-46.

1958 *Man, Morals, and History: Today's Legacy from Ancient Times and Biblical Peoples* (New York: Harper & Brothers).

Mero, F.

1978 'Hydrology', in Serruya 1978a: 87-102.

Merrill, S.

1881a *East of the Jordan* (New York: Charles Scribner's Sons).

1881b *'Galilee' in Picturesque Palestine, Sinai, and Egypt: With Numerous Engravings on Steel and Wood from Original Drawings by Harry Fenn and J.D. Woodward* (ed. Sir C.W. Wilson; New York: D. Appleton).

1881c *Galilee in the Time of Christ* (Boston: Congregational Publishing).

1908 *Ancient Jerusalem* (New York: Arno, reprint 1977).

Meshorer, Y.

1966 'Coins of the City of Gadara Struck in Commemoration of a Local Naumachia', *Sefunim* 1: 28-31.

Meyers, E.M.

1976 'Galilean Regionalism as a Factor in Historical Reconstruction', *Bulletin of the American Schools of Oriental Research* 221: 93-101.

1979 'The Cultural Setting of Galilee: The Case of Regionalism and Early Judaism', *Aufstieg und Niedergang der römischen Welt: Geschichte und Kultur Roms im Spiegel der neueren Forschung* II 19, 1 (ed. H. Temporini; Berlin: W. de Gruyter), pp. 686–702.

1985 'Galilean Regionalism: A Reappraisal', in *Approaches to Ancient Judaism: Theory and Practice. V, Studies in Judaism and its Greco-Roman Context* (ed. W.S. Green; Brown Judaic Studies, 32; Atlanta: Scholars Press), pp. 115-31.

1997 'Jesus and His Galilean Context', in *Archaeology and the Galilee: Texts and Contexts in the Graeco-Roman and Byzantine Periods* (ed. D.R. Edwards and C.T. McCollough; University of South Florida Studies in the History of Judaism; Atlanta: Scholars Press), pp. 57-66.

Meynersen, S.F.

2001 'The Tiberias Gate of Gadara, Umm Qays:Reflections concerning the Date and its Reconstruction', *Annual of the Department of Antiquities of Jordan* 45: 427-32.

Milken, R.L.

1992 *The Land Called Holy: Palestine in Christian History and Thought* (New Haven: Yale University Press).

Millar, F.

1969 'P. Herennius Dexippus: The Greek World and the Third Century Invasions', *Journal of Roman Studies* 59: 12-29.

Mionnet, T.E.

1973 *Description des médailles antiques, grecques et romaines* (9 vols.; Graz: Akademische Druck- und Verlagsanstalt).

Mittmann, S.
  1970   *Beiträge zur Siedlungs- und Traditionsgeschichte des nördlichen Ostjordan-landes* (Wiesbaden: Otto Harrassowitz).
Montague, E.P.
  1849   *Narrative of the Late Expedition to the Dead Sea, from a Diary by One of the Party* (Philadelphia: Carey & Hart).
Montgomery, J.A.
  1918   'The American School of Oriental Research', *Art and Archaeology* 7: 173.
  1919   'The American School of Oriental Research in Jerusalem', *Bulletin of the American School of Oriental Research* 1 (December): 4.
  1920   'Needs of the School', *Bulletin of the American School of Oriental Research* 2 (February): 9-10.
Moore, S.D.
  2006   *Empire and Apocalypse: Postcolonialism and the New Testament* (Sheffield: Sheffield Phoenix Press).
Moreland, M.
  2007   'The Inhabitants of Galilee in the Hellenistic and Early Roman Periods,' in Zangenberg, Attridge and Martin 2007: 133-59.
Morgan, T.
  1738–40   *The Moral Philosopher* (3 vols.; London: Printed for the author, 2nd edn).
Morley, D., and K. Robins
  1990   'No Place like Heimat: Images of Home(land) in European Culture', *New Formations* 12: 1-23.
Mosse, G.L.
  1988   *The Culture of Western Europe: The Nineteenth and Twentieth Centuries* (Boulder, CO: Westview Press, 3rd edn).
  1964   *The Crisis of German Ideology* (New York: Grosset & Dunlap).
Moulton, W.J.
  1926–27   'The American Palestine Exploration Society', *Annual of the American Schools of Oriental Research* 8: 55-78.
Mylona, D.
  2003   'Fishing in Late Antiquity', in *Zooarchaeology in Greece: Recent Advances* (ed. E. Kotzabopolou, Y. Hamilakis, P. Halstead, C. Gamble and P. Elefanti; British School at Athens Studies, 9; London: British School at Athens), pp. 103–10.
  2008   *Fish-Eating in Greece from the Fifth Century B.C. to the Seventh Century A.D.: A Story of Impoverished Fishermen or Luxurious Fish Banquets?* (BAR International Series, 1754; Oxford: Archaeopress).
Nasier, A. (trans.)
  2003   *Three Impostors* (Whitefish, MA: Kessinger).
Nebenzahl, K.
  1986   *Maps of the Bible Lands: Images of Terra Sancta through Two Millennia* (London: Time Books).
Notley, R.S.
  2007   'Et-Tell Is Not Bethsaida', *Near Eastern Archaeology* 70: 220-30.
Nun, M.
  1989a   *The Sea of Galilee and its Fishermen in the New Testament* (Kibbutz Ein Gev, Israel: Kinnereth Sailing).

1989b   *Sea of Galilee: Newly Discovered Harbours from New Testament Days* (Kibbutz Ein Gev, Israel: Kinnereth Sailing, rev. edn).

1996   *The Land of the Gadarenes: New Light on an Old Sea of Galilee Puzzle* (Kibbutz Ein Gev: Sea of Galilee Fishing Museum).

1999   'Ports of Galilee: Modern Drought Reveals Harbors from Jesus' Time', *Biblical Archaeology Review* 25.4: 18-31, 64.

Oakman, D.E.

1992   'Was Jesus a Peasant? Implications for Reading the Samaritan Story (Luke 10:30-35)', *Biblical Theology Bulletin* 22: 117-25.

Obenzinger, H.

1999   *American Palestine: Melville, Twain and the Holy Land Mania* (Princeton, NJ: Princeton University Press).

Orni, E., and E. Efrat

1971   *Geography of Israel* (New York: American Heritage Press, 3rd rev. edn).

Orr, J.

1903   *David Hume and his Influence on Philosophy and Theology* (Edinburgh: T. & T. Clark).

Otwell, J.H.

1958   'In Memoriam Chester C. McCown', *Pacific School of Religion Bulletin* 37.1 (March): 2.

Peck, J.M.

1992   'Rac(e)ing the Nation: Is There a German 'Home'?', *New Formations* 17: 75-84.

Pedraza, H.

1986   *Winston Churchill, Enoch Powell and the Nation* (London: Cleveland Press).

Penner, T.

2005   'The Challenge from Within: Reading Räisänen against Dominant Methodological Discourse', in *Moving beyond New Testament Theology? Essays in Conversation with Heikki Räisänen* (ed. T. Penner and C. Vander Stichele; Publications of the Finnish Exegetical Society, 88; Helsinki: Finnish Exegetical Society; Göttingen: Vandenhoeck & Ruprecht), pp. 1-31.

2008   'Die Judenfrage and the Construction of Ancient Judaism: Toward a Foregrounding of the Backgrounds Approach to Early Christianity', in *Scripture and Traditions: Essays on Early Judaism and Christianity in Honor of Carl R. Holladay* (ed. P. Gray and G. O'Day; Supplements to *Novum Testamentum*, 129; Leiden: E.J. Brill), pp. 429-`55.

Peters, J.P.

1918a   'Jerusalem Redeemed: The Ancient Holy City and its Place in History', *American Review of Reviews* 57 (January): 47-58.

1918b   'Spiritual Meaning of Jerusalem's Deliverance', *Literary Digest* (February): 31-32.

1919   'Inheritors of Canaan', *Asia* 19: 1229-36.

Petersen, W.L.

1992a   'Ebionites, Gospel of the', in *The Anchor Bible Dictionary* (ed. D.N. Freedman; 6 vols.; New York: Doubleday), II, 261-62.

1992b   'Nazoraeans, Gospel of the', in *The Anchor Bible Dictionary* (ed. D.N. Freedman; 6 vols.; New York: Doubleday), IV, 1051-52.

Popkin, R.
1991 'Translator's Introduction to Pierre Bayle', in *Historical and Critical Diction-ary: Selections* (Indianapolis: Hackett), pp. viii-xl.
1996 'Spinoza and Bible Scholarship', in *The Cambridge Companion to Spinoza* (ed. D. Garrett; Cambridge: Cambridge University Press).
2003 *The History of Scepticism: From Savonarola to Bayle* (Oxford: Oxford University Press, rev. and expanded edn).

Powell, J.E
1977 *Wrestling with the Angel* (London: Sheldon Press).
1991 'Genesis of the Gospel', *Journal for the Study of the New Testament* 42: 5-16.
1992a *Reflections: Selected Writings and Speeches of Enoch Powell* (London: Bellew).
1992b 'Interview with Anne Brown, BBC Radio, 13 April 1986', in Powell 1992a: 27-38.
1992c 'A National Church (1981)', in Powell 1992a: 72-76.
1992d 'To the Annual General Meeting of the West Midlands Area Conservative Political Centre (Birmingham, 20 April, 1968)', in Powell 1992a: 161-69.
1994 *The Evolution of the Gospel* (New Haven: Yale University Press).

Purcell, N.
1995 'Eating Fish: The Paradoxes of Seafood', in *Food in Antiquity* (ed. J. Wilkins, D. Harvey and M. Dobson; Exeter: University of Exeter Press), pp. 132-49.
2003 'Fishing', in *The Oxford Classical Dictionary* (ed. S. Hornblower and A. Spawforth; Oxford: Oxford University Press, 3rd rev. edn), p. 599.

Putnam, R.D.
2000 *Bowling Alone: The Collapse and Revival of American Community* (New York: Simon & Schuster).

Queen, E.L., II
1996 'Ambiguous Pilgrims: American Protestant Travelers to Ottoman Palestine, 1867–1914', in *Pilgrims & Travelers to the Holy Land* (ed. B.F. Le Beau and M. Mor; Omaha, NE: Creighton University Press).

Ragg, L., and L. Ragg
1907 *The Gospel of Barnabas* (Oxford: Clarendon Press).

Ravikovitch, S.
1970 'Geomorphology: Soil Map', in *Atlas of Israel: Cartography, Physical Geography, Human and Economic Geography, History* (Jerusalem: Survey of Israel, Ministry of Labour, 2nd English edn), II, 3.

Reed, J.L.
1995 'The Social Map of Q', in *Conflict and Invention: Literary, Rhetorical and Social Studies on the Sayings Gospel Q* (ed. J.S. Kloppenborg; Valley Forge, PA: Trinity Press International), pp. 17-36.
2000 *Archaeology and the Galilean Jesus: A Re-Examination of the Evidence* (Harrisburg, PA: Trinity Press International).
2007 *HarperCollins Visual Guide to the New Testament: What Archaeology Reveals about the First Christians* (New York: HarperOne).
2008 'Galilean Economics from a Demographic Perspective: The Role of Mortality, Morbidity, and Migration', Unpublished paper presented at the annual meeting of the Society of Biblical Literature, Boston, Massachusetts.

Reider, J.
    1987   'Bibliography of the Works of Max Leopold Margolis', in Greenspoon 1987:
            165-78.
Reifenberg, A.
    1947   *Soils of Palestine: Studies in Soil Formation and Land Utilisation in the Medi-*
            terranean (London: Thomas Murby, 2nd rev. edn).
Reimarus, H.S.
    1972   *Apologie oder Schutzschrift für die vernünftigen Verehrer Gottes* (2 vols.; ed.
            Gerhard Alexander; Frankfurt: Insel).
    1897   'Unmöglichkeit einer Offenbarung, die alle Menschen auf eine gegründete Art
            glauben könnten', in *Gotthold Ephraim Lessings sämtliche schriften*, XXII
            (ed. K. Lachmann and F. Muncker ; Berlin: J.G. Goschen), pp. 316–58.
Renan, E.
    1927   *The Life of Jesus* (New York: Modern Library).
Renfrew, J.M.
    1973   *Palaeoethnobotany: The Prehistoric Food Plants of the Near East and Europe*
            (Studies in Prehistory; London: Methuen).
Retief, F., and L. Cilliers
    2004   'Malaria in Greco-Roman Times', *Acta Classica* 47: 127-37.
Rhodes, A.
    1976   *Propaganda* (New York: Chelsea House).
Richardson, P.
    2002   'What Has Cana to Do with Capernaum?' *New Testament Studies* 48: 314-31.
Robinson, E.
    1856   *Later Research in Palestine and in the Adjacent Regions: A Journal of Travels*
            in the Year 1852. Drawn up from the Original Diaries with Historical Illustra-
            tions, with New Maps and Plans (Boston: Crocker & Brewster).
Robinson, E., and E. Smith
    1841   *Biblical Researches in Palestine, Mount Sinai, and Arabia Petrea* (Boston:
            Crocker & Brewster).
Rohrbaugh, R.L.
    1993   'A Peasant Reading of the Parable of the Talents/Pounds: A Text of Terror?'
            Biblical Theology Bulletin 23: 32-39.
Rosenan, N.
    1970a   'Climate: Temperature', in *Atlas of Israel: Cartography, Physical Geography,*
            Human and Economic Geography, History (Jerusalem: Survey of Israel, Min-
            istry of Labour, 2nd English edn), IV, 1.
Rosenberg, A.
    1902   'Socialism in Ancient Israel', *Arena* 28: 37-44.
Rousseau, J.J.
    1984   'Discourse on the Origin and Foundations of the Inequality', in *A Discourse*
            *on Inequality (*trans. Maurice Cranston; Oxford: Oxford University Press), pp.
            55-171.
Rousseau, J.J., and R. Arav
    1995   *Jesus and his World: An Archaeological and Cultural Dictionary* (Minneapo-
            lis: Fortress Press).
Rubin, S.
    1978   'Meteorology: Precipitation', in Serruya 1978a: 69-86.

Rubin, S., A. Israeli, Z. Gat, L. Klebaner, Y. Mishaeli and U. Lev-Ami
   1992   *Israel: Geo-Climatic Regions* (Bet Dagan: Israeli Meteorological Service).
Running, L.G., and D.N. Freedman
   1975   *William Foxwell Albright: A Twentieth Century Genius* (New York: Morgan).
Rushdie, S.
   1992   *Imaginary Homelands: Essays and Criticism 1981–91* (London: Granta Books).
Ryan, T.
   2009   *Pierre Bayle's Cartesian Metaphysics: Rediscovering Early Modern Philosophy* (New York: Routledge).
Safrai, Z.
   1994   *The Economy of Roman Palestine* (London: Routledge).
Said, E.
   2003   *Orientalism* (London: Penguin, reprinted with a new Preface).
Sallares, R.
   2002   *Malaria and Rome: A History of Malaria in Ancient Italy* (Oxford: Oxford University Press).
Sanders, E.P.
   1977   *Paul and Palestinian Judaism* (London: SCM).
   1985   *Jesus and Judaism* (Philadelphia: Fortress Press).
   1993a *The Historical Figure of Jesus* (London: Allen Lane).
   1993b 'Jesus in Historical Context', *Theology Today* 50: 429-48.
   2002   'Jesus' Galilee', in *Fair Play: Diversity and Conflicts in Early Christianity. Essays in Honour of Heikki Räisänen* (ed. I. Dunderberg, K. Syreeni and C.M. Tuckett; Supplements to *Novum Testamentum,* 103; Leiden: Brill), pp. 3-41.
Sapir, B., and D. Ne'eman
   1967   *Capernaum (Kfar-Nachum): History and Legacy, Art and Architecture* (Tel Aviv: Historical Sites Library Interfaith Survey of the Holy Land).
Saulcy, L.F. de
   1976   *Numismatique de la terre sainte: description des monnaies autonomes et impériales de la Palestine et de l'Arabie Petrée* (Sala Bolognese: Forni).
Sawicki, M.
   2000   *Crossing Galilee: Architectures of Contact in the Occupied Land of Jesus* (Harrisburg, PA: Trinity Press International).
Schama, S.
   1999   'Simon Schama's Top Ten History Books', guardian.co.uk, 10 December 1999: http://www.guardian.co.uk/books/1999/dec/10/top10s.history.books.
Schattner, I.
   1973   'Physiography', in *Geography* (Israel Pocket Library; Jerusalem: Keter Books) 24–93.
Scheidel, W.
   2001   *Death on the Nile: Disease and the Demography of Roman Egypt* (*Mnemosyne* Supplements; Leiden: Brill).
Schleiermacher, F.
   1975   *The Life of Jesus* (ed. and with introduction by J.C. Verheyden; Philadelphia: Fortress Press).
Scholz, S.
   2010   'Lederhosen Hermeneutics: Toward a Feminist Sociology of German White Male Old Testament Interpretations', in *Crossing Textual Boundaries: A Fest-

schrift for Professor Archie Lee in Honor of his Sixtieth Birthday (ed. N. Tan and Z. Ying; Hong Kong: Divinity School of Chung Chi College), pp. 334-53.

Schottroff, L.

1975   'Gewaltverzicht und Feindesliebe in der urchristlichen Jesustradition', in *Jesus Christus in Historie und Theologie: Neutestamentliche Festschrift für Hans Conzelmann zum 60. Geburtstag* (Tübingen: Mohr), pp. 197-221.

Schottroff, L., and W. Stegemann

1978   *Jesus von Nazareth–Hoffnung der Armen* (Stuttgart: W. Kohlhammer).

Schumacher, G.

1890   *Northern Ajlun* (London: Palestine Exploration Fund).

Schürer, E.

1979   *A History of the Jewish People in the Age of Jesus Christ (175 B.C.–A.D. 135),* II (trans. and ed. Geza Vermes, Fergus Millar, Matthew Black with Pamela Vermes; Edinburgh: T. & T. Clark, rev. edn).

Schweitzer, A.

1906   *Von Reimarus zu Wrede: Eine Geschichte der Leben-Jesu-Forschung* (Tübingen: Mohr).

1911   *The Quest of the Historical Jesus: A Critical Study of its Progress from Reimarus to Wrede* (London: A. & C. Black, 2nd edn).

1931   *The Mysticism of Paul the Apostle* (London: A. & C. Black).

1998   *The Quest of the Historical Jesus: A Critical Study of its Progress from Reimarus to Wrede* (Baltimore: John Hopkins University Press).

2000   *The Quest of the Historical Jesus: First Complete Edition* (ed. John Bowden; London: SCM Press).

Scott, B.B.

1989   *Hear Then the Parable: A Commentary on the Parables of Jesus* (Minneapolis: Fortress Press).

Seetzen, U.J.

1854   *Reisen durch Syrien, Palästina, Phönicien, die Transjordan-Länder, Arabia Petraea und Unter-Aegypten,* I (ed. F. Kruse with Prof. Hinrichs and G.F.II. Müller; Berlin: Georg Reimer; reprinted, Hildesheim: Georg Olms, 2004).

1859   *Reisen durch Syrien, Palästina, Phönicien, die Transjordan-Länder, Arabia Petraea und Unter-Aegypten,* IV (ed. F. Kruse and H.L. Fleischer; Berlin: Georg Reimer; reprinted, Hildesheim: Georg Olms, 2004).

Segal, A.

2004   'Hippos-Sussita of the Dekapolis', *Minerva* 15.5: 23-25.

Semler, J.S.

1780   *Beantwortung der Fragmente eines Ungenannten, insbesondere vom Zweck Jesu und seiner Junger* (Halle: Erziehungsinstitut, rev. edn).

Serruya, C.

1978a   *The Kinneret* (Monographie Biologicae; The Hague: W. Junk).

1978b   'The Lacustrine Environment: General Background', in Serruya 1978a: 123-46.

Shepherd, N.

1987   *The Zealous Intruders: The Western Rediscovery of Palestine* (San Francisco: Harper & Row).

Sherlock, T

1729   *Tryal of the Witnesses of the Resurrection of Jesus* (London: Printed for J Roberts).

Shroder, J.F., and M. Inbar
  1995 'Geologic and Geographic Background to the Bethsaida Excavations', in *Bethsaida: A City by the North Shore of the Sea of Galilee*, I (ed. R. Arav and R.A. Freund; Kirksville, MO: Truman State University Press), pp. 65-98.
  2009 *Contextualizing Gender in Early Christian Discourse: Thinking beyond Thecla* (London and New York: T. & T. Clark/Continuum).
Silberman, N.A.
  1982 *Digging for God and Country: Exploration, Archeology, and the Secret Struggle for the Holy Land, 1799–1917* (New York: Alfred A. Knopf).
  1997 'Nationalism and Archaeology', in *Oxford Encyclopaedia of Archaeology in the Near East*, IV (ed. E. Meyers; Oxford: Oxford University Press), pp. 103-12.
Silk, M.
  1984 'Notes on the Judeo-Christian Tradition in America', *American Quarterly* 36: 65-85.
Simon, R.
  1689 *Critical History of the Text of the New Testament: Wherein Is Firmly Establish'd the Truth of Those Acts on which the Foundation of Christian Religion Is Laid* (London : printed for R. Taylor).
Singer, A.
  2007 *The Soils of Israel* (Berlin: Springer).
Smith, C. Delano
  1990 'Maps as Art and Science: Maps in Sixteenth Century Bibles', *Imago Mundi* 42: 65-83.
Smith, E.
  1883 *Researches of the Rev. E. Smith and H.G.O. Dwight in Armenia: Including a Journey through Asia Minor and into Georgia and Persia, with a Visit to the Nestorian and Chaldean Christians of Oormiah and Salmas* (Boston: Crocker & Brewster).
Smith, G.A.
  1984 *The Historical Geography of the Holy Land Especially in Relation to the History of Israel and the Early Church* (London: Hodder & Stoughton).
  1901 *The Historical Geography of the Holy Land Especially in Relation to the History of Israel and of the Early Church* (London: Hodder & Stoughton, 13th edn).
  1910 *Historical Geography of the Holy Land Especially in Relation to the History of Israel and of the Early Church* (London: Hodder & Stoughton, 16th edn).
Smith, G.B.
  1919 'Making Christianity Safe for Democracy' *Biblical World* NS 53: 3-13, 133-45, 245-58, 408-23, 493-507, 628-39.
Smith, H.B., and R.D. Hitchcock
  1863 *The Life, Writings, and Character of Edward Robinson, D.D., L.L.D.* (New York: Anson D.F. Randolph).
Smith, J.Z.
  1982 *Imagining Religion: From Babylon to Jonestown* (Chicago: University of Chicago Press).
  1990 *Drudgery Divine: On the Comparison of Early Christianities and the Religions of Late Antiquity* (Chicago: University of Chicago Press).

1993 [1978]   *Map Is Not Territory: Studies in the History of Religion* (Chicago: University of Chicago Press).

2004   *Relating Religion: Essays in the Study of Religion* (Chicago: University of Chicago Press).

Smith, W.C.

1978   *The Meaning and End of Religion* (London: SPCK).

Smylie, J.E.

1963   'Protestant Clergymen and American Destiny: Prelude to Imperialism, 1865–1900', *Harvard Theological Review* 56: 297-311.

Snodgrass, K.

2008   *Stories with Intent: A Comprehensive Guide to the Parables of Jesus* (Grand Rapids: Eerdmans).

Sperling, S.D.

1992   *Students of the Covenant: A History of Jewish Biblical Scholarship in North America* (Confessional Perspectives Series; Atlanta: Scholars Press).

Spinoza, B.

1998   *Theological-Political Treatise* (trans. S. Shirley; Indianapolis: Hackett).

Stanhill, G., and J. Neumann

1978   'The General Meteorological Background', in Serruya 1978a: 49-58.

Stanley, A.P.

1871   'Introduction', in *The Recovery of Jerusalem* (ed. W. Momson; London: Bentley), pp. i-xxiv.

Stemberger, G.

1979   *Das klassische Judentum: Kultur und Geschichte der rabbinischen Zeit (70 n.Chr.–1040 n.Chr.)* (Munich: Beck).

Strauss, D.F.

1879   *A New Life of Jesus* (London: Williams & Norgate).

Stubbe, H.

1911   *An Account of the Rise and Progress of Mahometanism* (ed. H.M.K Shairani; London: Luzac).

Sugirtharajah, R.S.

2002   *Postcolonial Criticism and Biblical Interpretation* (Oxford: Oxford University Press).

2008   'Catching the Post or How I Became an Accidental Theorist', in *Shaping a Global Theological Mind* (ed. D.C. Marks; Aldershot: Ashgate), pp. 163-76.

Sukenik, E.L.

1935   *The Ancient Synagogue of el-Hammeh (Hammath-by-Gadara): An Account of the Excavations Conducted on Behalf of the Hebrew University, Jerusalem* (Jerusalem: Mass).

Swift, J.

1713   *Mr C---s's Discourse of Free-Thinking, put into plain English, by way of abstract for use of the Poor* (London: Printed for John Morphew).

Talbert, C.H. (ed.)

1971   *Reimarus: Fragments* (London: SCM Press).

Thayer, J.H.

1895   'Presidential Address', *Journal of Biblical Literature* 14: 16.

Theissen, G.

1989   *The Gospels in Context: Social and Political History in the Synoptic Tradition* (Minneapolis: Fortress Press).

1973 'Wanderradikalismus: Literatursoziologische Aspekte der Überlieferung von Worten Jesu im Urchristentum', *Zeitschrift für Theologie und Kirche* 70: 245-71.

1977 *Soziologie der Jesusbewegung: Ein Beitrag zur Entstehungsgeschichte des Urchristentums* (Munich: Chr. Kaiser Verlag).

1979 *Studien zur Soziologie des Urchristentums* (Tübingen: Mohr).

1989 *Lokalkolorit und Zeitgeschichte in den Evangelien: Ein Beitrag zur Geschichte der synoptischen Tradition* (Novum Testamentum et orbis antiquus, 8; Göttingen: Vandenhoeck & Ruprecht).

Theissen, G., and A. Merz
1998 *The Historical Jesus: A Comprehensive Guide* (Minneapolis: Fortress Press).

Thomson, W.M.
1859 *The Land and the Book: or, Biblical Illustrations Drawn from the Manners and Customs, the Scenes, and Scenery of the Holy Land* (2 vols.; New York: Harper & Brothers).

1888 *The Land and the Book: or, Biblical Illustrations Drawn from the Manners and Customs, the Scenes and Scenery of the Holy Land* (London: T. Nelson & Sons).

Timm, Stefan (ed.)
2005 *Das Onomastikon der biblischen Ortsnamen: Edition der syrischen Fassung mit griechischem Text, englischer und deutscher Übersetzung* (Berlin: W. de Gruyter).

Tindal, M.
1730 *Christianity as Old as the Creation: or the Gospel a Republication of the Religion of Nature* (London).

Toland, J.
1999 *Nazarenus* (ed. Justin Champion; Oxford: Voltaire Foundation, University of Oxford Press).

Vaage, Leif E.
1992 'The Son of Man Sayings in Q: Stratigraphy and Significance', in *Early Christianity, Q and Jesus* (ed. J.S. Kloppenborg and L.E. Vaage; Semeia, 55; Atlanta: Scholars Press).

1994 *Galilean Upstarts: Jesus' First Followers according to Q* (Valley Forge, PA: Trinity Press International).

2007 'Beyond Nationalism: Jesus "the Holy Anarchist"?' Paper read at Det teologiske fakultet/Universitet i Oslo on 7 June 7.

2010 'Beyond Nationalism: Jesus "the Holy Anarchist"?', in *Jesus beyond Nationalism: Constructing the Historical Jesus in a Period of Cultural Complexity* (ed. H. Moxnes, W. Blanton, and J.G. Crossley; London: Equinox).

Vander Stichele, C., and T. Penner
2009 *Contextualizing Gender in Early Christian Discourse: Thinking beyond Thecla* (London and New York: T&T Clark/Continuum).

Van Dyke, H.
1908 *Out-of-Doors in the Holy Land. Impressions of Travel in Body and Spirit* (New York: Charles Scribner's Sons).

Van Rensselaer, J.T.
1905 'The Identity of Socialism and Christianity', *Arena* 34: 39-44.

Vermes, G.
1973 *Jesus the Jew* (Philadelphia: Fortress Press).

Vincent, J.H., J.W. Lee and R.E.M. Bain
1894   *Earthly Footsteps of the Man of Galilee* (New York: N.D. Publishing).
Vogel, L.
1993   *To See a Promised Land* (University Park, PA: Pennsylvania State University Press).
Wachsmann, S.
1990a   'Literary Sources on Kinneret Seafaring in the Roman-Byzantine Period', in *The Excavations of an Ancient Boat in the Sea of Galilee (Lake Kinneret)* (ed. S. Wachsmann; Jerusalem: Israel Antiquities Authority), pp. 111-14.
Wagner-Lux, U., E.W. Krueger, K.J.H. Vriezen and T. Vriezen-van der Flier
1978   'Bericht über die Oberflächenforschung in Gadara (Umm Qes) in Jordanien im Jahre 1974', *Zeitschrift des deutschen Palästina-Vereins* 94: 135-44.
1979   'Bericht über die Oberflächenforschung in Gadara (Umm Qes) in Jordanien im Jahre 1974', *Annual of the Department of Antiquities of Jordan* 23: 31-39.
Wagner-Lux, U., and K.J.H. Vriezen
1987   'Gadara', in *Der Königsweg: 9000 Jahre Kunst und Kultur in Jordanien und Palästina* (Rautenstauch-Joest Museum Köln vom 3. Oktober 1987 bis 27. März 1988; Mainz am Rhein: Philipp von Zabern), pp. 267-72.
Warren, Colonel Sir C.
1901   'Gadara', in *Dictionary of the Bible* (ed. J. Hastings; New York: Charles Scribner's Sons), II, 79-80.
Weber, T.M.
1991   'Gadara of the Decapolis: Tiberiade Gate, Qahawat el-Far'oun and Bait Rusan: Achievements in Excavation and Restoration at Umm Qais 1989–1990', in *The Near East in Antiquity: German Contributions to the Archaeology of Jordan, Palestine, Syria, Lebanon and Egypt*, II (ed. Susanne Kerner; Amman: Goethe-Institut/German Protestant Institute for Archaeology/Al Kutba), pp. 123-33.
1996   'Gadarenes in Exile: Two Inscriptions from Greece Reconsidered', *Zeitschrift des deutschen Palästina-Vereins* 112: 10-17.
1997   'Thermal Springs, Medical Supply and Healing Cults in Roman-Byzantine Jordan', in *Studies in the History and Archaeology of Jordan* (ed. G. Bisheh, M. Zaghland and I. Kehrberg; Amman: Amman Department of Antiquities of Jordan), pp. 331-38.
1999   'Thermalquellen und Heilgötter des Ostjordanlandes in römisher und byzantinischer Zeit', *Damazener Mitteilungen* 11: 433-51, plates 57-60.
2002   *Gadara–Umm Qēs*. I, *Gadara Decapolitana: Untersuchungen zur Topographie, Geschichte, Architektur und Bildenden Kunst einer 'Polis Hellenis' im Ostjordanland* (Abhandlungen des Deutschen Palästinavereins, 30; Wiesbaden: Otto Harrassowitz).
2007   'Gadara and the Galilee', in Zangenberg, Attridge and Martin 2007: 449-77.
Weinstein, J.
1967   *The Decline of Socialism in America 1912–1925* (New York: Monthly Review Press).
Weksler-Bdolah, S.
1998   'Tel Nov', *Exploration and Surveys in Israel* 18: 8.
Whelan, R.
1989   *The Anatomy of Superstition: A Study of the Historical Theory and Practise of Pierre Bayle* (Oxford: Voltaire Foundation, University of Oxford).

White, H.
1973 *Metahistory: The Historical Imagination in Nineteenth-Century Europe* (Baltimore: Johns Hopkins University Press).

Whitehair, C.W.
1918 'An Old Jewel in the Proper Setting: An Eyewitness's Account of the Reconquest of the Holy Land by Twentieth Century Crusaders', *National Geographic* Magazine (October): 325-44.

Whitelam, K.W.
2007 'Lines of Power: Mapping Ancient Israel', in *To Break Every Yoke: Essays in Honor of Marvin L. Chaney* (ed R.B. Coote and N.K Gottwald; Sheffield: Sheffield Phoenix Press), pp. 40-79.
2008 'The Land and the Book: Biblical Studies and Imaginative Geographies of Palestine', *Postscripts: The Journal of Sacred Texts & Contemporary Worlds* 4: 71-84.
2010 'Resisting the Past: Ancient Israel in Western Memory', in *Between Evidence and Ideology: Essays on the History of Ancient Israel Read at the Joint Meeting of the Society for Old Testament Study and the Oud Testamentisch Werkgezelschap Lincoln, July 2009* (ed. B. Becking and L. Grabbe; Oudtestamentische studiën; Leiden: E.J. Brill), pp. 199-211.

Wilken, R.L.
1992 *The Land Called Holy: Palestine in Christian History and Thought* (New Haven: Yale University Press).

Williams, J.G.
1999 *The Life and Times of Edward Robinson: Connecticut Yankee in King Solomon's Court* (Biblical Scholarship in North America, 19; Atlanta: Society of Biblical Literature).

Wilson, C.W.
1871 'The Sea of Galilee', in *The Recovery of Jerusalem* (ed. W. Morrison; London: Bentley), pp. 337-87.
1881 *Picturesque Palestine, Sinai, and Egypt* (ed. C.W. Wilson; 2 vols.; New York: D. Appleton).

Wilson, E.
1895 *In Scripture Lands: New Views of Sacred Places* (New York: Charles Scribner's Sons).

Wolf, C.U.
1962 'Nomadism', in *The Interpreter's Dictionary of the Bible* (Nashville: Abingdon Press), III, 559-60.

Woolf, S. (ed.)
1996 *Nationalism in Europe, 1815 to the Present: A Reader* (London: Routledge).

Woolston, T.
1729 *A Sixth Discourse on the Miracles of our Saviour, in View of the Present Controversy between the Infidels and Apostates* (London: Printed for the author).

Wright, N.T.
1992 'Quest for the Historical Jesus', in *The Anchor Bible Dictionary* (ed. D.N. Freedman; 6 vols.; New York: Doubleday), III.
1996 *Jesus and the Victory of God* (London: SPCK).

Wuellner, W.
1967 *The Meaning of "Fishers of Men"* (New Testament Library; Philadelphia: Westminster Press).

Zangenberg, J.
    2001   *Magdala am See Gennesaret: Überlegungen zur sogenannten 'mini-sina-goga' und einige andere Beobachtungen zum kulturellen Profil des Ortes in neutestamentlicher Zeit* (Kleine Arbeiten zum Alten und Neuen Testament, 2; Waltrop: Verlag Hartmut Spenner).
    2003   'Magdala – Reich an Fisch und reich durch Fisch', in Fassbeck *et al.* 2003: 93-98.
Zangenberg, J., H.W. Attridge and D.B. Martin (eds.)
    2007   *Religion, Ethnicity, and Identity in Ancient Galilee: A Region in Transition* (Wissenschaftliche Untersuchungen zum Neuen Testament, 210; Tübingen: Mohr Siebeck).
Zangenberg, J., and P. Busch
    2003   'Hippos und Gadara – Ein Hauch von Welt am See', in Fassbeck *et al.* (2003), pp. 117-29.
Zohary, D.
    1969   'The Progenitors of Wheat and Barley in Relation to Domestication and Agricultural Dispersal in the Old World', in *The Domestication and Exploitation of Plants and Animals: Proceedings of a Meeting of the Research Seminar in Archaeology and Related Subjects Held at the Institute of Archaeology, London University* (ed. P.J. Ucko and G.W. Dimbleby; London: Gerald Duckworth), pp. 47–66.
Zohary, M.
    1962   *Plant Life of Palestine: Israel and Jordan* (Chronica Botanica, 33; New York: Ronald Press).

INDEX OF REFERENCES

INDEX OF AUTHORS

Lightning Source UK Ltd.
Milton Keynes UK
UKOW031055141211

183774UK00001B/20/P